Topics in Down Syndrome

CLASSROOM LANGUAGE SKILLS for CHILDREN with DOWN SYNDROME

A Guide for Parents and Teachers

Libby Kumin, Ph.D., CCC-SLP

Woodbine House ◆ 2001

Cover Illustration: Lili Robins

First edition

All rights reserved. Published in the United States of America by Woodbine House, Inc., 6510 Bells Mill Road, Bethesda, MD 20817 www.woodbinehouse.com

Library of Congress Cataloging-in-Publication Data

Kumin, Libby.
   Classroom language skills for children with Down syndrome : a guide for parents and teachers / Libby Kumin.—1st ed.
      p. cm.
   Includes bibliographical references and index.
   ISBN 1-890627-11-9 (pbk.)
   1. Mentally handicapped children—Education. 2. Mentally handicapped children—Means of communication. 3. Down syndrome. 4. Language arts. I. Title.

LC4616.K86 2001
371.92'8—dc21

                                                         2001026732

Manufactured in the United States of America

10   9   8   7   6   5   4   3   2   1

DEDICATED TO:

Dr. Herbert and Berniece Kumin, who respect and support knowledge and form the foundation of my commitment to others

Dr. Martin Lazar, who helps me continue to grow as a scholar and as a person

Dr. Jonathan Lazar, who makes every day a joyous celebration

Table of Contents

Acknowledgements

I care deeply about infants, toddlers, children, adolescents, and adults with Down syndrome and their families, and I bring to my work a passionate effort. There are many people who have influenced me, some people who have helped me and continue to help me in my work, and a few people who form a strong circle of support around me. First, my parents, Herbert and Berniece Kumin have been there for me from day one. They have helped me and have served as examples of people who strive to make the world a more caring, responsive place for all people. My husband, Martin, has given me encouragement and love, and is always in the background helping things run smoothly. My son, Jonathan, has given me great joy. His enthusiasm is a sunny background for living life. I cherish the love and caring of Mollie Lazar, Joel and Sandra Lazar, and Milton and Phyllis Shuch. They all nurture my soul and spirit.

My professional colleagues, Lisa Schoenbrodt and the faculty of the department of Speech-Language Pathology, and the administrators, faculty, and staff at Loyola College have provided a supportive community in which I have grown as a professional. Cheryl Councill and Mina Goodman are my valued colleagues who have been with me from the beginning of the clinical language intervention program at Loyola for individuals with Down syndrome. Together, we have developed a dynamic, effective program that has helped so many families through the years. My colleagues in the professional community have influenced my thinking. I want to especially thank William Cohen, Marilyn Bull, Bonnie Patterson, Sheila Cannon, Sheila Hebein, Dennis McGuire, Diane Bahr, Pat Winders, and Len Leshin for memorable discussions about the many issues facing families and their children with Down syndrome. Thanks also to Joan Medlen for her valuable insights and resources regarding communication partners, dual diagnosis, and augmentative communication.

Thanks to Jessica Pearsall, Cindy Casten, Kitti and Michael Drops, and the families who shared their children's worksheets and photographs, as well as to Adelaide Martin, Cindy McCathran, and Rhoda Stackhouse for their assistance in collecting photos of children at school. Thanks to Terry Johnson and Sally Long at Mayer-Johnson for their speedy and gracious response in providing permission to use, and access to, the Picture Communication Symbols used on many worksheets. Thanks to the team at Woodbine House, especially Susan Stokes and Brenda Ruby. I appreciate their questions, comments, diligence, and attention to detail.

There is a larger circle, the Down syndrome community, which has influenced my work. It is such a pleasure to work alongside you, to see you at conferences, to brainstorm, to hug, to laugh, and to cry with you. Many of you I talk with often; others I have spoken with only briefly. Your commitment and caring for me and for each other has affected me greatly.

Introduction

The elementary and middle school years are times of growth, learning, and achievement. Children with Down syndrome master many new skills, both academic and social, during these years.

Communication and language are an integral part of every school day. During the day, your child may greet the school bus driver, complete early morning routines such as saying the Pledge of Allegiance, copy down assignments, complete worksheets, read a story, follow the teacher's instructions for writing a composition, talk with other children in the class, greet the lunchroom staff, work in a cooperative group, follow written instructions for a science experiment, follow oral instructions for dismissal routines, and say good-bye to friends, teachers, and the bus driver. When your child returns home, she needs to tell you something about the day, retrieve and complete homework for the next day, and gather any worksheets, projects, and materials needed for the next day at school.*

Clearly, there are many language demands during and after the school day. For children with typical development, these language skills essential for school success may be learned without concentrated focus. For children with Down syndrome, however, we need to identify essential language skills so that we can provide assistance, when necessary, to help them learn and use the skills they need to succeed in school.

This book presents a framework for analyzing and describing the language needs in school. I have tried to provide ideas and techniques that can be used for many children with Down syndrome to help them master the language of the curriculum, language of instruction, language of the hidden curriculum, language of testing, language of routines, and the language of social interaction.

Communication is important in school settings, and in daily living. I have described a variety of resources, materials, and techniques to help children with Down syndrome with classroom language skills. For children who are unable to use speech as their primary communication system, there is information on assistive technology equipment, augmentative and alternative communication, materials, and other resources that can help.

---

* We use the personal pronouns "he" and "she" alternately by chapter throughout this book, so as not to imply that all children with Down syndrome are either male or female.

Worksheets at the ends of chapters and in the appendix can be used to help you and the IEP team plan your child's individual program to help her meet her educational goals. Ideas in the book can stimulate you to think about the different kinds of assistance that can be used to help your child. In the Resource Guide, you will find a directory of organizations, websites, and companies that can provide information, support, and commercial products useful to families of children with Down syndrome. The Appendix contains forms that will be helpful in planning for collaborative meetings with the school staff and speech-language pathologist.

This book is meant to be used by families, teachers, special educators, and speech-language pathologists. It is meant to help you and your child as you progress through the school years. It will be most helpful to families whose children are in elementary or middle school, but some of the information may be useful to parents of students in high school.

I have known many of you for a long time. The children whom I began to work with as infants are graduating from high school now. What a pleasure to attend those graduation ceremonies and parties! I have gotten to know many more of you through my writing. Many parents used my book *Communication Skills in Children with Down Syndrome* to help their infants, toddlers, and young children develop language and speech skills. Those children are now of elementary school age, and there are many additional communication skills that they need to master to succeed during the school years. This book examines the language your child needs for school success, and provides many suggestions for helping her achieve those skills.

Every child has unique talents and interests. Children have different learning styles, and different needs. The ideas and suggestions in the book are meant to be customized by you and the teachers and therapists working with your child, to match your child's gifts and challenges. One size does not fit all. Read the book. Mark those areas that are useful for you now. Make notes in the margins. Put stars next to what resonates with you; the suggestions that excite you. Fill-in the worksheets and planning sheets. Make use of the information. Put it to use to help your child. Make it a living, working document for your child. That's what makes all of my effort in writing the book worthwhile.

CHAPTER 1

An Overview of Language Needs in Schools

Children are nurtured within their families. They are part of a community. But, most of children's waking hours are spent in school. Children have a job, and they have a workplace. Their job is achieving success in an educational setting and their workplace is school.

Just as adults are expected to meet certain annual goals in their jobs, children are expected to meet annual goals in mastering the curriculum for their school year. They are expected to achieve measurable progress each year, according to scores on classroom tests and standardized tests. They may be allowed to demonstrate progress through a portfolio of their work over time. They are rated several times each year through grades and comments on their report cards. This is true for typically developing children and for children with Down syndrome.

Adults have some control when choosing their professions and choosing their specific jobs and job settings. Adults can choose their area of work based on their strengths. So, adults who do not perform well in mathematics would not usually choose to be accountants. Adults who are not strong in visual and spatial skills would probably not choose to be architects. Adults who do not work well under the pressure of deadlines would not choose to be journalists. Also, in many jobs, adults can bring in consultants to supplement their own strengths. When a manager needs to design a brochure for his company, he brings in a specialist from within the company or a consultant from outside the company who can provide the visual design and layout expertise. In daily life, adults may also bring in consultants. We seek out an accountant who prepares our tax returns, a roofer who fixes the roof when it is leaking, and a landscaper who prunes the trees.

Unlike adults, school children are not allowed to choose their occupation (i.e., student) or their subject areas based on their strengths, maximizing the chance that they will excel at their job. A ten-year-old can't say, "I am good at reading, but math problems are hard for me, so I will call in a math specialist to complete my assignments." Nor can children choose not to deal with the language requirements within the classroom, such as communicating with teachers and peers and following instructions. Language is the foundation for educational success, because language is the basis for learning in school. This is especially hard for children with Down syndrome, who usually have difficulty with language skills.

We expect typical children to master the material in all subjects to at least a passing level on report cards at grade level. We also expect typical children to perform well in each subject and, increasingly, to pass state- or county-wide exams in order to move on to the next grade, or to receive a high school diploma.

Expectations for children with disabilities, in contrast, are in flux. In the past, special education focused on goals for functional life skills, but did not usually include many academic goals. Thanks to recent amendments to the Individuals with Disabilities Education Act (IDEA), however, there is a new focus on progress in the regular educational curriculum, and on the supports and modifications needed for educational achievement. This represents an opportunity for children with disabilities—including Down syndrome—to master many educational skills, and to move beyond former expectations.

Children with Down syndrome, through individualized education programs (IEPs), can call on consultants to help them with things that are difficult for them. Teachers, parents, and SLPs can act as consultants for children with DS, helping devise ways for them to learn many skills that, in the past, were thought to be beyond their ability. They can help children by adapting the curriculum to make it easier to master the subject matter. They can modify oral and written instructions so that children will understand what they are supposed to do. They can design worksheets and tests so that children will be able to show what they have learned. Families with children with disabilities can access help—and this is a good thing in particular for kids with DS, who usually have significant problems with language.

Different children learn in different ways. In the past twenty years, most children with Down syndrome have learned in a special education setting. The smaller classes and personalized attention by special educators who have knowledge and experience undoubtedly benefited many students with Down syndrome. But, in most special education classes, there are children with a wide variety of disabilities, and with a wide range of skills. As a result, sometimes children who initially did not have behavior problems began imitating the inappropriate behavior of classmates. In some special education classes, there were low expectations, with the primary goal being to help children learn the activities of daily living. On the other hand, special education classes generally have fewer students, and the teachers have more time to focus on functional skills.

What Is Inclusion?

Many children with disabilities such as Down syndrome are able to learn to read and to master academic subjects. They live in the community and have relationships with other children and adults. So, there has been a movement toward inclusion—toward including children with disabilities in the regular education classroom in the local neighborhood school, to the greatest extent possible. Inclusive schooling is the practice of including everyone in the learning community, and ensuring that every student's needs are met. Inclusion does not necessarily mean that the child with Down syndrome in the class is learning the same material

as the other children in the class. But it does mean that the child with Down syndrome is part of that class. He is a member of the community in that classroom and contributes to that class.

For different children with Down syndrome, the least restrictive environment (LRE) can mean different things. For one child, it may be the regular education classroom for the entire school day. For another child, it may mean five hours a day in the regular classroom and one hour a day in a resource room getting extra help with writing and spelling. For another child, it may mean four hours a day in the regular classroom and two hours daily in pull-out therapy sessions that are needed to reach IEP goals. (Speech therapy may occur in the classroom, or may be pull-out therapy in a separate room.) For still another child, the LRE may be a self-contained special education classroom for academics, and inclusion with typical students for lunch, recess, art, and music.

Communication Needs in Inclusive Settings

For children with Down syndrome to make good progress in communication skills, they need:

- a reason to communicate,
- strong communication models,
- opportunities to practice communication skills,
- a system with which to communicate.

As long as the classroom setting is designed so that there is a reason to communicate and there are opportunities to communicate with teachers, other children, and school personnel, an inclusive setting can offer all these opportunities for communication growth. One important reason is that the typical children in the classroom are good communication models for their classmates with disabilities. In inclusive classrooms, friendships often develop that provide communication opportunities both inside and outside the classroom. Another important reason is that most of what goes on in the regular education classroom is related to communication and language. Most school curricula focus on linguistic and logical/mathematical skills, in the subjects of reading, language arts, and math. Textbooks and testing procedures rely heavily on language abilities in speaking and writing, listening, and following spoken instructions. Classroom interactions, class assignments, and daily instruction rely heavily on verbal interaction skills. Even the instructions for lining up and for boarding the bus rely on language. So, there are many opportunities to practice language skills.

There are published lists of school survival skills (e.g., *Wisconsin Day Care Survival Skills, Wisconsin Kindergarten Survival Skills, Hawaii Kindergarten Survival Skills*) that provide information on which specific communication skills teachers view as important for early school performance. The skill that is most frequently listed is "Follows general rules and routines."

Communication skills that have been identified as important to school success in the early school years are:

- Follows general rules and routines.
- Expresses wants and needs.
- Understands and complies with specific directions given by an adult.
- Takes turns.
- Interacts verbally with peers.
- Interacts verbally with adults.
- Focuses attention on speaker/eye contact.
- Has good listening skills.
- Knows and recognizes his name.

Some of the language and pragmatics (social interactional language) skills that children are expected to have mastered during the later elementary school years are:

- Understands and follows classroom routines.
- Able to deviate from the routines when necessary.
- Participates in peer routines at lunch, recess, and in class.
- Able to interact verbally and socially with peers.
- Knows how to introduce and sustain topics.
- Understands turn-taking rules.
- Takes turns appropriately in conversation.
- Knows how to request a turn.
- Uses appropriate greetings for different situations.
- Able to follow teacher instructions.
- Able to follow long, complex directions.
- Able to decode and understand the teacher's cues.
- Able to answer questions.
- Able to share information.
- Understands the teacher's expectations for performance in an activity.
- Understands the teacher's expectations for the form and complexity of a response.
- Able to request clarification when direction is unclear.
- Able to repair conversational breakdowns.

In addition, educators have lists of other skills that are needed for school success. The skills cluster in the areas of appropriate behavior, following rules and routines, organizational skills, completing assignments well and in a timely manner, learning strategies, test-taking strategies, interpreting graphics, and using textbooks and reference books effectively. Not surprisingly, language has a major impact on each of these areas, too. In this book, chapters will consider the impact of language in each of these areas, and what we can do to help children succeed.

Clearly, there are many reasons and opportunities for children with Down syndrome to practice and improve communication skills in an inclusive setting. These opportunities can lead to great communication growth, but they can also present significant challenges for students with Down syndrome. The next section discusses how these challenges can complicate inclusion.

Language and Communication Strengths and Challenges for School-Aged Children with Down Syndrome

Children with Down syndrome experience a wide range of communication skills, strengths, and challenges. There is no one typical pattern of development of speech and language for all children with Down syndrome. Usually, however, there are some speech and language skill areas that are more advanced and continue to develop into adolescence and adulthood (e.g., vocabulary) and other areas that are less advanced and present more difficulty (e.g., forming longer phrases and sentences, speech intelligibility). As a result, children with Down syndrome generally are not at an equal point across speech and language areas. For example, a child who is using vocabulary at a five-year-old level may be using grammatical structures at a three-year-old level, but may comprehend language at a six-year-old level.

Not only do children with Down syndrome develop different speech and language skills at different rates, but their speech and language skills often lag behind their cognitive skills. That is, language and knowledge may not be at the same developmental level. In fact, children with Down syndrome often have more difficulty with language skills, and especially with speech and intelligibility skills, than would be predicted by mental age and cognitive testing.

TYPICAL SPEECH, LANGUAGE, AND HEARING CHALLENGES

Although this section discusses some of the factors that can affect speech and language in children with Down syndrome, it is important to remember that each child has his own group of communication strengths and challenges. Also, specific problems with communication, such as with speech intelligibility, can affect different children differently. For example, in some children, problems with intelligibility may occur due to a soft voice and unclear speech related to low muscle tone. In other children, the difficulties might be with motor planning for speech and fluency (stuttering). In still others, intelligibility may be affected by speaking rapidly and leaving off the final sounds in words. In addition, difficulties with grammar may or may not be present and contribute to difficulties with intelligibility.

Below are descriptions of the major strengths and challenges in speech, language, communication, and hearing that may occur in children with Down syndrome, together with information about how these problems affect inclusion:

Relative Difficulties with Language. Children with Down syndrome have more difficulty with language than with other developmental skills. Specifically, we generally see slower development in the area of language relative to cognitive

or motor development. This can have a far-reaching impact on a student's success in school, since learning in school is based on language. We use language to follow directions in class. We use language to learn from textbooks and worksheets. We use language to take tests, answer questions in class verbally, and write—that is, we use language to let the teacher know that we have learned the material.

Receptive-Expressive Gap. Within the channels and areas of language, comprehension is usually more advanced than production. This is sometimes known as the receptive-expressive gap. It can be difficult to measure expressive language, because we are usually testing using speech. Speech presents many difficulties for children with Down syndrome. It is possible that language comprehension appears higher because it is measured by pointing or by following directions or by demonstrating understanding, whereas language production is measured by speaking. Because children with Down syndrome have difficulty with expressive language, teachers often underestimate what they know and understand. In inclusion, we need to find ways in which students with Down syndrome can demonstrate their understanding, despite problems with expressive language—such as by answering multiple choice questions instead of writing essays.

Relative Strengths and Weaknesses. Some areas of language are easier for children with Down syndrome to master than others. Semantics (vocabulary) mastery is easier to learn and generally more advanced than morphosyntax (grammar and structure). In inclusion, children with Down syndrome may have specific difficulty with grammar exercises. Lots of practice and exercises that require recognizing the correct answer (multiple choice) rather than generating it may be helpful. The child with Down syndrome should be able to master much of the vocabulary used for each subject, as well as vocabulary needed for conversation. Research on individuals with Down syndrome has shown that vocabulary continues to grow into adulthood. Inclusion in the regular classroom, as well as in community activities, promotes vocabulary development by providing good models, and by providing opportunities for learning new vocabulary and using vocabulary in conversation.

Hearing Loss. Most children with Down syndrome have some degree of hearing loss. The most common type of hearing loss for children with Down syndrome is a fluctuating conductive hearing loss. That is, it varies in severity from time to time in the same child, and is related to fluid in the ears (otitis media with effusion). It has been estimated that 60-90 percent of children with Down syndrome have some hearing loss related to fluid accumulation (Kavanagh, 1994; Roizen, 1997). There is growing evidence that a history of early fluctuating hearing loss affects speech and language development in any child, so it is important to treat the condition and to minimize the effects of the hearing loss. Some children also experience a sensorineural hearing loss, which is a more permanent hearing loss.

With either type of hearing loss, it may be more difficult for the child with Down syndrome to hear instructions being given in class, especially when there are extraneous noises, such as kids moving their chairs, air conditioning noises, hall noises. This can be solved in a number of ways. Preferential seating which allows the child to sit near the teacher may be used. Amplification systems of various types may be used in the classroom. One or several children can be linked into the same system, and these systems have been found to be helpful. The parents, pediatrician, audiologist, speech-language pathologist, special education teacher, and regular classroom teacher can all work together to help maximize the child's ability to hear in class.

Speech Intelligibility. Intelligibility of speech is a problem for many children with Down syndrome, especially when talking with unfamiliar listeners. Specific factors affecting intelligibility may include low muscle tone in the mouth area, difficulties with jaw movements, motor planning difficulties for speech, rapid rate of speech, and fluency difficulties.

Every child with Down syndrome needs to be able to communicate effectively. Speech therapy and an oral motor exercise program can enable many children to speak understandably. But, if your child cannot be easily understood, an augmentative communication system can be designed to complement and supplement the speech that your child can use. Picture cards, an alphabet board, or a computer-based system are different kinds of systems that can be used. Augmentative communication systems are not only for people who cannot speak at all. They can be used to supplement the speech that you have so that you can communicate everything that you need to communicate. Chapter 12 provides information on how you can work with professionals to ensure that your child has an effective communication system that can meet his communication needs.

Auditory Learning Weaknesses. In children with Down syndrome, the visual channel (sight) is usually a stronger channel for learning than the auditory channel (hearing). It is harder for children to follow verbal instructions than pictured or written instructions in class. Learning to read can help children with Down syndrome progress in language, as well as move forward educationally. Reading from text and using the computer may have a positive impact on language learning. Visual cues and organizers can be used to help children learn in class.

Cognitive Impairment. The degree of cognitive impairment (mental retardation) has an impact on speech-language learning, because language is related to abstract concepts. Mental retardation also affects memory, making it harder to remember multi-part instructions or grammar rules. It also affects word retrieval, or the ability to come up with the word you need when you need it, which makes it harder to use language for speaking.

Despite these difficulties, children with Down syndrome can continue to progress in communication throughout childhood and into adulthood. Language-enriching experiences can occur at school, at home, in community settings, and in the work environment. Inclusion in school and in community activities presents many opportunities for communication practice and enhances communication skills. Later chapters will explain how to address communication-related problems during the school years, to ensure that children with Down syndrome make maximum progress.

Are Specific Communication or Learning Skills Required for Inclusion?

The Individuals with Disabilities Education Act (IDEA) states that students with disabilities should be: "educated with children who are not disabled, and special classes, separate schooling or other removal of children with disabilities from the regular educational environment occurs only when the nature or severity of the disability is such that education in regular classes with the use of supplementary aids and services cannot be achieved satisfactorily." (Part B, Sec. 612 (a) (5) (A)). Although this is a strong mandate for full inclusion, some school systems have not embraced inclusion as warmly as others.

Sometimes, parents of children with Down syndrome are told that the school does not have the personnel to meet the child's needs in a regular classroom, or that the child's needs can only be met in a special education class or in a separate school. Other times, parents are told that their child's speech and language is not adequate to learn in the regular classroom.

The law is very specific in mandating "the use of supplementary aids and services" to help students achieve in the regular classroom. If a child is nonverbal, assistive technology can be used to provide a "voice" for him and enable him to participate in the regular education classroom. In addition, a child cannot be refused placement at his neighborhood school because the school does not currently offer the services that he needs to succeed in an inclusive setting. For example, if a child is determined to need a one-on-one aide or a certain level of speech therapy, the school must provide those services rather than insisting that the child go to a

school that already offers them. On the other hand, if the child has severe receptive language difficulties that would prevent him from understanding the language being used in class, even with supplementary aids and services, it may be difficult for him to learn in a regular classroom.

The fact that children with Down syndrome may learn differently and need more support in the classroom than typical children do is absolutely not a valid reason for excluding them from inclusive classrooms. In reality, every child has a unique learning style. Some children memorize the explorers' names, dates, and places of exploration most effectively through studying their notes or textbook. Other children find that drawing a diagram, copying over their notes, or tape recording their notes is more effective. Some children will learn the information if it is part of a jingle, rhyme, or rap song, and others will use dance steps or movements to help them remember the information. Amplification of sound and seating in the front of the room may maximize learning for some children, but impede the learning of other children. Some children work best in groups, while others achieve more working on their own.

One of the benefits of inclusion is that it focuses on individual learning styles and what assistance each child needs to succeed in school. This is helpful for all children—typically developing children, children with learning disabilities, *and* children with Down syndrome. It sets our minds thinking about how children learn best. It challenges us to modify and adapt the curriculum to help children learn, rather than insisting on one style of learning for all children. When children work in teams, the different skills that they bring to the task strengthen the cooperative team effort. See Chapter 5 for more information on learning styles.

Is Inclusion the Right Choice for Your Child?

Individual decisions as to whether the least restrictive environment for a child is an inclusive classroom must be left to the IEP team. But, most children with Down syndrome do well being included with neighborhood children in the local school. The National Down Syndrome Society sponsored a large study that demonstrated that inclusion had many positive benefits for children with Down syndrome (Wolpert, 1996). The National Down Syndrome Congress, in a 1997 position statement on inclusive education concludes that "quality inclusive education . . . should be a readily available and accessible option for every student with Down syndrome." And John Rynders and J. Margaret Horrobin, noted educators of children with Down syndrome, describe the social and communication gains in children and adolescents who have been educated in the mainstream in their book *Down Syndrome: Birth to Adulthood* (1996).

Perhaps most compelling are the findings of a study conducted by Sue Buckley, educator and researcher at the Sarah Duffen Centre, University of Portsmouth (England). In a study in Hampshire, England, Buckley found that the expressive language skills of teenagers with Down syndrome in mainstream (inclusive) settings were on average two and a half years ahead of their peers who were in special education schools (Buckley, 1999). On reading and writing measures, the mainstreamed teenagers were three years and four months ahead of the students in special education.

Building Language Skills for Classroom Success

There are a variety of language demands within the classroom and in the broader school setting. Identifying the language needs is the first step towards working on strengthening those skills. I have found that there are six areas of communication that are needed for success in regular classroom inclusion settings:

1. The Language of the Curriculum,
2. The Language of Instruction,
3. The Language of the Hidden Curriculum,
4. The Language of Testing,
5. The Language of Classroom Routines,
6. Social Interactive Communication.

Each of these areas is explained briefly below, and discussed in detail in one of the following chapters.

<table>
<tr><td>

THE LANGUAGE OF THE CURRICULUM

</td><td>

The language of the curriculum focuses on the vocabulary and language level of the material included in the curriculum for each subject. That is, what specific language concepts does the child need to know to master the objectives for a given subject (second grade social studies, fourth grade science, etc.)? There are differences from one subject to another. There are also differences between different grade levels. For example, a first grade textbook is much more likely to have pictures and other visual cues than is an eighth grade textbook. A science textbook is more likely to have diagrams and charts than a literature book is.

</td></tr>
</table>

How can we describe the language of the curriculum and help the child learn the concepts that he needs? We can describe the language of the curriculum for a specific grade in a specific subject by answering the following questions:

1. What concepts are included in the subject area? (e.g., what concepts are being taught in third grade social studies?)
2. What vocabulary words are used?
3. What is the language level of the textbooks used?
4. Are there differences in language difficulty between subject areas?(Is the language level similar for science, reading, and social studies? Does science have more unfamiliar words than reading?)

The people answering these questions should be the professionals who are designing the curriculum for that grade. Ideally, since language is so integrally involved with learning the curriculum, the speech-language pathologist and the special educator should follow up on this information and design exercises, worksheets, and experiences that will help the child learn the concepts that he needs in order to learn what is expected of him in each subject.

In reality, I have spoken with many parents who have been told that the classroom teacher and the specialists do not have time to make lists of vocabulary words and concepts, and it is left to the parent to review the textbooks and make those lists, and then to send the material to the teacher. Parents have also been told, "I don't know how to test whether your child knows the science unit on clouds. Why don't you make up a test that you think he will be able to do, and I will give it to him." This should not happen. Chapter 4 will present strategies that may help prevent this kind of situation. In a good inclusive classroom, helping your child with language skills needed for subject areas is a collaborative effort for the classroom teacher, special educator, speech-language pathologist, classroom aide, and family members.

<table>
<tr><td>

THE LANGUAGE OF INSTRUCTION

</td><td>

The language of instruction is the language used to teach and learn within the classroom. It includes the channels used, such as speech or writing. For example, does the teacher provide oral instructions? Short or long strings of directions? Does the teacher provide written instructions? Do the instructions stay on the blackboard or are they erased quickly? Does the teacher provide pictured or diagramed instructions? What terms are used in teaching and in learning in that classroom? Are there differences between the way that different subjects are taught?

</td></tr>
</table>

Science and physical education are usually more hands-on and provide many more contextual cues during instruction. Social studies and language arts generally involve more lecture, fewer visual cues and models, and more use of *decontextualized*

language—language in which there are no environmental cues for teaching. In science, when the teacher is talking about a seed, the child is likely to be looking at or holding a seed. In social studies, when the teacher is talking about the colonists, there are many fewer cues in the environment. This decontenxtualized language is much more difficult for children with Down syndrome. Through the use of visual organizers, which will be discussed in later chapters, it is possible to provide the child with visual cues and a framework with which to understand the material that is being taught.

Questions that need to be answered to learn more about the language used for instruction include:

- What terms are used in teaching and learning in that classroom?
- What terms are used for each subject area of instruction?
- Can your child follow the teacher's instructions? If not, what is interfering with your child's ability to follow the instructions?

In the primary grades, terms used for instruction might include *underline, circle,* and *draw a line*. In later elementary school, terms might include *cause and effect, factors that influence, action and response*. These terms can be taught and practiced so that the child can answer the questions that are being asked in class. Visual cues and samples of correct answers can be used to help him understand what is being asked. Even if the child knows the answer, if he does not understand the language of instruction, he may not get credit for what he knows. For a child with Down syndrome, getting the answer right may involve not only knowing which word begins with a /b/, but knowing that you need to underline that word.

THE LANGUAGE OF THE HIDDEN CURRICULUM

The hidden curriculum is never explained to students or parents. It is not purposely hidden; it is largely unconscious and out of our awareness, and even out of the conscious awareness of the teachers themselves. Students who do well in a particular class have mastered the hidden curriculum, but even they may not be able to identify the factors that contributed to their success.

The hidden curriculum is what you need to do in a specific class with a specific teacher to be a successful student. Just as students are different, teachers are different, too. Very rarely do teachers tell you, "Here's what you need to do to succeed in my class." For example, when children are asked to write a composition about pets, how many sentences is the teacher expecting? How much detail does she expect? Does she want you to write about pets in general, or about your pet? Teachers will spend a long time teaching how to head the paper, and where to write your title, but they will not often provide specific information on what their expectations are. You only find that out when you get your grade. Teachers may act on the hidden curriculum unconsciously, but may not be directly conscious of their hidden curriculum and may not be able to clearly explain it. They know what they consider to be a good paper, but they rarely explain that.

In elementary school, children are with the same teacher for the entire school year. By the end of the year, students generally have a better idea of what the teacher expects than they did at the beginning of the year. Even at that time, students who have not done well in the class may still not know what is expected. In middle school and high school, students may not be in a teacher's class more than one period a day. If someone asks about that teacher, the student may say, "I've never had her before. I don't know what to expect."

Questions that need to be answered include:

- How should a student answer questions in class?
- What should be included in a good answer?
- How should you answer questions in written assignments?
- What counts most with this teacher—complete, comprehensive answers, creativity, memorization, neatness, being on time with assignments?

Every teacher considers some factors more important than others— when you learn about the hidden curriculum, you are gaining information about what these factors are. Once you gain information, checklists and other organizers can be used to help your child succeed.

THE LANGUAGE OF TESTING

There may be some overlap between the language of instruction and the language of testing, especially in the lower grades. The major difference is that the language of testing is highly *decontextualized*—that is, there are few, if any cues in the context to help you figure out what the material is about. On tests, there are generally no illustrations and no manipulatives. The words stand alone, and you need to interpret and respond to those words with no cues.

In elementary school, the language of testing may include questions on reading comprehension, topic sentences, appropriate titles for a story, analogies, and word problems. Specific terms such as *underline, circle, mark within the lines* may be used in giving instructions for the test. When the language of testing is identified, it can be worked on in therapy and in the classroom, to help children achieve on tests. Accommodations and modification for testing will also be discussed in Chapter 9.

THE LANGUAGE OF CLASSROOM ROUTINES

The language of classroom routines is involved with following directions and with speaking and behaving appropriately in class. Classroom routines might include getting to class on time; sitting in your seat ready to work; beginning a task, staying on task, and completing a task; shifting tasks as indicated by the teacher; working within a cooperative learning group; lining up and dismissal procedures; and lunch, assembly, and fire drill procedures. It might also include how to respond to a teacher's request, when and how to ask for assistance, how to indicate that you don't understand the task or the instructions, when to talk and when not to talk, and how to work in cooperative learning groups.

The language of classroom routines will be most difficult for children at the beginning of the school year. Routines often involve long strings of instructions that may be difficult for children with Down syndrome to follow. But, routines are repeated frequently, so there are visual models and many opportunities for practice. Sometimes, a buddy system works well when routines are first being learned. Classroom aides can be of great help in mastering the routines.

SOCIAL INTERACTIVE COMMUNICATION

Social interactive communication includes communication with peers and all school personnel (including teachers, administrators, cafeteria workers, maintenance staff, bus drivers) in the classroom, at lunch, recess, and on the school bus.

To maximize social communication, some questions that need to be answered are:

- How does the child interact with peers?
- What communication system is used?
- What maximizes communication?
- What interferes with communication?
- Does the child use social greetings, start conversations?
- Does the child take turns in conversations? Stay on topic?
- Where does the child communicate best? With whom?
- Does the child use eye contact? Appropriate gestures? Appropriate facial expressions? Maintain appropriate distance between people?

Conclusion

In this book, we will focus on language skills that are needed for classroom success. We will discuss the language needs for different subjects, different grade levels, and different teachers. We will discuss the IEP process for speech-language pathology services, and what needs to be included in the IEP. We will provide home activities and materials to help you help your children learn. We will also provide planning guides and forms that families can use as part of the IEP process. Later chapters will provide information on assistive technology and alternative communication systems that can help your child communicate. Language is the foundation of learning in school. This book will focus on how to build a language foundation that promotes classroom participation and learning.

REFERENCES

Buckley, S., Bird, G., Sacks, B., & Archer, T. (2000). The development of teenagers with Down syndrome in 1987 and 1999: implications for families and schools. *Down syndrome News and Update, 2* (in press).

Buckley, S., Bird, G., Sacks, B., & Archer, T. (2000). A comparison of mainstream and special school education for teenagers with Down syndrome: effects on social and academic development. *Down Syndrome Research and Practice, 7* (in press).

Chisler, J. & Oaks, R. (1995). *The collaboration companion*. Moline, IL: Lingui-Systems.

Damico, J. (1987). Addressing language concerns in the schools: the SLP as consultant. *Journal of Childhood Communication Disorders, 11,* 17-40.

Fowler, A. E. (1995). Linguistic variability in persons with Down syndrome: research and implications. In Nadel, L. & Rosenthal, D. (1995). *Down syndrome: Living and learning in the community*. New York: Wiley-Liss, 121-131.

Kavanagh, K. T. (1994). Ear, nose, and sinus conditions of children with Down syndrome. In Van Dyke, D.C, Matthias, P., Eberly, S.S. & Williams, J. *Medical & surgical care for children with Down syndrome: A guide for parents*. Bethesda, MD: Woodbine House, 155-174.

Kumin, L. (1999). Comprehensive speech and language treatment for infants, toddlers, and children with Down syndrome. In Hassold, T. J. *Down syndrome: A promising future, together*. New York, NY: Wiley-Liss, 145-153.

Kumin, L. (1996). Speech and language skills in children with Down syndrome. *Mental Retardation and Developmental Disabilities Research Reviews, 2,* 109-116.

Kumin, L. (1995). Speech and language skills in children and adolescents with Down syndrome. New York, NY: National Down Syndrome Society.

Miller, J.F., Leddy, M. & Leavitt, L. A. (1999). *Improving the communication of people with Down syndrome*. Baltimore, MD: Paul H. Brookes.

National Down Syndrome Congress (1997). A position statement on Inclusive Education for Students with Down syndrome.

Roizen, N. (1997). Hearing loss in children with Down syndrome: A review. *Down Syndrome Quarterly, 2,* 1-4.

Rynders, J. & Horrobin, M. (1996). Down syndrome: birth to adulthood: giving families an EDGE. Denver, CO: Love Publishing.

Shott, S. (2000). Down syndrome: Common pediatric ear, nose, and throat problems. *Down Syndrome Quarterly, 5,* 1-6.

Wolpert, G. (1996). The educational challenges inclusion study. New York, NY: National Down Syndrome Society.

CHAPTER 2

The Communication Team

What Is the Communication Team?

Communication happens all of the time in school and in daily life. Communication does not only occur in the speech-language pathology room. That means that we can't work on communication just in a separate speech-language pathology room. Teachers, aides, other children in the classroom, the bus driver, other children on the bus, the cafeteria people, the office staff, and the school administrators are all communicating with your child. They are members of the larger circle of communication that surrounds your child at school. Depending on your child's activities in the community, a variety of adults and children also support your child's communication efforts outside of school.

But, within the school setting, there is a more specialized group of professionals that form your child's communication team. They have the expertise to help your child with specific skills needed for speech and language. The speech-language pathologist is part of the communication team. Other members may include the occupational therapist who works on postural control that is needed for speech, the psychologist who helps measure your child's cognitive level, and the audiologist who measures your child's hearing and suggests amplification as needed. They are the professionals who serve on the IEP planning team to help plan an individualized supportive program to help meet your child's educational needs.

The Role of The Speech-Language Pathologist at School

As the professional who is trained to diagnose and treat difficulties with receptive and expressive language and speech, the speech-language pathologist (SLP) is one of the most important members of your child's communication team. The SLP is trained to observe and analyze individuals, two-person groups, and larger groups communicating. Consequently, she can observe your child in the classroom and suggest adaptations, modifications, and assistance with language in the classroom.

At school, the SLP's role on your child's communication team is dictated by the Individuals with Disabilities Education Act (IDEA), the federal special education law. This is because, under IDEA, speech therapy is classified as a "related service." The latest amendments to IDEA, enacted in 1997, define related services as services needed for the child to progress in the regular education setting with reference to the general curriculum. (This is in contrast to earlier versions of IDEA, in which related services were defined as those services needed by the child in order to benefit from special education.)

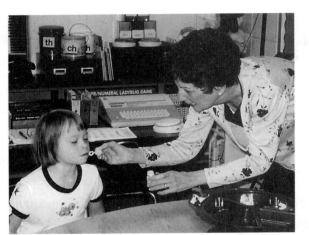

Under the law, school-based speech therapy is not designed to meet all of your child's communication needs. The goal of IDEA is not to maximize your child's skills or to allow her to continue therapy until she has achieved her highest communication potential. Instead, therapy is provided to help children develop the skills they need to progress in the classroom. This can be a source of conflict between parents—who believe that their children *need* speech therapy to develop the best possible communication skills—and school personnel—who know that school systems have certain eligibility requirements to qualify for services. In short, your child may need speech and language services even when your child is not "eligible" for services through the schools. And she may need more frequent and intensive speech therapy than she qualifies for under the law. Need and eligibility are two different issues. See "What If Your Child Is Not Receiving School-Based Therapy," below, as well as Chapter 7 for more information on eligibility.

Many different speech and language areas may be the focus of treatment. But again, in order for your child to receive treatment for these problem areas, they must be determined to affect your child's progress in the regular educational curriculum. It seems as if this requirement has made it easier to get *language* services, but more difficult to get *speech and intelligibility* services. Speech and language treatment may focus on many areas, including:

- listening skills
- auditory memory
- receptive language
- following directions
- vocabulary
- grammar
- expressive language
- answering questions appropriately
- increasing the length of sentences
- speech intelligibility
- articulation
- voice
- fluency
- conversational skills
- written language skills
- social language skills
- metalinguistics (being able to talk about language)

In addition, SLPs are becoming increasingly involved in helping students with reading and writing, because of their knowledge of language learning. Reading and writing are closely connected with spoken language, especially in the early grades where the words used for reading and writing are all familiar words that the child has heard in her environment. According to the American Speech-Language-Hearing Association, "Spoken and written language have a reciprocal relationship, such that each builds on the other, to result in general language and literacy competence, starting early and continuing through childhood into adulthood" (ASHA, 2001, p. 17). SLPs may work closely with teachers in planning a literacy program, identify children at risk for reading and writing problems, prevent some problems by fostering language development and working on preliteracy skills (such as reading from left to right, sound-to-letter correspondence), and assess and treat reading and writing problems (ASHA, 2001).

An example of a need that the school SLP may *not* be able to work on with your child is speech intelligibility. Children are often denied services related to improving speech intelligibility on the grounds that intelligibility problems do not prevent them from moving ahead in the general curriculum. However, intelligibility of speech (how easily your child's speech can be understood) *is* a major problem for children with Down syndrome, as noted by many researchers (Miller, 1988; Miller, Leddy & Leavitt, 1998) and by parents (Kumin, 1994) and needs to be worked on in therapy for most children with Down syndrome.

Many factors influence intelligibility, and these factors can be worked on and improved through speech therapy. Low muscle tone (hypotonia) in the oral and facial area, muscle coordination difficulty, and oral motor planning difficulty are three factors that frequently affect intelligibility in children with Down syndrome. Unfortunately, however, school system guidelines consider how the child's speech and language problem affects her progress in the regular educational curriculum. If it cannot be proven that the difficulties in intelligibility affect progress in the curriculum, services will not be provided solely on the basis of these difficulties. (However, the child may be eligible for speech and language therapy due to other difficulties that do affect progress in the curriculum.) See Chapter 3 for information about how school systems determine eligibility for speech and language therapy and what you can do if your child is not determined to be eligible.

How Speech Therapy Is Provided at School

How can the SLP work with your child in the schools? There are a variety of *service delivery models*—that is, ways in which speech-language pathology services can be provided. Service delivery includes where and in what size group therapy will be conducted. Frequency of service is another factor that must be determined. For service delivery, the SLP may use individual or group treatment. Small group treatment (2-4 children) is typical in the school setting. Individual therapy is rare, and if it is used, is often for a short 15-20 minute period once weekly.

Children may be seen in a separate treatment room; this is known as "pull-out" therapy. Some treatment rooms are light and colorful and have storage space for many materials. Other treatment rooms are former broom closets, and all of the SLP's materials are stored in her canvas bag which she carries with her from school to school.

Children may also be seen for treatment in the regular classroom. This is known as "in-class" or "push-in" therapy. Children may be seen in a corner of the classroom or several children may be seen at once. The SLP may also be involved in presenting lessons about communication to the entire class. For instance, she may give a lesson on using your voice properly, not shouting and abusing it.

SLPs may also be involved on a consultative basis. That means that they do not see your child directly for treatment, but they serve as a resource for the teacher when she has questions about your child's speech and language, or for the IEP team in planning for your child.

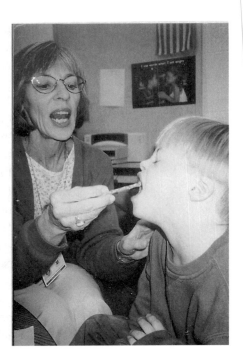

PULL-OUT THERAPY

Until recently, speech-language pathology services were usually provided in a separate room, in individual or small group settings within the class day. Using this model, children are taken out of the classroom for therapy. The time for therapy is chosen so as to least interfere with activities within the classroom, so that children do not need to miss a major subject.

Pull-out therapy may involve individual or small-group treatment. Groups work well for some types of treatment. For example, if we are working on conversational skills or giving and following instructions, it is best to work with two to four children in a small group. If we are working on specific exercises for the facial muscles, groups only work well if each child in the group has similar problems. If one child is doing tongue exercises, another is doing lip exercises, and a third is practicing elevating the palate muscles, working together in a group will not be helpful. It will turn into three individual therapy sessions taking place at the same time in the same room, with perhaps ten minutes devoted to each child. I have also observed groups in which one child is working on the /f/ sound, another is working on auditory discrimination of /s/ and /sh/ (hearing the differences between sounds), and a third child is working on difficulties related to overly nasal speech. Again, there will actually be three individual therapy sessions taking place during the "group" session.

Individual pull-out therapy is currently out of favor with some professionals, and especially with educators. One reason is that educational administrators favor serving large numbers in class rather than one child at a time. Pull-out group therapy, however, is still the most frequently used type of service delivery. According to ASHA's 2000 Schools Survey, "Each week, a typical school-based ASHA-certified speech-language pathologist spends an average of 23 hours providing services using traditional pull-out, 2 hours using a collaborative consultation, and 1 hour using a classroom-based/curriculum-based model" (ASHA, 2001).

One of the problems with pull-out therapy is that it is based on a *remediation model*. Pull-out therapy is usually used to remediate (fix) existing problems but not to prevent potential ones. So, the SLP would work on a sound such as /s/ only when your child was significantly delayed in producing that sound according to age and developmental norms. The IEP for pull-out therapy is based on deficits found during an annual evaluation, and is reactive rather than proactive. Pull-out therapy is used when scores demonstrate that your child is significantly behind, or has failed. This means that if your child progresses well, and does not score far enough below the cut-off test scores, she might lose eligibility for services. This presents a catch-22 situation for parents, who are pleased that their child is making progress, but concerned about losing speech and language services.

Another problem with group pull-out therapy is that it is often difficult to schedule a group of children so that none of them miss important classwork, while at the same time, ensuring that all children in the group have speech difficulties that are similar and can be worked on in a group.

Theoretically, there is no reason that pull-out therapy could not be used to prevent speech and language problems, but it historically has not been used in that way. It has been based on remediation of an existing problem that meets the eligibility requirements for school speech-language pathology services.

ALTERNATIVES TO PULL-OUT THERAPY	Inclusion and the emphasis on progress in the regular educational curriculum have had a major impact on the role of the speech-language pathologist in the schools, and in the way that special services are delivered to children in the schools. Currently, there is a trend for speech-language therapy to be provided through in-class therapy, otherwise known as classroom-based intervention or the collaborative consultation/team-based approach.

Classroom-based intervention usually means in-class services. But, it may also be used to mean that the content of therapy and the materials used in therapy focus on what the child needs to succeed in the classroom. *Collaborative consultation* means that the speech-language pathologist and the classroom teacher work together to help the child with communication skills that are needed for success in the classroom. These methods are most successful when they are used in combination, as needed, as the basis of the child's program.

IN-CLASS THERAPY

Some school systems provide only in-class therapy services. In other school systems, when parents ask about having speech-language pathology services provided in class, they are met with blank stares. Although the IEP is meant to be individualized for each child, where service is delivered appears to be handled in a global way, with county or district school systems deciding on a system-wide basis how services will be provided.

In-class therapy is sometimes provided at a regular spot with a table and chairs in the back or on the side of the classroom. Or, the SLP may move around the room and work with your child at her desk or in a learning centers area. The SLP may work with your child alone, or may conduct a lesson that includes a small group of children, or sometimes even the whole class. The idea is that therapy is brought directly into the classroom—the place where your child spends the day—to focus on academic learning experiences and communication opportunities as they occur.

Classroom-based therapy may be the job exclusively of the speech-language pathologist (the same as with pull-out therapy), or it may be based on active and ongoing collaboration between the classroom teacher and the speech-language pathologist. It is certainly more successful when the intervention involves not only cooperation, but collaboration between the speech-language pathologist and the classroom teacher.

One of the benefits of classroom-based therapy is that it involves groups of children within the class. This helps provide models of good communication skills and facilitates interactions between all of the children in the class, including the children with Down syndrome. A classroom-based lesson may be given to the whole class, discussing greetings, or staying on topic, or facial expressions. "Instruction which aims, through modeling, feedback, and practice to make students aware of the social graces and language conventions involved in successfully working and playing with others, would in itself be of great value to students with Down syndrome" (Farrell & Elkins, 1994/95, p. 272). Interactive language involves at least two people, and it is more natural to work with two peers communicating, rather than for the SLP to serve as a communication partner.

Another benefit of classroom-based therapy is that the SLP can observe first-hand what the language requirements of the classroom are. For example, how does the teacher give instructions? ask questions?

A drawback of classroom-based therapy is that there are many distractions within the room. Classrooms are noisy, and speech may be occurring when there are other activities going on at the same time. It can be difficult for your child to focus on a speech session when the rest of the class is doing something else. For push-in therapy to be successful, your child needs to be able to attend to the task despite distractions.

In my opinion, classroom-based therapy does not lend itself to certain types of therapy—for example, therapy for motor planning problems for speech. But, classroom-based therapy need not be the only service delivery model used. Remember that the IEP must be individually designed for your child's needs. If your child needs a combination of classroom-based and individual therapy, that should be provided (in the best of worlds!) in the schools, or through a combination of school-based and outside therapy. For more information about addressing speech-language needs through the IEP, see Chapter 4.

COLLABORATIVE CONSULTATION

When the term collaborative consultation is used in relation to speech-language pathology, it refers to the collaboration between the speech-language pathologist and the classroom teacher. It is a team approach to speech and language intervention in which the speech-language pathologist and the classroom teacher share in decision making and in working on the speech and language goals for your child.

Collaborative consultation enables professionals to share expertise with each other to better help their students. Classroom teachers can carry over language lessons within other areas of the curriculum, and speech-language pathologists can provide information on how to modify the specific assignments or requirements for a child based on her language needs. For this method to succeed, it is essential that the SLP and teacher both understand how speech and language are connected to reading and writing. They need to understand that "language does not take place for only the 30-45 minute time period the speech-language pathologist is in the classroom" (Achilles et al, 1991, p. 155).

One major benefit of collaborative consultation is that speech and language is not relegated to a brief time slot in a separate room. Instead, it can be integrated within the classroom and the curriculum, and become more a part of your child's daily life. By observing the SLP, classroom teachers can learn how to modify the way they provide information and to provide feedback in a way that supports their students' communication needs. (Prelock et al, 1995, p. 290). For her part, the speech-language pathologist can use her skills not only for direct service in therapy, but also to examine the language needs of your child in the classroom. To succeed in using this approach, the speech-language pathologist needs "to inspect curriculum goals and/or objectives, assess daily classroom routines, become familiar with classroom demands" (Magnotta, 1991, p. 150). The SLP must also identify the many language needs within the curriculum that are hidden. These may include the need to be able to hear, process, and respond to three-stage commands, or the language expectations that a teacher has when she asks essay questions on a test. (See Chapter 8 for more on the hidden curriculum.) In addition, the SLP can assess your child's communication needs in the classroom related to:

- the formal curriculum
- prior knowledge that is needed to understand the curriculum
- the teacher's expectations
- the language of testing
- communication as classroom behavior
- communication interaction with teachers
- communication interaction with peers

In practice, it can be difficult for teachers and SLPs to find the time to collaborate effectively, although many teachers and SLPs strive to make this happen against all odds. It is rare that administrators set aside one period a day of planning time for the classroom teacher and SLP to collaborate. According to the ASHA Schools Survey 2000, SLPs spend only one hour per week on collaborative consultation during regular school hours. But, I have heard of many dedicated professionals who work together over lunch, or who jog together after school, or even do their grocery shopping together, to carve out some time when they can talk together and plan how to best help the children with whom they work.

Collaborative consultation needs to be based on mutual professional respect, respect for the child's family, and sharing of information. It can be difficult if egos or turf battles intervene. Sometimes the teacher feels that the SLP is invading her turf, or that she is free to leave and take a free period when the SLP appears to work in the classroom. Collaboration can only be successful if there is strong administrative support. In addition, the degree of collaboration needs to be discussed in detail at the beginning of the year. If your school system supports collaboration, celebrate the effort. Have luncheons, dessert parties, or bring in bouquets of the first Spring flowers. If your school system does not support collaborative efforts, advocate to make the collaboration happen.

CONSULTATIVE SERVICES

Sometimes the SLP does not work with a child directly, but is available to help school staff on a consultative basis. Consultative service may be used when your child is not eligible for direct service because her communication problems are mild, or when the SLP is monitoring progress but does not feel that direct service is needed. It should never be used because the SLP has too big a caseload, and does not have room for your child on her caseload. It should never be used to fit more children in when the SLP does not have time.

"Consultative services" can mean a variety of things for your child. Consultation may mean frequent observations of your child in the classroom and ongoing consultation with you and the teacher. One example might be when your child is able to use pronouns in therapy and just needs practice carrying over that skill to speaking and writing in class and at home. Consultation may also mean once-a-term hallway conferences between the SLP and teacher to discuss broad issues such as "How's Kerry doing in class?" This would never be sufficient for any child.

If consultative service is being discussed for your child, be sure that the IEP is very specific and contains a detailed implementation plan. The IEP should include the frequency with which the SLP will observe your child and meet with the teacher and what measurements will be used to determine whether the consultative service is meeting your child's needs. Will the SLP only consult with the teacher if asked? Will the SLP get reports from the teacher? Will the SLP observe your child directly? How will the SLP and the family communicate and how often? Will there be a home-based component to the services? Can you, as the parents, initiate a consultative visit if you see a problem when your child is doing homework? Is there a written contingency plan for starting direct services for your child if consultative services are not enough?

Which "Model" Is Best for Your Child?

Both pull-out and in-class therapy are widely used in the schools. Most school systems use one or the other. My professional opinion is that each type of treatment has benefits, and that the type of treatment should meet the needs of your individual child, not be used system-wide. For example, in-class therapy may be preferable for your child if she has goals related to learning the vocabulary, concepts, and language of instruction that is used in the class, since the SLP will have access to the textbooks and worksheets that your child is using. In-class therapy is also useful for students who need to practice conversational skills, such as staying on topic, as there are always communication partners available for practice. But, pull-out therapy is preferred for oral-motor exercises or intelligibility work, which require individual focus and attention, away from the distractions of the classroom.

When classroom-based, curriculum-related collaborative consultation is used, your child might receive a combination of in-class and pull-out therapy. She may receive individualized therapy, as well as therapy in the context of small group or whole class lessons. Her needs would be met by a team of professionals. When your child needs more work in a specific area, follow-up can be provided by any of

the specialists—including the classroom teacher—through homework, class work, or group or individual pull-out therapy.

Collaborative consultation can occur in special education settings, as well as in inclusive settings. Some parents prefer special education settings because more specialists are available, and they are usually available in one place. They see themselves as members of a team who are used to consulting and working with one another.

As a parent, you may or may not have much say as to what type of service delivery model will be used. According to the ASHA 2000 Schools Survey, in most cases (87 percent) the individual SLP determines the type of service delivery model. But, more than half of the approximately 3000 respondents (58 percent) indicated that a team also determines the model to be used.

The bottom line is that the service delivery model that is used should meet the needs of your child in therapy.

What Does ASHA Say about the Different Therapy Models?

In Spring 1996, The American Speech-Language-Hearing Association published a position statement on inclusive practices for children and adolescents with communication disorders. The ideas put forth are important and can be helpful in continuing to secure the individualized services that your child needs. It is ASHA's position that:

"An array of speech, language, and hearing services should be available to support children and youths with communication disorders. Inclusive practices consist of a range of service-delivery options that need not be mutually exclusive. They can include direct, classroom-based, community-based, and consultative intervention programming. Factors contributing to the determination of individual need include the child's age, type of disability, communication competence, language and cultural background, academic performance, social skills, family and teacher concerns, and the student's own attitudes about speech, language, and hearing services.

"ASHA recognizes that the provision of speech, language, and hearing services in educational settings is moving toward service delivery models that integrate intervention with general educational programming, often termed inclusion. Inclusion has numerous strengths, including natural opportunities for peer interaction, and available research suggests cautious optimism regarding its effectiveness in promoting communication abilities...." (ASHA, 1996, p. 35).

Other Members of the Communication Team

The role of the speech-language pathologist in helping your child develop communication skills has been explored in detail above. The team effort needed to support your child with Down syndrome, however, may include a wide range of professionals, including you, the parent, and the classroom teacher. Thanks to IDEA 97, special education and related services are now seen as a collaborative support system that brings services to the child to support her in the regular classroom and help her progress in the general curriculum. Other members of your child's IEP team who may help support her communication efforts include:

Classroom Teacher. This teacher is the frontline educator who works with your child on a daily basis. The classroom teacher has knowledge of the requirements of the curriculum, and is experienced in working with individual children and groups of children. The classroom teacher(s) would be involved in helping with language and speech in the classroom if your child is fully included in the elementary or middle school. Some classroom teachers could be involved if there is a mixture of inclusion and special education in the elementary or middle school years.

Special Education Teacher. The special education teacher is the specialist who identifies and analyzes your child's special needs as they relate to the academic curriculum, and to how she functions in the classroom. The special educator might suggest adaptations to classroom assignments to help your child master skills, or design a program to improve classroom behavior. In full inclusion, the special education teacher serves as a consultant to the classroom teacher, and is often involved in adapting materials. If your child is in a special education classroom, the special educator would be the classroom teacher.

Classroom Aide or Paraprofessional. Inclusive classrooms that include more than one student with disabilities may have an aide assigned to the classroom who helps the teacher or "floats" around to assist any students who are struggling in class. This individual may also be referred to as an instructional assistant. The aide may adapt worksheets; copy, collate, and hand out assignments; and assemble materials for projects. Generally, school systems do not have specific educational requirements for aides, although they may be required to attend orientation sessions or classes related to their responsibilities.

Personal Aide. Your child might also have a one-on-one or personal aide who may "shadow" your child in all classroom activities, or only selected activities. This aide is assigned directly to one child based on documented special education and/or communication needs. Responsibilities of the aide could include: to adapt materials and worksheets on a daily basis for an individual child; to interpret instructions given verbally by the teacher or on written class work; to physically help a child who has difficulties with mobility, stability, self-care skills, etc.; to help the teacher and children in the class understand the child who has severe speech intelligibility problems; or to monitor and maintain an augmentative communication device so that it meets the daily communication needs of a child. Whether or not your child needs a personal aide will be determined by her IEP team. See Chapter 3.

Communication Aide/SLP Assistant. The communication aide (CA) or SLP assistant helps the child with language and speech activities under the guidance and supervision of the speech-language pathologist. This is a new specialty designation. In the 2000 Schools Survey conducted by ASHA, 75 percent of the SLPs surveyed indicated that no SLP assistants are employed by their school.

The CA may work with the child on practice exercises (such as on grammar and vocabulary), and may be involved in adapting materials and in creating picture worksheets. The CA works under the supervision of the SLP in ongoing treatment, but cannot prescribe and develop the treatment plan. Sometimes, the classroom aide functions as a communication assistant for the child.

Since the SLP aide or assistant is a new job title, states are currently determining the educational requirements and clinical experience requirements for the SLP-A. Your state or school system may not use SLP aides, and children may receive all speech and language therapy from a speech-language pathologist.

Audiologist. The audiologist is the professional who diagnoses problems in hearing and provides treatment. Audiologists can measure how well your child hears sounds and words. If your child is found to have a hearing problem, the audiologist might recommend preferential seating (close to the teacher); amplification devices, such as auditory trainers or classroom amplification systems; and therapy, referred to as aural habilitation. Audiologists work closely with otolaryngologists (ENTs), who medically diagnose and treat problems of the ear. Some school systems have audiologists on their professional staffs. At other times, an audiologist may be called in as a consultant, or you may see a private audiologist and have the reports sent to the IEP team.

Physical Therapist. The physical therapist analyzes and treats difficulties in gross motor skills, including balance and equilibrium, sitting, standing, and walking. The PT will address muscle strength, endurance, and range of motion. If your child has difficulty walking in line or standing, well balanced, for long periods of time, the physical therapist might be called in to consult with the team.

Occupational Therapist. The occupational therapist analyzes and treats difficulties with fine motor skills including positioning, sensory integration, manual dexterity, and neuromuscular function. If your child has difficulty sitting in the existing classroom chairs, the OT might consult with the team to provide better seating. If your child has difficulty with writing and written assignments, the SLP and OT would work together with your child on an ongoing basis. The SLP would be involved in helping your child with the language involved in writing, such as the parts of speech that need to be included in a sentence. The OT would be involved in helping your child with eye-hand coordination, grasp, and other physical processes involved in writing.

Psychologist. The psychologist can administer and analyze cognitive, intelligence, and behavioral tests; interpret behavior; and provide insight into your child's cognitive, behavioral, and emotional functioning. A psychologist can use nonverbal intelligence tests so that your child's intelligence test scores will not be lowered by language difficulties and perhaps more accurately reflect your child's cognitive ability. See Chapter 3 for more information.

Counselor or Guidance Counselor. The counselor works with individuals or groups to address behavioral and social concerns within the classroom. The counselor or psychologist may be involved in planning positive behavioral support programs. Also, because many behavior problems are believed to result from frustrations due to an inability to communicate, the SLP should work closely with the counselor and psychologist.

Nurse. The school nurse can interpret medical history, provide information on medications that your child is currently taking, and administer and monitor medications during school hours. The nurse is often the professional who provides vision and hearing screenings for children in the school, although children with Down syndrome will require more in-depth evaluations from trained medical specialists (ophthalmologists and otolaryngologists).

Social Worker. If the school conducts home visits, the social worker is usually the professional who visits the home, reports on family dynamics, family strengths, needs, and concerns. The social worker often has knowledge regarding funding sources such as for augmentative communication devices.

Reading Teacher. Reading teachers may be involved in teaching reading to all children, or may get involved only if a child has a reading problem. The reading teacher may be involved in programs to assess reading readiness, and in prescriptive treatment which matches different reading approaches to children based on their needs and skills. With the current focus on basic skill mastery, some school systems have created programs in which reading specialists, rather than the classroom teachers, teach reading to children in the primary grades. For example, Montgomery County, Maryland, has a program called the Reading Initiative designed to ensure that all children are reading well by the end of second grade. Reading specialists join with the classroom teachers in teaching reading to groups of fifteen or fewer children, allowing students to get more individualized attention.

Music Therapist. The music therapist may use rhythm, performance, and listening activities to assist the child in developing skills. The therapist may also suggest background music that will help the child to focus and learn. It is rare to find a music therapist in regular education settings. Sometimes, the music teacher will function in this role. It is more likely to find a music therapist as part of the team in special education.

Adaptive Physical Education Teacher. These teachers use specialized equipment and activities to improve motor development and coordination. Adaptive PE may be based on individual exercise programs, as well as group sports activities. You are more likely to find Adaptive PE teachers in special education programs. Many children with Down syndrome are included in regular P.E. with their nondisabled peers and do not require a physical education teacher as part of the IEP planning team.

ENSURING THAT THE TEAM WORKS AS A TEAM

As Chapter 4 explains, your child's Individualized Education Program (IEP) will specify which goals, objectives, and benchmarks each professional is responsible for helping your child achieve. In some cases, this will seem obvious. For example, the speech-language pathologist is the one who will work on helping your child learn how to answer "wh" questions.

Sometimes, it is not obvious which professional will have the responsibility and how the implementation plan will be monitored. For example, if your child needs adaptations of classroom materials, such as picture multiple choice answers on worksheets, who is responsible for making up these worksheets every day? Is it the special educator, the speech language pathologist, the classroom teacher, the classroom aide, or the communication aide? When the responsibilities are not spelled

out, too often the parents are left to fill the gaps. Many parents have told me that they are the ones adapting materials on a daily basis. How about communication between school and home? Who will write and send a daily log? How and how often will the parents respond? This type of daily task can slip between the cracks easily. These types of responsibilities need to be spelled out very clearly in the IEP.

What happens when the specialists don't work as a team? Ideally, your child should have a case manager or service coordinator (depending on the school system job titles, other designations may be used) who facilitates the team members working together. But this doesn't always work smoothly. Many specialists are assigned to several schools, and are in any particular school one or two days per week. The team members' schedules are often different so that they are not in the same school on the same days. This makes it difficult to meet.

The large caseloads, paperwork requirements, and the need for frequent documentation and recordkeeping make professionals feel overwhelmed and swamped. In the ASHA 2000 Schools Survey, SLPs reported that burdensome amounts of paperwork (88 percent) and lack of time for planning, collaborations, and meetings (81 percent) are their greatest problems. Professionals who go from school to school may use their briefcase as their office. Some have laptop computers that enable them to centralize records, but others have access to records only on the days that they are in that particular school. Often, parents are left to coordinate the information and let each specialist know what the other is doing.

Sometimes, children are receiving services inside and outside of school. In these cases, parents become the primary conduit of information between school service providers and private service providers. At the Loyola College Speech and Language Center where I work, we exchange reports with school SLPs on a semiannual basis, the clinic SLP visits the child's school and home, and the school SLP visits the clinic and observes. On a weekly basis, however, the parent is the main source of information. For children in our program receiving sensory integration services through a private practice, it is about the same. There is regular communication between professionals, but the most frequent communication is between the parents and the professionals at each center.

The form at the end of this chapter can help you keep track of the many members of your child's communication team, as well as who is responsible for doing what.

REFERENCES

Achilles, J., Yates, R. R. & Freese, J. M. (1991). Perspectives from the field: Collaborative consultation in the speech and language program of the Dallas Independent School District. *Language, Speech and Hearing Services in Schools, 22,* 154-55.

American Speech-Language-Hearing Association (1996). Inclusive practices for children and youths with communication disorders: Position statement and technical report. *ASHA, 38* (Suppl. 16, pp. 35-44).

American Speech-Language-Hearing Association (2001). 2000 schools survey. (An Executive Summary of this survey is available at http://professional.asha.org/slp/schools_exec_sum.pdf)

Ferguson, M. L. (1992). Implementing collaborative consultation: An introduction. *Language, Speech and Hearing Services in Schools, 23,* 361-62.

Kumin, L. (1994). Intelligibility of speech in children with Down syndrome in natural settings: Parents' perspective. *Perceptual and Motor Skills, 78,* 307-13.

Magnotta, O. H. (1991). Looking beyond tradition. *Language, Speech and Hearing Services in Schools, 22,* 150-51.

Miller, J. F. (1988). The developmental asynchrony of language development in children with Down syndrome. In L. Nadel (Ed.), *The Psychobiology of Down syndrome* (pp. 315-44). Cambridge, MA: The MIT Press.

Peters-Johnson, C., Hoffman, P. & Norris, J. (1992). *Whole language intervention for children with articulation and language disabilities.* Rockville, MD: American Speech-Language-Hearing Association

Prelock, P. A., Miller, B. L. & Reed, N. L. (1995). Collaborative partnerships in a language in the classroom program. *Language, Speech and Hearing Services in Schools, 26,* 286-92.

Will, M.C. (1986). Educating children with learning problems: A shared responsibility. *Exceptional Children, 52,* 411-415.

Planning Form for the Communication Team

Name _____   Date _____

Who will serve on your child's communication team? Include names.

_____ Speech-Language Pathologist _____

_____ Classroom Teacher _____

_____ Special Education Teacher _____

_____ Communication Aide _____

_____ Classroom Aide _____

_____ Audiologist _____

_____ Physical Therapist _____

_____ Occupational Therapist _____

_____ Feeding Specialist _____

_____ Psychologist _____

_____ Guidance Counselor _____

_____ Nurse _____

_____ Social Worker _____

_____ Reading Teacher _____

_____ Music Therapist _____

_____ Adaptive Physical Education Teacher _____

_____ Other _____

Who will serve as consultants to the communication team?

_____ Pediatrician _____

_____ Specialized Physicians _____

_____ ENT _____

_____ Other _____

continued ▶

In school, who will be responsible for:

Adapting materials _____

Helping your child understand classroom instructions _____

Helping your child communicate with other children in class _____

Home-to-school communication _____

Other _____

Who else supports your child's communication?

At home: _____

_____

_____

_____

_____

_____

In school: _____

_____

_____

_____

_____

_____

In the community: _____

_____

_____

_____

_____

_____

CHAPTER 3

Evaluation and Eligibility for Speech-Language Services

Before the speech-language pathologist can become a part of your child's communication team at school, the school has to find your child eligible for speech and language therapy. Before this can happen, your child's speech and language abilities must be evaluated, and the following questions must be answered:

1. Is there a communication disorder affecting your child's speech and language?
2. Is the communication disorder affecting your child's ability to learn in the classroom?
3. Is your child eligible for related services according to the guidelines of the local educational agency (LEA) (usually the county or district school system)?

IDEA stipulates that when a child is first being considered for special education services, he must be evaluated "in all areas of suspected disability." This statute should ensure that speech and language are always tested in children with Down syndrome. Parents should not be told that "in our district, we don't test speech until the child is talking," or "in our district, we test speech at age three for all children with Down syndrome." Since most children with Down syndrome are delayed in speech development, communication should always be considered an area of "suspected disability."

Evaluation Procedures

If your child has not previously received special education services through the public school, he will need to undergo a comprehensive evaluation or assessment in all areas of learning and development in which he might need special education support. For instance, he may be given evaluations in cognitive, speech-language, fine motor, and gross motor skills. These evaluations will determine whether he has difficulties in these areas that would have an "educational impact" on him, and whether he therefore needs therapies, classroom modifications, instructional support, or other assistance to succeed at school. If he is already receiving special education services through the school system, his skills will periodically be re-evaluated to determine whether his needs have changed so that he now needs more or less support. If performed by the school, these evaluations will be done at no charge to you, the parent.

Since this book is about communication skills for children with Down syndrome, we will focus on how the speech and language portion of your child's evaluation should ideally be conducted. For information about evaluations in general, you may want to refer to the book *Negotiating the Special Education Maze: A Guide for Parents and Teachers* by Winifred Anderson et al (Woodbine House, 1997).

If possible, speech and language evaluation should be conducted over several sessions in a familiar environment with familiar people. Ideally, parents should be able to observe too, and let the SLP know whether the communication abilities your child demonstrates during the evaluation represent his true abilities.

Studies have shown that children with communication difficulties perform more poorly with unfamiliar examiners than with familiar examiners (Fuchs et al, 1985). A one-session evaluation in an unfamiliar setting with unfamiliar examiners is unlikely to give an accurate picture of your child's typical language performance. This is frustrating for parents and professionals. Often, professionals are allowed a limited amount of time (such as two hours or one day) to conduct an evaluation, score the test batteries, and present the results to the family. This situation is most likely to occur with the first evaluation, or if your LEA uses a county diagnostic center for testing, rather than the speech language pathologist in the neighborhood school who knows your child.

If your child must be evaluated by unfamiliar people in an unfamiliar setting, then supplement the evaluation with videotapes (preferable) or audiotapes of your child engaged in communication at home, with siblings, friends, and grandparents. This can become part of the evaluation portfolio (see below) and can be available to the speech- language pathologists to help document your child's functional communication abilities. And be sure that observations and insight are provided by the regular education classroom teacher. IDEA 97 specifically allows for material provided by the parents and teachers to be included in the evaluation. This information is most difficult to have included at the initial evaluation, because you, your child, and the testers are all new to each other.

Try to go to the testing center beforehand with your child to familiarize him with the setting, and bring familiar toys or books with you on the day of the evaluation. You want the testing environment to be as natural a situation as possible. Collaboration between parents and professionals is essential to an accurate evaluation.

AREAS EVALUATED

A comprehensive speech and language evaluation should include assessment of:

- **speech:** your child's verbal output,
- **oral-motor:** The strength and coordination of muscles in the mouth and face used for speech,
- **receptive language:** your child's understanding of language through hearing and reading,
- **expressive language:** your child's language output through speech and writing, as well as pragmatics skills, how your child uses his communication skills to interact with others.

For school-aged children, evaluation should also include language and literacy skills, and curriculum-based language skills. It is important to explore how your child's communication skills affect his function in the classroom setting.

In addition, referrals should be made for audiological (hearing) evaluation and otolaryngological (ear, nose, and throat) evaluation. Children with Down syn-

drome are at high risk for ear infections and middle ear fluid, which can lead to hearing problems, and research has demonstrated that hearing ability affects success in the classroom. Hearing testing should be conducted on a regularly scheduled basis, and should include assessment of middle ear function and fluid in the ear, pure tone testing (hearing testing of a variety of sound frequencies), speech reception (testing ability to identify words that are heard accurately), and central auditory processing (testing the ability to understand and make sense out of what is heard).

If needed, your child may also be referred for other evaluations. For example, he may be referred to a neurologist if he is having difficulty processing information from the environment. Such a neurological evaluation might be recommended if your child does not seem to understand or respond to speech or gestures, or is easily overwhelmed by the sights, sounds, smells, and other sensations in his environment. Your child could also be referred to an occupational therapist for an evaluation of his sensory integration skills if he seems to crave or avoid certain sensory experiences (touch, spinning, high places) or seems to have sensory overload or difficulties processing sensory information.

These evaluations can help pinpoint problems that may be interfering with your child's speech and language skills. Remember, speech and expressive language are "output systems" based on input from vision, hearing, touch, and other sensations, as well as on interpretation of that sensory information. Consequently, problems with making sense out of sensations received from the environment can contribute to communication problems.

After your child's initial speech and language evaluation, he will likely be evaluated again many times over his school career. These reevaluations may or may not be as comprehensive as the initial evaluation, depending on why they are being done. Here are some reasons reevaluations may be done:

- to determine whether your child continues to have a disability requiring special education or related services;
- to determine his present levels of performance and educational needs;
- to determine whether he needs any additions or modifications to the therapy he is receiving to enable him to reach his IEP goals;
- as pre- and post-tests to determine the effectiveness of a therapy technique;
- to document what your child has learned;
- for entrance to specialized programs, such as for children who have difficulty with auditory memory.

Before any reevaluations are conducted, you have a right to ask the SLP what will be evaluated and why, and to ask that results be discussed with you. For initial testing, it is likely that you will be consulted and need to sign permission forms, but reevaluations are often done as therapy progresses, and parents may not be consulted or informed that testing is being done. It is important for parent to have that information, and to be able to provide feedback. What if the testing was done when your child was not feeling well? Would this testing be accurate? What if the testing was done on the morning of a school trip and your child was very excited about the trip and refused to perform on the test? What if the test results show that your child can now use five-word sentences? You need to know that information in order to expect more from him at home. You need to know what is happening and you need to know the results of the testing. You can ask that the IEP stipulate that you be informed of any reevaluations.

TYPES OF TESTS USED

Since the focus of this book is on language for classroom success and school inclusion, we will not go into a detailed discussion of speech and language evaluation. You should know, however, that IDEA requires that testing be done in your child's usual mode of communication, which may include sign language or augmentative communication. The following brief overview is intended to help you understand some of the more effective ways of testing communication skills in children with Down syndrome.

FORMAL TESTS

Standardized Tests. Standardized tests are often used in evaluating speech and language abilities. When a test is standardized, it means that the test has *validity* (it measures what it is supposed to measure), *reliability* (scores are consistent), a standard set of instructions and standard administration procedures, standard scoring, and provides norms. Norms are comparison scores that are used to measure your child's performance against the performance of a group of children of the same age or grade who served as comparison subjects when the test was being developed. The major problem with norms is that they are scores of typically developing children, not children with Down syndrome. So, when the examiner compares your child's scores (a child with Down syndrome) with the norms (scores for children with typical development), the test result may or may not be relevant. Although we have some physical development norms (height, weight, and head circumference), we do not, at this time, have norms for psychological, educational, and speech and language tests for children with Down syndrome.

Standardized tests present some difficulties for children with Down syndrome, because standard instructions mean that the examiner may not be able to repeat the instructions, or rephrase them, or allow extra time. Psychologists tell us that you cannot violate the rules of standardized tests, so if adaptations are made, the scores are no longer considered valid. And if the norms with which your child's scores are being compared are not norms for children with Down syndrome, the scores may not be meaningful. This explains why the test results that you, as parents, are given often seem so out of sync with your child's performance in daily life. For example, you might be told that your five-year-old's scores are at the level of a three-year-old—that his language output and speech, or ability to verbalize similarities and differences or copy block designs (on an intelligence test) are at the level of a typically developing three-year-old. But what does that really mean?

Criterion Referenced Tests. These tests evaluate how your child performs on a specific set of skills, such as auditory memory or the ability to identify the number of words in a sentence or the number of syllables in a word. Unlike norm-referenced tests, they do not compare your child's performance to other children's. They merely determine what your child is and is not able to do.

Criterion referenced tests are helpful in educational planning because they usually document which skills your child has mastered as well as which skills need to be mastered. If we describe the results on a criterion referenced test, rather than just giving a score, these results can be meaningful. So, criterion referenced tests can often serve as guidelines for not only what skills your child has, but what he needs to learn next. The results can help in planning treatment.

INFORMAL ASSESSMENT

The purpose of informal testing is to observe and evaluate what your child actually does to communicate. Here is where teacher observations and videotapes can be used to provide a picture of your child's skills in his natural environment. Informal assessment can also be used to evaluate your child's attention and on-task behavior. Some school systems rely more heavily on formal tests, while others place more emphasis on actual performance. According to the school SLP survey conducted by the American Speech-Language-Hearing Association, 85 percent of school systems across the United States have entrance and exit criteria for eligibility for speech and language services. Most rely on formal or criterion based test scores.

There is growing recognition that formal testing does not always provide an accurate picture of a child's actual daily communication skills. In a testing situation, children with Down syndrome may respond inconsistently, shift their attention rapidly, or be difficult to motivate. Their responses may also be affected by problems with memory, hearing, vision, or motor skills. Also, as mentioned earlier, they generally do not do their best when testing is conducted by unfamiliar examiners in unfamiliar surroundings. And, even familiar examiners are caught in a difficult situation when test results and their real-life observations do not agree. For example, the test results might show that your child cannot identify the color green, but the SLP knows that he just identified "green" in a classroom unit on trees. School speech-language pathologists may work with a child for several years and may therefore have excellent individual and classroom observations of his actual communication skills.

Portfolio Assessment. Portfolio assessment is emerging as an important trend in evaluations. Rather than using one testing session to evaluate your child's skills, a folder is maintained of his progress over time, with samples of his work in language arts or social studies or communications skills. Other terms used to describe this method are *authentic assessment* or *the new assessment.* (Assessing real samples of the child's skills *is* authentic assessment, but in popular usage, this type of evaluation, which usually includes portfolio assessment, is referred to as portfolio assessment.)

Portfolio assessment involves collecting and evaluating multiple representative samples of your child's work. It is similar to the portfolios that artists and graphic design specialists have always carried to interviews to demonstrate their skills, and to the manila folders that teachers use during school meetings to show parents examples of their child's academic performance. Portfolios contain authentic examples of your child's communication abilities in various situations, and also show problems encountered and progress made over time.

The specific samples to be included in the portfolio may be mandated by the school system or the speech and language or special education program, or they may be individually designed. Video or audio tape recordings of the student speaking or reading, writing samples, logs and journals, classroom tests, and projects may be part of the portfolio. Anecdotal examples and home and school checklists may also be part of the portfolio. Portfolios may also include results of formal tests and observations, as well as self-evaluation and peer evaluation, and parent evaluation or parent reaction to a student's schoolwork.

What to include in the portfolio folder is one of the major decisions to be made. There may be several folders comprising a student's portfolio, such as a home folder, school folder, and self-esteem folder. A *collection portfolio* or a *working portfolio* includes all work output from the child. A *display portfolio* or *showcase portfolio* includes samples of the best work only.

A report of your child's progress can be made and learning goals and strategies can be determined based upon the portfolio. Authentic assessment grades the child on his progress, not on a comparison with another child's performance and not on a normal bell curve. Portfolio assessment can involve the student in self-evaluation. The student often fills out a reflective evaluation form, and chooses the items to be included in the display or showcase portfolio. These activities help the student take ownership of his portfolio and the work included in it. A sample of a portfolio self-reflection is included on the next page.

Not only can portfolios be used to document ongoing progress, they can also be used to demonstrate your child's skills to unfamiliar teachers and administrators. Remember that IDEA 97 now permits parent feedback and information to be included in the evaluation and considered for placement and related services decisions. So, if you are faced with an unfamiliar examiner or with teachers or administrators who do not believe that they can meet your child's needs or that your child can succeed in an inclusive setting, use a portfolio to demonstrate your child's skills. You might want to include a video of your child interacting in Sunday School, worksheets from preschool or previous school years, or samples of your child's writing on a report, a poem, or even a self-made Mother's Day card. If your child uses a computer, you might include some word processed material.

Speech and Language Portfolio

Student's Name: _____

Grade Level: _____

What are you working on in Language Arts in class? _____

_____

_____

_____

What are you working on in speech-language therapy? _____

_____

_____

_____

What is included in this portfolio?

                Class worksheets _____   Homework _____

                   Class projects _____   Audiotapes _____

                       Videotapes _____   Other _____

For each sample of work, describe why you chose to include it in your portfolio!

1._____

_____

2._____

_____

3._____

_____

4._____

_____

5._____

_____

The portfolio can be used when your child enters the school system, when he changes school levels, or when he is going to attend a new school. It is a way of introducing your child and highlighting his abilities. Because it demonstrates how much your child can do, you can use it to help you advocate for inclusion.

Curriculum/Work Objectives Mastery. Curriculum/work objectives mastery is another trend in evaluation. Rather than trying to determine what test score is needed to succeed in a regular education class, the special education teacher or other staff member analyzes the curricular demands, as designated in the IEP. What skills does your child need to succeed in learning the curriculum in school? Given your child's abilities and needs, what supports and modifications may he need to help him master those skills? Speech and language therapy is one of the supports that may be needed. Testing or portfolio assessment can then be used to document the progress your child makes in mastering the curricular skills.

Whole Language Assessment. This is another trend in the schools. Rather than focus an evaluation on the elements of speech and language traditionally evaluated by SLPs, all components of language (including speaking, reading, writing, and understanding) are assessed. This is helpful for children with Down syndrome who are likely to be more advanced in understanding and reading than they are in speaking. Whole language assessment cannot usually be used to determine a child's eligibility for speech therapy, but it can be used to figure out effective language strategies to use with your child in class and in speech therapy sessions.

Dynamic Assessment or Diagnostic Therapy. In dynamic assessment, the child is seen for multiple sessions for a short trial period of therapy. This trial period is designed to determine whether the child improves after guided learning and what methods will be effective for this child.

In Ohio, for example, school districts can conduct Intervention-Based Multifactored Evaluation projects (IBMFEs) based on a problem-solving, diagnostic therapy approach. An intervention plan is developed for the child based on the curriculum and the child's needs in the classroom. The interventions are then used as short-term diagnostic therapy. "If the interventions work for the child, there is usually no need to test the child and label them. If the interventions don't work they may be changed and/or modified. If they still don't work of if they are too difficult to maintain in the regular classroom, the child will be referred for testing" (*Parents' Guide to MFE's,* p. 23).

Checklists and Developmental Scales. Finally, a recognition is emerging that parents know a great deal about their child's communication and that speech and language evaluation is a collaborative effort. Language tests that include parents' evaluation of their child's language as an integral part of the test include:

- *Environmental Language Inventory* (MacDonald and Horstmeier),
- *Communication & Symbolic Behavior Scale* (Wetherby & Prizant),
- *Learning Accomplishment Profile* (Sanford & Zelman),
- *MacArthur Communicative Development Inventories* (Fenson et. al.),
- *Language Development Survey* (Rescorla), and
- *Sequenced Inventory of Communication Development* (Prather et al.).

Checklists and observation forms that are developed by the teacher and/or speech-language pathologist can also be used by parents to provide feedback regarding their child's speech and language and educational functional level. They can be used to document the progress that occurs with speech-language pathology treatment and with progress in the classroom. For example, parents may be able to report that their child is using longer sentences at home, or is indicating that he doesn't know what to do when he does not understand the instructions that have been given. This feedback is helpful in designing and modifying treatment programs.

EVALUATING NONVERBAL CHILDREN

Many schools will say they can't evaluate your child's speech and language skills if he doesn't have any speech. Is that true?

There is a difference, as we have previously discussed, between speech and language. If your child can understand and follow instructions, receptive language tests (such as the *Peabody Picture Vocabulary Test* and the *Receptive One-Word Picture Vocabulary Test*) can be used. These tests can give an idea of how much single-word vocabulary your child is able to understand. If your child is using sign language or an augmentative system, testing can be done using those systems. The goal is to describe how your child communicates, and how successful he is with using expressive language, as well as receptive language. So, language output (expressive language) can be evaluated as long as your child has a usable language system.

Speech, (including articulation, voice, loudness, etc) cannot be evaluated until your child is speaking using sounds and word approximations. However, the precursors to speech (respiration skills, sound production skills) can be evaluated for any child. A speech evaluation could investigate reasons that a child is not speaking, such as hearing loss or dyspraxia. The school can conduct a speech-language evaluation for any child to describe what the child is doing to understand the language in his world, and to communicate with his world.

UNDERSTANDING TEST RESULTS

After your child's evaluation, IDEA requires that you be given a written copy of the evaluation results.

Feel free to ask questions so that you understand what the test results mean. Good questions to ask include:

- What does this test measure?
- What is the format of the test?
- How many sections and different types of questions are asked?
- Can you show or tell me examples of each type of question asked?
- What does my child's score mean?
- What problems do the test results highlight?
- What therapy, supports, modifications follow from the results?

The Eligibility Decision

Your child's speech and language evaluation may be the basis for the decision as to whether your child receives speech and language services, as well as the amounts and types of services that he qualifies for.

Many schools use a discrepancy rating to determine whether a child is eligible for speech-language therapy. That means that in order to receive speech and lan-

Evaluations and Labels

Some people view the goal of a speech and language evaluation as to diagnose and label the problem. The difficulty is that "labels" in the area of special education often put the child on a long road that does not lend itself easily to change. Labels may be limiting and lower expectations. "Labels have a way of drawing our attention away from understanding the individual as a complex and competent person. Rather, what we see is reinterpreted within the stereotypes associated with the particular disability category" (Kliewer and Biklen, 1996).

When labels are used for a child with Down syndrome, they usually highlight that child's problems and weaknesses, not his strengths. A diagnostic evaluation should highlight both, and should explore the best channels and approaches for that child so that treatment can be planned to address the difficulties he is experiencing.

My own view of evaluation can perhaps be summed up best in the words of Jason Kingsley, a young man with Down syndrome who co-wrote a book called *Count Us In*: "Do the things that you *can* do...." [That's what I see as the purpose of evaluation—to see what your child can do and what is difficult for him] "...and learn the things that you *can't* do. When you learn the things that you *can't* do, it then becomes the things you *can* do" (Kingsley and Levitz, 1994, p. 180). That's what I see as the purpose of therapy—to help your child learn to do the things that are difficult for him. Evaluation and therapy are part of the same process leading to more effective functional speech and language skills.

guage services, the child's language test scores and intelligence test scores must be at different levels. If the child's language scores are at the same level as her mental age intelligence test scores, she can be denied services. The justification is that her language function is commensurate with her intelligence level. The problem with this approach is that many intelligence tests are based on language and use language for the questions and answers. Thus, language test scores and standardized intelligence test scores are more than likely to be highly correlated.

Another approach to determining eligibility has been to use a developmental model in which your child's test results are compared to those of typically developing children at that chronological age. Usually, the school has specific entrance and exit criteria to qualify for speech and language services. For example, your child may need to score one year below chronological age, or two standard deviations below norms for the age to qualify for services. Services may not be continued if your child's scores, based on annual assessment, improve so that they are age appropriate. Sometimes, chronological age level is used and sometimes mental age level is used to determine eligibility through this formula.

Both of these approaches to determining eligibility place parents in a Catch-22 situation. In situation 1, since cognitive testing is often based on language ability (both in understanding and following test instructions and in answering questions verbally), it is no surprise that cognitive levels and language levels may appear similar. In situation 2, your child can only receive services when he is below expected levels (certain cut-off scores). So, if your child improves, he can be denied services, and services will only begin again when his test scores fall a specific amount below age level.

If your child is denied services on the grounds that his language skills are commensurate with his intelligence, request that the psychologist administer a nonverbal intelligence test and that the speech-language pathologist administer a complete language battery. This may help establish that there *is* a discrepancy between his language and cognitive abilities. See the section on "What If Your Child Is Denied School-Based Therapy," below, for more information.

In some, but not all, states, children aged 3-9 may be found eligible for special education and related services, including speech-language therapy, solely on the basis of having a "developmental delay." IDEA allows, but does not *require,* this provision. In school districts that allow this provision, children qualify for services if they are found to have a developmental delay in physical, cognitive, communication, social or emotional, or adaptive development. In states that use this eligibility criteria, it is usually easy for children with Down syndrome to qualify for speech-language therapy, since most have at least some developmental delay at this age. To find out whether your state allows young children to qualify for services under the developmental delay criteria, ask for a copy of your state's special education regulations from the State Department of Education. Libraries, especially law libraries, should also have copies of the regulations.

For children who are aged 14 and above, another way to qualify for speech therapy is as a transition service. Beginning at this age, students' IEPs must list the services they need to prepare for their transition to the workplace or postsecondary education. If your child has speech and language problems that will affect his abilities to succeed on the job, then therapy should be provided to address these problems.

What If Your Child Is Denied School-Based Therapy?

If the school system says that your child with Down syndrome is not eligible to receive speech and language therapy, and if you feel that your child needs services, there are three possible alternatives. One is to continue to advocate for services. A second alternative is to seek private speech and language services in another center or setting. A third alternative is to seek resources and information from professionals, workshops, and publications and to try to help your child at home.

When you are denied school services, talk with the SLP and the IEP team to determine what would make your child eligible for services. It is important to understand the reason for denial. Ask the SLP and/or the service coordinator about the criteria for determining whether services will be provided in your LEA (local educational agency—usually the county school district).

Your child's program must legally be determined by his needs, not by the diagnosis of Down syndrome. So, if the SLP tells you, "We don't give therapy to children with Down syndrome who are under three years old," or "Children with Down syndrome have pull-out therapy for twenty minutes once a week," know that both of these statements violate the guidelines in IDEA 97. Your child's speech and language program must be individually designed. Your child cannot be turned down for speech and language services based on the diagnosis of Down syndrome. Your child can only be turned down because he, as an individual, is not eligible for services based on the school's interpretation of the federal legislation.

Sometimes children with Down syndrome are denied services (or adequate services) on the grounds that the school system "just doesn't have enough speech-language pathologists." A variation on this is "We can't hire enough SLPs even though we try." This is the school system's problem, not your problem. If your child qualifies for services, but there is a shortage of speech-language pathologists, check whether the school system will pay for therapy in another facility, such as a hospital or university clinic.

TEST RESULTS THAT DON'T SHOW A "NEED" FOR SERVICES

Another reason that therapy is denied is that test results show that your child's language and cognitive function are at the same level. If there is no discrepancy, the SLP may tell you that therapy will not help since your child's language level is right where it should be, at his cognitive level. A typical situation is that of seven-year-old Ken, who is not currently receiving speech therapy in school because they say that his speech and language are at the same level as his cognitive ability.

How can you respond to this denial of service? The first step is to separate out cognitive skills and speech/language skills. Most intelligence tests are heavily lan-

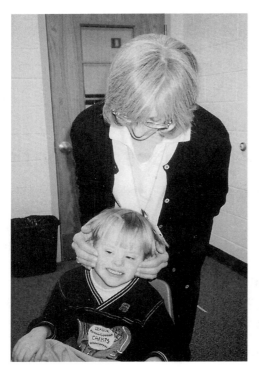

guage-based, relying on oral directions and verbal or written responses to many items. Many children have been denied speech and language services because their language test scores are at the same level as their intelligence scores. If you used a language-based test to test cognitive abilities, it would make sense that the language and IQ scores would be similar because you would be relying on many of the same skills on both tests.

Nonverbal Intelligence Tests. Request that your child be tested with a nonverbal intelligence test. There are two nonverbal cognitive tests that are often used by psychologists. They are widely accepted as measures of intelligence.

The Comprehensive Test of Nonverbal Intelligence (CTONI) can be used to test children from ages six years to eighteen years. This test measures six different types of nonverbal reasoning ability. No oral responses, reading, or writing are required. There are two subtests in each of three ability areas. The areas are analogical reasoning, categorical classification, and sequential reasoning. In addition to standard scores, percentiles, and age equivalents, the test results in nonverbal intelligence quotient, pictorial nonverbal intelligence quotient, and geometric nonverbal intelligence quotient. The norms are provided in one-year intervals, so missing several questions may result in a score one year lower. Your child would need good visual perceptual skills in order to complete the items on the test.

The Revised Leiter International Performance Scale (Leiter-R) tests from ages two to seventeen years. The Leiter was revised in 1997 and has many subtests. It is designed as a nonverbal intelligence and cognitive abilities test. The norms, although they were based on typically developing children, are presented in smaller intervals, so a more precise score is available than with the CTONI. Norms are available for chronological ages two to twenty-one years, so the test can be used throughout your child's school career. It includes twenty subtests in the general areas of reasoning skills, visualization skills, memory skills, and attention skills, and thus can provide a broad profile of cognitive skills. The test provides IQ scores, percentiles, grade equivalents, and age equivalents. The test has a high correlation with the Wechsler Intelligence Scale for Children (WISC), which is the IQ test that most schools routinely administer to children.

Two other tests that are sometimes used are the Matrix Analogy Test and the Universal Nonverbal Intelligence test (UNIT). Both are not used as frequently, or accepted as widely, as the CTONI and the Leiter-R.

Speech and Language Tests. You should also request a complete battery of speech and language tests. For many children with Down syndrome, the results of the separate intelligence testing and language testing will show a discrepancy. Research has indicated that many children with Down syndrome have language impairment that is greater than would be expected by mental age scores. Often services are denied based on the assumption, following language-based cognitive testing, that language is at the same level as cognition. However, if you can demonstrate that your child's language level is lower than his cognitive level, services cannot be denied based on this factor.

WHEN TESTING DOESN'T SHOW A DISCREPANCY

It is possible that testing will not show a discrepancy. Then, your child can be denied speech and language therapy on the grounds that he has similar functional levels in language and cognition.

Unfortunately, discrepancy formulas are still widely used to determine who qualifies for speech-language services. This is the case even though IDEA 97 stipulates that related services are supposed to be provided to help a child progress in the regular education curriculum. A survey by the American Speech-Language-Hearing Association (2001) found that in 85 percent of school districts across the United States, entrance and dismissal criteria are used to determine student eligibility for speech-language pathology services. In 55 percent of the cases, entrance and exit criteria are adopted district-wide; in 39 percent of the cases, the criteria are adopted state-wide. Almost all of the speech-language pathologists responding to the survey (97 percent) reported that the criteria are based on standardized tests. SLPs also report using descriptive measures/nonstandardized tests (82 percent).

So, even though psychologists tell us that the scores for children with Down syndrome should not be compared with the norms for typically developing children and even though portfolio assessment and observational data systems are available, standardized tests are still the most widely used measure for determining eligibility for services (ASHA, 2001).

It is important for your family, teachers, and the speech-language pathologists to work together to document your child's need for services. Although there is still a major reliance on standardized test information, remember that nonstandardized and descriptive measures can be used to supplement the test score information. It may be possible to argue that your child needs better speech/language skills to succeed in inclusion, regardless of his standardized test scores. After all, the major criteria for speech and language services under IDEA 97 is that the services are needed to help the child progress in the regular educational curriculum. The need can be demonstrated by showing samples of your child's work in class and documenting the problems that he is encountering in class that are based on language and speech difficulties. For example, your child may need to improve his ability to follow instructions or may need help learning vocabulary in specific subject areas such as science.

The 1997 amendments to IDEA strengthened the role of the family in providing input, and participating in planning and monitoring the child's IEP. By law, your family must be able to be involved as a member of the IEP team that determines whether your child qualifies for services. Determination of eligibility shall be made "by a team of qualified professionals and the parent of the child." (IDEA, 614, 4, A). Initial evaluation and reevaluations must take into consideration, in addition to tests, "evaluations and information provided by the parents of the child, current classroom-based assessments and observations, and teacher and related service providers [SLP comes under this category] observation." The legislation mandates that classroom-based assessments and input from parents, teachers, and specialists such as the speech-language pathologist, be included in the evaluation process. So, there is legislative support for greater collaboration and joint decision making.

Alternatives to School-Based Therapy

During the elementary school years, most of a child's waking hours revolve around school, homework, school projects, and other activities related to school. Because their child has such a full schedule, many parents rely on the school as the sole provider of speech and language help. There are several problems with doing this, including the fact that your child may not receive consistent and ongoing therapy due to school eligibility criteria. One year, your child may be eligible for services, but the next year, his progress or test scores may make him ineligible.

Always remember that the schools are not the only source of speech and language services for your child. If you feel that your child needs services, get an independent speech and language evaluation that is based on "need," rather than "eligibility." Community-based clinics, university training programs (college clinics), hospital-based clinics, and private practitioners also provide speech-language pathology services. Some parents have arranged for private speech-language pathology services (outside of school hours) with the speech-language pathologist from the school. Some school systems do not allow their specialists to see children from their school caseload through private practice. However, if this is allowed, it may be an ideal situation, since the SLP knows your child and your child is familiar with the SLP. This may be an especially good option during summer vacation if extended year services are not available.

The cost of private speech therapy may be a factor, but many centers have reduced fees, a sliding fee scale, or scholarship assistance. Some health insurance policies cover speech and language intervention, but other insurers cover only speech and language assessment or a limited number of treatment sessions. Insurance companies may require reevaluation at certain intervals and have other stipulations. Unlike with physical and occupational therapy, referral and/or a prescription from a physician is not required for speech-language pathology services. Many pediatricians, ENTs, and other physicians will recommend speech-language therapy, but you can also seek an evaluation and/or treatment by self-referral or by recommendation of a parent or professional.

If you think your child needs speech-language pathology services, explore every option to provide those services for him. Remember, your child's communication skills are the foundation of his education.

References

Anderson, W., Chitwood, S. & Hayden, D. (1997). *Negotiating the special education maze: A guide for parents and teachers.* Bethesda, MD: Woodbine House.

ASHA 2001 Survey. *See citation in Chapter 2.*

Brown, L., Sherbenou, R. & Johnsen, S. *Test of nonverbal intelligence,* 3rd edition (TONI-3). Austin, TX: PRO-ED.

Fuchs, D., Fuchs, L, Powers, M., Daily, A. (1985). Bias in the assessment of handicapped children. *American Educational Research Jouranl, 22,* 185-97.

Kingsley, J. & Levitz, M. (1994). *Count us in.* New York: Harcourt-Brace.

Leiter, R.G. & Arthur, G. *Leiter-R international performance scale.* Wood Dale, IL: C.H. Stoelting Co.

Parents' guide to MFE's (multifactored evaluations). Columbus, OH: Ohio Coalition for the Education of Children with Disabilities.

Wolf, D.P. (1990). Portfolio assessment: Sampling student work. *Educational Leadership, 46,* 4-10.

CHAPTER 4

Planning for a Communication Support Program: Your Child's IEP

Most children with Down syndrome qualify for special education services, and they will have an individualized education program (IEP). As you probably know, an IEP is a written contract that states what the public school system agrees to do to help a child with disabilities benefit from her education. If your child is in an inclusive setting, it is essential for her IEP to spell out how her speech and language needs will be supported in the classroom. This chapter offers suggestions to help you in the planning and implementation of the IEP to ensure that your child's IEP provides the communication support she needs.

What Must Be Included in the IEP?

The requirements for IEPs are specified in the Individuals with Disabilities Education Act, IDEA 1997, otherwise known as Public Law 105-17. This is the federal law that guarantees children with disabilities a free, appropriate public education in the least restrictive environment. The most recent amendments to the law assume that the least restrictive environment is the regular education classroom, unless a child is unable to make progress in the general education curriculum there. Under the law, special education and "related services" such as speech and language pathology are viewed as supports to help children progress in regular education settings.

For every area of need, including speech and language, your child's IEP must include information on:

- ***Present levels of performance (PLOP)***—What are your child's current strengths and needs in academic and developmental areas? For speech and language, the documentation of PLOP includes the results of standardized tests, classroom observations, and portfolio assessment described in Chapter 3. Parent input, as well as teacher input should be included.

- **Measurable goals and objectives**—What your child is working to achieve, in all areas of need (see below for more information). This should include short-term, as well as long-term objectives.
- **How will progress be measured?** How will we know if the student has achieved her goals? What will we use as measurements to monitor the child's progress?
- **Statement of special education and related services**— What services will your child receive, where, and when. For example: individual speech and language therapy, provided

twice a week for thirty minutes at a time, once in the classroom and once in the therapy room. Remember, the scheduling and frequency of services must be keyed to your child's unique needs, and not based on some arbitrary formula such as: "We provide 30 minutes of speech therapy twice weekly in groups for children with Down syndrome." Likewise, putting your child in group therapy because the SLP says, "I don't have time in my schedule to see children individually" is not a legitimate reason. Chapter 3 describes the range of settings in which therapy can be provided in a public school setting. In addition, if your child is in private school, IDEA 97 provides that "services may be provided on the premises of private, including parochial schools." [sec 612 (a) (10)].

- **Supplementary aids and services**—Supports that your child needs to function in the classroom. This may include a classroom aide or a personal aide, or specialized equipment such as a classroom amplification system or an auditory trainer.
- **Program modifications**—How teaching methods, curriculum, classroom setting, or other elements will be adapted to help your child succeed in reaching his goals. See Chapters 6 and 7 for more information.
- **Supports for school personnel**—Training or assistance that will help professionals involved with your child teach her more effectively. This may include continuing education such as a workshop about children with Down syndrome, in-service classes to teach sign language to teachers and aides, or a resource library of books and materials. See below for more information.

Ensuring SLP Input at Your Child's IEP Meeting

If you want to make sure that your child's IEP provides the communication support she needs in the inclusive classroom, it would be logical to expect the SLP to attend the IEP planning meeting, wouldn't it? However, under IDEA, these are the only people who are required to be on a child's IEP team:

- parent,
- regular educator,
- special educator, or, if appropriate, at least one special education provider of the child,
- person who can interpret evaluation information,
- professional representing the school district who knows the general curriculum and has information on the resources that will be available to help the child.

If your child's primary disability is a speech impairment and the only special education service she receives is speech-language therapy, then the SLP might be expected to attend as "the special education provider of the child." In kindergarten and the primary grades, some children with Down syndrome are receiving speech and language services as their only special education service. In that case, the SLP should be the special educator to attend IEP meetings. Otherwise, the speech-language pathologist is not required by federal law to attend the IEP meeting. But if the SLP is not present, how can the meeting be a *team* planning meeting?

If your child receives speech and language services through the school, it is your right to specifically request that the SLP attend your child's IEP meeting, and be an integral part of the planning process. If this is not possible, the SLP would submit your child's speech and language goals to the team before the meeting. You should also try to talk with her before the meeting. It is especially important to try to get the SLP to attend the IEP planning meeting if you expect the team to object to certain communication-related services you will be requesting at the meeting—for instance, increased therapy services, or a change in service delivery from pull-out to push-in. Also make sure the SLP attends if you think the team might find your child ineligible for speech services and deny the services. Sometimes, it is difficult to reschedule the meeting, but it is worth it to have the SLP in attendance if she will help advocate for your child.

Planning Meaningful Communication Goals and Objectives

Your child's IEP must contain overall annual goals as well as short-term instructional objectives for every area of need identified on her IEP. The annual goals are just that—goals or new skills that your child is expected to achieve, or make significant progress toward achieving, in the course of a year. Annual goals are general. They will usually be stated in the form: "To understand and use the vocabulary concepts appropriate for third grade."

Some examples of speech and language goals during the school years are:

- To improve comprehension vocabulary;
- To understand comparative and superlative concepts;
- To follow three-stage commands;

- To follow multistage school directions;
- To master vocabulary for a specific subject (science, community helpers);
- To improve lip closure and decrease tongue protrusion;
- To understand the meaning of conversational idioms;
- To learn to use requests;
- To improve the understanding and use of synonyms;
- To improve the use of pronouns;
- To understand and use regular and irregular past tense verbs;
- To increase the mean length of utterance (MLU) in conversational speech;
- To increase intelligibility of speech.

The short-term objectives are measurable intermediate steps toward the annual goals which may be accomplished over a period of weeks or months. Short term objectives break the skills described in the annual goal down into the components needed to master that skill. For example, under the above goal "To learn to use requests," a short-term objective for one child might be "Bob will be able to ask for help when he does not understand the instructions 80% of the time." A short-term objective for another child might be "Beth will ask the teacher or aide when she needs help 50% of the time." A short-term objective for still another child might be "Stephanie will hold up her sign asking for help when she does not understand how to do a worksheet 70% of the time." The following chapters include examples of goals and objectives for specific areas of need that children with Down syndrome often have related to the language of the curriculum, language of instruction, etc.

Instead of, or in addition to short-term objectives, your child's IEP might include benchmarks, or major milestones. (IDEA mandates that either short-term goals or benchmarks be included in the IEP.) Benchmarks establish expected performance levels, stating the amount of progress that your child is expected to make in a specific time period. For example, if a long-term goal on your child's IEP is "To improve the use of pronouns," a benchmark might be: "Student will use "mine" instead of "mines" 80% of the time by the end of the first grading period, October 24." An IEP team may use short-term objectives or benchmarks, or may choose to use a combination of the two depending on the nature of the annual goals for the specific child.

CHOOSING GOALS RELATED TO PROGRESS AT SCHOOL

The criteria for choosing communication goals and objectives are based on several factors. The first is *functionality*. That is, is this a skill that your child needs to learn? Will learning the skill benefit your child? Another factor is *practice opportunities*. Will your child have many opportunities to practice the skill in school and at home? Having many opportunities is crucial to helping your child *generalize* a skill to different situations—that is, to be able to use the skill in different settings and situations. Another consideration is *age appropriateness*. Is this goal at your child's level based on her mental and/or chronological age? Generally, it is more important for goals to be appropriate to a child's chronological age when she is younger, but as she reaches middle-school age, goals may need to be geared more to her mental age. This really depends on the child and the difficulty of the material she is working on.

Although some parents can come up with dozens of communication goals they would like their child to achieve, the school system's bottom line is whether the speech and language services are needed to help your child benefit from the regular education curriculum. There are many IEP meetings that deadlock over this point, but school speech language therapy was designed to address problems with school progress. It was not designed and is not provided to help your child reach the highest level of communication ability possible. So, there will be times when you feel that your child "needs" and would benefit from therapy for specific difficulties, but you will be told that services cannot be provided for that problem. This is often a point of contention in the area of speech intelligibility. Children with Down syndrome might *need* services to become more intelligible, but be considered ineligible because the school does not believe that speech intelligibility difficulties affect progress in the regular educational curriculum.

The speech-language pathologist works with the IEP team to identify the relationship between the child's speech and language difficulties and "any adverse effect on the ability to learn the general curriculum....The team relies on the evaluation results to determine both a student's *need* for service and the student's *eligibility* for special education and related services on the basis of federal legislative mandates, state regulations and guidelines and local policies and procedures" (ASHA, 2001). Know the guidelines for your state department of education and local school system. Be sure that the speech-language pathologist is following the eligibility guidelines set by the local school system and the federal legislation. Families and professionals need to work together to ensure that the legislation meets the needs of children with special needs.

QUESTIONS TO ASK ABOUT GOALS AND OBJECTIVES

The following questions can help you determine whether communication objectives and activities are appropriate for your child:

Does the activity allow her to participate more fully or to achieve more in the classroom setting? For example, if worksheets are modified so that your child can respond using multiple choice answers instead of fill-ins, she may be able to show that she has learned the material. She is able to participate more fully in the classroom activity.

Will achieving the objective and mastering the skills make a difference in your child's school life? For example, if a speech goal is to have Jimmy greet teachers, peers, and school staff at appropriate times during the day, how will this affect his school life? Achieving this goal will enable Jimmy to interact with others in school. Once he learns greetings and is comfortable using them, the skills will probably generalize to other situations, such as at home and in the community. Jimmy will greet the minister and his friends at Sunday school. He will greet the ice cream man, and the workers in the bakery. The skill of using social greetings will make a difference in his life. (Although the IEP is only concerned with how mastering the skill will affect progress in the regular educational curriculum, the skills learned will usually have a positive impact in other settings, as well.)

What if the goal is a more complex and advanced skill, such as increasing sentence length to five or more words? The first determination is **can your child master this skill?** Can her speech output and intelligibility support the use of five-word sentences? Would using longer sentences help her succeed at school?

Probably. She might be able to answer reading/listening comprehension questions more accurately in history and language arts to let the teacher know that she understands the material. She might be able to explain why she needs assistance with assignments, instead of merely feeling frustrated.

Will mastering the skills open up new opportunities for your child? Now? In the future? At home? In school? In the community? For children in later elementary and middle school years, activities relating to following directions are important. For example, if the goal is that eleven-year-old Jessie will be able to ask for clarification when she does not understand instructions 60 percent of the time, will this goal open up new opportunities? In fact, when this skill is mastered, it *should* open up many new opportunities at school, at home, and in the community. When Jessie can ask for clarification, she is more likely to correctly complete the activity, whether that activity is finishing a worksheet for school, or finishing a crafts project for Girl Scouts. The skill of asking for help and clarification can also open up opportunities in the future for Jessie. It is a skill that is important to success in the workplace.

Although the IEP is concerned with progress in regular education, the transition plan for adolescents does take into consideration future needs in the workplace and the community. So, it is possible for parents to make the case that mastering a skill will help their child in the future.

INCORPORATING GOALS AND OBJECTIVES INTO THE SCHOOL DAY

Once the IEP goals and objectives for communication are determined, use a planning matrix form to figure out how your child's goals can be facilitated during the school day. A sample matrix form is included on the next page.

Look at the classroom schedule, and then look at the IEP goals. Can your child work on this objective in class? Can she work on the objective in certain subjects, but not others? at certain times, but not others? For example, she can work on social conversation at lunch and recess, but not during math. What kind of support, adaptation, or modification will she need to work on this goal? Does she need personal assistance to reach the goal? Should the assistance come from an adult classroom aide or a peer tutor? Will she need to work on an alternative task during a specific time during the day?

If possible, request that the schedule matrix be attached to your child's IEP. The matrix will probably need to be filled out in the Fall, at the beginning of the school year, after the daily schedule in the class has been determined (not the previous Spring when your child's IEP will likely be signed). If your child's IEP includes a goal for home-to-school communication (see below), a short-term objective could be that the educational planning matrix be sent home by the end of the first month of school.

MAKING SURE GOALS AND OBJECTVES ARE ACHIEVED

Even when the best IEP goals are written, it is important to keep a steadfast watch on the implementation of the plans. Your child's IEP must include information about how her progress toward achieving goals will be measured. This can be done in two ways:

1. The team can write measurable objectives, and include the criteria that will be used to determine whether your child has reached them. For example, the criteria for achieving the objective of

IEP Planning Matrix

Name _____ Grade _____

Date _____

I. Language IEP Goals

_____

_____

_____

_____

_____

_____

_____

II. Schedule

SUBJECT AREA	GOALS TO BE TARGETED	HOW ADDRESSED

III. Accommodations

_____

_____

_____

_____

_____

_____

IEP Planning Matrix (sample)

Name ___BJ___   Grade ___3rd___

I. Language IEP Goals

  1. Uses verbal greetings with peers

  2. Uses verbal greetings with adults

  3. Follows classroom routine rules

  4. Comprehends verbs

  5. Takes 2 turns in conversation with peers

  6. Takes 2 turns in conversation with adults

  7. Uses 5 word sentences in speech and writing.

II. Schedule

SUBJECT AREA	GOALS TO BE TARGETED	HOW ADDRESSED
1. A.M. Opening Routines	1, 2, 3,	— Aide will prompt BJ to use greetings with peers/adults — BJ will use a visual cue reminder in the form of pictures to help him remember the morning routine rules
2. Spelling	3, 4, 7	— Picture cue for rules — BJ will choose correct verb to use in sentences for spelling — BJ will write 5 word sentences for spelling homework
3. Reading / Language Arts	3, 4, 6, 7	— Picture cue for rules — Teacher will prepare verb practice sheets so BJ can circle the correct verb or can choose correct verb from word bank — The teacher will talk to BJ about the story and take 2 turns

continued ▶

4. Music	2, 3, 6	— BJ will greet music teacher — Picture cue for rules — Music teacher will talk with BJ
5. Lunch	1, 2, 3, 5, 6	— Peer budy will include BJ at lunch and have a conversation — BJ will use picture cue boards to remember cafeteria rules
6. Recess	1, 2, 3, 5, 6	— Aide will promote and model child /adult conversation — Peer buddy will promote peer conversation with focus on at least 2 conversation turns — Picture cue for rules
7. Social Studies	3, 5, 6, 7	— Picture cue for rules — In cooperative group, peer buddy will converse with BJ about social studies assignment — Aide will converse with BJ — BJ will use pacing board to cue sentence length
8. Math	3	— Picture cues for rules
9. Physical Education	3, 4, 5, 6	— Picture cue for rules — Understands verbs in PE instruction — Peer buddy will have conversation with BJ during PE
10. Dismissal	1, 2, 3, 4	— Aide and peer buddy will help with greetings — Picture cue for rules — Comprehend instructions with verbs

III. Accommodations

    a. Classroom aide to promote language skills

    b. Special education aide responsible for adapting work sheets

    c. Seating at front of room

    d. Seating next to peer buddy

    e. Multiple choice (2 choices) or word bank vocabulary on class worksheets and homework

mastering verb tenses might be that your child can successfully use the past tense verb 3 out of 4 times, or with 75% success.
2. The team can write benchmarks giving a specific date when your child is expected to have mastered a particular skill necessary to reach the goal. For example, the objective listed above would be a benchmark if it specified the date by which your child should be using the past tense correctly.

Remember, IDEA 97 requires the use of short-term objectives *or* benchmarks. School systems may choose to use either, both, or a combination as needed to monitor progress of a specific child.

The IEP will also list any tests that have been used to measure progress or that will be used during the period that the IEP is in effect (usually one year).
It will also list supplementary aids and services, training for teachers, etc. that will be needed to implement the IEP.

Home-to-School Communication Plans

Parents are usually not in school daily or even weekly. Many parents find that it is difficult to find out what is going on in the classroom or in pull-out therapy. Here is how one mother describes a typical scenario:

Matthew is in first grade and is receiving speech therapy in school. When we had the IEP meeting, the speech-language pathologist seemed very friendly and speech was written into the IEP. My problem is that when I try to contact her, she does not respond. I sent a note to school six weeks ago because I wanted to know how Matthew was doing in speech. I waited two weeks and when I did not receive a response, I wrote again. After three weeks, I called the school but she was in therapy, and did not return my call. Finally, after six weeks, I spoke to the special education teacher, and asked her to find out what they were working on in speech, and how my son was doing.

Then, I got a call from the speech-language pathologist. She apologized for not calling sooner, and told me a little bit about what they had been doing in speech. She said Matthew was doing well. She did not suggest anything that we could do at home to help. I want to be of help, but how can I get her to let me know what to do? She also was noncommittal when I asked when she would call me again. She said that she was so busy now that she was in the classroom for therapy and still doing pull-out therapy that it would be difficult for her to call. "I'm only one person," she said and I could hear the frustration in her voice.

The best way to monitor your child's progress with speech and language goals is to be in regular communication with the speech-language pathologist. How do you make that happen? IDEA 97 specifies that home-school communication plans can be written into the IEP. The IEP can include specific plans for how communication will occur between teachers and related services personnel and others in school and between the school and home.

Beginning with your child's first IEP, it is a good idea to include a specific goal to promote parent-professional communication and cooperation. See the example below.

Sample Goal to Promote Parent-Professional Communication

Goal:
- To provide a means for speech-language pathologist-parent communication on a regular basis.

Short-term objectives:
- The SLP and parents will communicate through a written journal at least once weekly.
- The SLP will provide information on the child's sessions and home activities.
- The parents will provide feedback on home practice, progress, and problems and report on family activities that might serve as the basis for conversations in therapy sessions.

Face-to-face meetings are often difficult for speech-language pathologists and parents to schedule on a regular basis. But, if you are a volunteer at school or if you carpool and are at school on a regular basis, this may be possible. If not, communication can take place by phone, e-mail, notebook journal, tape recordings, etc. Many parents tell me that e-mail is a very satisfying way to stay in contact with the classroom teacher, special education teacher, and speech-language pathologist on a frequent, often daily basis. Other parents use journal sheets in a notebook that describe briefly what happened during the day at school. This can help provide cues so that you can ask your child specific questions about the day at school. We all know that the generic question, "What did you do at school?" or "What did you do in speech today?" gets a general answer such as "nothing" or "stuff." So we really can't rely on our children to give specific information about the day.

A notebook page can take many forms. For younger children, the teacher, SLP, classroom aide, or communication aide can fill out a form to inform parents about what went on in school that day. This type of form enables parents to ask their child direct questions instead of the more general unproductive "What happened in school today?" and to get some answers and discuss the child's day. An example of this type of "School-to-Home Daily Log" is on the next page.

A similar form can be used by families to give the teacher and SLP information about what the child did at home. An example of this type of form is on page 59.

School-to-Home Daily Log

Student's Name: _____   Today's Date: _____

Today in class we worked on: _____
_____

My Class Buddy was: _____

At lunch, I sat with: _____

My behavior was: _____

My work was: _____

I have homework in: _____

I am currently working on the following projects: _____
_____

My strengths today were: _____
_____

My problems today were: _____
_____

Comments from home: _____
_____

News from home: _____
_____

Home-to-School Daily Log (sample)

Last night at home . . .

dinner	For dinner I ate _____
television	On TV I watched _____
people	Our company was _____
play	I played _____
bedtime	I went to bed at _____
wake-up	This morning I woke up at _____
breakfast	For breakfast I ate _____
play	This morning I played _____

A log can also address your child's specific IEP goals and inform parents about progress at school related to those goals. See below for a weekly form that focuses on IEP goals.

If your child has a communication aide or if there is a classroom aide who can copy or take off the computer picture symbols such as the Picture Communication Symbols© made with Boardmaker software™ (Mayer-Johnson), your child may be able to participate in completing the daily log. She may choose the pictures that represent the activities that she engaged in during the school day. She may also, independently or with the assistance of an aide or a peer buddy, be able to write down what she did during the day. You will still need to rely on the teacher and the specialists to report on her progress and to give detailed information on what information was given in class.

For an example, see the next page.

HOME PROGRAMS

When a child with Down syndrome is in early intervention, her parents are often observers and/or participants in the program and know what their child is working on in therapy. When their child transitions to preschool and school-aged services, they are less likely to observe and be part of the speech and language sessions. No matter what your child's age is, however, it is essential

IEP Goals Weekly Log (sample)

Eric's Progress for the Week of _____

Eric held the pencil appropriately	yes _____	no _____
Eric traced the letters of his name	yes _____	no _____
Eric traced alphabet letters	yes _____	no _____
Eric greeted the teacher in morning	yes _____	no _____
Eric said hi to 2 other students	yes _____	no _____
Eric walked up the stairs using alternating feet	yes _____	no _____
Eric checked out 2 books from the school library	yes _____	no _____
Eric read the title of the 2 books	yes _____	no _____
Eric identified initial letters in words	yes _____	no _____
Eric used he and she appropriately	yes _____	no _____
Eric answered questions in class	yes _____	no _____
Eric copied the homework from the board	yes _____	no _____
Eric shouted in class	yes _____	no _____
Eric lined up with his buddy	yes _____	no _____

Daily Log Using Picture Communication Symbols© (sample)

Today is: _____

What did Matthew eat for lunch today?

for you to have information about therapy sessions, so that you can follow through at home. Most young children with Down syndrome are not going to remember what they worked on in therapy for an hour or two a week at school and then take it upon themselves to practice it at home! If you, the parent, don't know what skills your child should be practicing, there is little or no chance that practice will take place.

Your child's IEP can stipulate the need for a home program. The home program may include follow-up activities to speech therapy sessions to be completed at home, and information sent to the parents on a regular (daily, weekly) basis. If a home program is specified in your child's IEP, the SLP can send home activities via a school-to-home communication system. And you could send back feedback on your child's progress in the home program via home-to-school

Language Home Program Practice Sheet (sample)

In class, Brittany is working on verbs and in speech therapy, we are practicing the same skills. Brittany is currently working on *-ing* verb endings. Can you practice the following words at home? You can do the action and ask "What am I doing?" or you can find pictures with her, and ask "What is s/he doing?" Practice once daily!

Verb	Day 1	Day 2	Day 3	Day 4	Day 5	Day6	Day 7
running							
jumping							
walking							
swimming							
sitting							
stretching							
bending							
opening							
closing							
twisting							
driving							
pushing							
pulling							

communication. See the previous page for an example of how a home program activity might be communicated to parents.

In summary, to ensure school-to-home communication and the implementation of a home program, be sure to include specific information regarding the following in your child's IEP:

- How will the family and the speech-language pathologist stay in contact?
- How frequently will this system be used?
- Will there be a home program of exercises and/or activities to reinforce the material being addressed in therapy sessions?
- How often will material be sent home?
- How will the family send back information to the speech-language pathologist regarding the home practice?

When the family and speech-language pathologist work together, everyone benefits!

Supplementary Aids and Services

During your child's IEP meeting, the need for "supplementary aids and services" will be addressed. Under IDEA, this refers to "aids, services, and other supports that are provided in regular education classes or other education-related settings to enable children with disabilities to be educated with nondisabled children to the maximum extent appropriate…." For some children, these might involve program modifications or adapted curricular materials. (These types of supplementary aids and services are discussed in Chapters 5-11.) For other children, there may be a need for an aide to help the child meet the demands of the classroom.

AIDES FOR CHILDREN WITH DOWN SYNDROME

How do school systems determine whether a child needs an aide? And would you child do better with a communication aide, personal aide, or classroom aide? The

case manager will rarely suggest that your child needs an aide. An aide is the most expensive type of support a district can provide, so most school systems are not anxious to provide that level of service. Parents, however, often ask for the assistance of an aide, because they think their child will have difficulty following instructions, communicating with teachers and peers, or completing regular assignments unless some modifications are made.

When parents request an aide, there are usually one of two responses from the IEP team:

1. The IEP team suggests that a classroom aide who may already be assigned to the classroom to work with other children could spend some time helping your child too. And in fact, this may be a workable option for some children with Down syndrome, depending on the child's needs, the aide's expertise, and how many other students the aide is assisting.

2. The team responds that if your child needs that intense level of support, she should be in a special education classroom. The flaw in this argument is that, under IDEA, children with disabilities are entitled to the supplementary aids and services that will help enable them to be educated with nondisabled peers to the maximum extent appropriate. A less inclusive placement is only supposed to be considered for a child *after* it has been determined that she cannot be educated with nondisabled peers with the help of supplementary aids and services.

TYPES OF AIDES

Depending on where you live, you may hear aides called by a variety of job titles, including communication aide, personal aide, one-on-one aide, classroom aide, instructional assistant, or paraprofessional. There are no real universal definitions of these positions. Every school district is different. In general, however, aides that children with Down syndrome may work with can provide three broad levels of assistance:

1. They can assist a number of children in the classroom, providing one-on-one assistance to individual children only as needed.
2. They can assist one child exclusively, for all or part of the day, during any activity in which she requires more help than the classroom teacher can provide.
3. They can assist one child with her communication needs only.

Classroom Aide. Whatever her title, this person may help in several classrooms or may be assigned to one classroom. She may help to set up materials, grade papers, help children understand how to do classwork, and tutor children who are having difficulty. She may be assigned to help a child with Down syndrome as part of her classroom responsibilities during the day.

Personal Aide. A personal or one-on-one aide works solely with one child. A child who has seizures or specific medical problems may require a personal aide. A child who cannot communicate verbally may need a personal aide. Parents may also advocate for a personal aide if they think their child needs close supervision due to behaviors such as wandering away from the classroom.

Communication Aide. A communication aide may be a personal aide or a classroom aide who is assigned to assist the speech-language pathologist in working with students on communication demands in the classroom. A communication aide may also be a speech-language pathology aide or assistant, or SLP-A. This is a new job description. Very few school systems use this designation at present, but it is a new career designation used by the American Speech-Language-Hearing Association. Currently, the education and experience levels for this position are under review at the state level.

All of these types of aides can help children with communication demands in the classroom in a variety of ways, including:

- using sign language with your child,
- interpreting the classroom instructions for your child,
- using an augmentative or alternative communication system such as PECS with your child,
- adapting materials for your child,
- developing the worksheets that your child needs for learning,
- communicating with parents, teachers, and the SLP about communication needs she observes in your child,
- serving as a communication partner for your child.

THE "RIGHT" AIDE FOR YOUR CHILD

How frequently or for how long does your child need an aide? This needs to be determined and documented in the IEP.

Some children may need an aide only in the morning and late afternoon to get materials organized for the day, and to help organize homework assignments in the afternoon. But, they may need the assistance throughout the year. Other children may need an aide for a short time in the Fall when they are getting back into the routine of school. Once the child learns the schedule and the rules of the classroom, a peer buddy may be able to help her. She may no longer need an aide. Children who need a great deal of modifications to classroom work, assistance communicating, or guidance in staying on task may need an aide every day for all or most of the day. So, the need will vary.

The specific schedule and responsibilities of the aide should be spelled out in your child's IEP under Supplementary Aids and Services.

The school system usually interviews and hires the aide. But, sometimes, parents find the aide. They may, for instance, ask someone who has done daycare with their child to become the aide, or ask an undergraduate student who has babysat for their child to become the aide. Unfortunately, it usually doesn't work that smoothly and aides can be difficult to find and retain.

Ensuring that the aide receives proper training may also be problematic. The school and/or the classroom teacher may have the responsibility for training the aide, but in reality, often no one trains the aide. They are left to learn about the child on their own or from parent-provided information. Many times, the parent not only recruits the aide, but also trains him or her. A high turnover rate can also be a problem. One mother told me that she had already trained four aides for her child this school year—and it was only February. It may be worthwhile to advocate for supports for your child's aide similar to those for the teacher, as described below.

Supports for Your Child's Teacher

There are many ways children with Down syndrome may receive speech therapy at school, including through *pull out, push in, collaborative consultation, or consultation.* (See Chapter 2.) The services your child receives should be appropriate for her needs, challenges, and learning styles. Generally, the more inclusive the

setting, the more your child will need the services of the speech-language pathologist for support. In special education settings, the classroom is usually designed to meet the special educational needs of the children in that classroom. In regular classroom settings, your child will need more speech and language support to learn in the classroom, and the regular classroom teacher will need more resource support by the speech-language pathologist to help understand your child's needs.

For the regular education teacher, this may be her first experience having a child with Down syndrome in her classroom. The special education teacher may have extensive experience with children with Down syndrome, or may have worked primarily with children with other disabilities. The teacher, special educator, and/or classroom aide (or other paraprofessionals) may or may not have worked with children with Down syndrome before. If they have not had extensive experience with children with Down syndrome, IDEA 97 provides funding for training. The funds are there; you need to be sure that they are used to train the people working with your child. Here are some examples of training that might be provided:

- If your child is using an augmentative communication system, the classroom personnel working with your child can receive training in how to program and maintain the equipment.
- If your child is using sign language, training in sign language can be provided for the teachers and paraprofessionals
- Local parent groups have met with special education administrators to suggest continuing education opportunities that can be provided for the staff.
- Family support groups and state agencies have partnered with the school system to bring in specialists who can train classroom teachers, assistants, and special educators in areas such as maximizing communication skills for children with Down syndrome. I, personally, have provided many two-day workshops on supporting communication in inclusion that have been funded with the collaboration of parent groups and the school system. Usually, the workshop has involved one day of professional training and one day of parent training. More parent groups are becoming proactive in working with the school systems in partnership.

Staff training needs can be written into the IEP under Supplementary Aids and Services. The case manager or service coordinator should be able to investigate training opportunities for the staff through the school system. If the case manager is not able to locate resources specific to Down syndrome, parents may provide referrals to agencies such as the local parent support group, the ARC, the National Down Syndrome Society and the National Down Syndrome Congress, which can suggest resources.

Putting the VIP in the IEP

One of the concerns often expressed by parents is that the professionals at the IEP meeting see their child as a diagnosis. They see Down syndrome, not an engaging seven-year-old who loves sports and music and often sings very loudly, and whose favorite foods are spaghetti and chocolate. The IEP meeting tends to focus on problems and deficits, not strengths and triumphs. To make the focus more positive, one parent told me that she starts every IEP meeting by asking, "Can you tell me something Tom does really well?"

How can you let the team members know what your child is really like? And how about school personnel who are not on the IEP team—the bus driver, the custodial staff, and the paraprofessionals? Don't they need to know more about Tina than that she's that girl with Down syndrome? What is the essence of Tina? How do you capture the spirit of that very important person? How do you let people know about Tina so that they are ready and able to look past the label?

One technique that works well is to develop a "Me Book," a personal portfolio describing your child. Some parents bring in the book for the teacher the week before school. Other parents bring the book to the IEP meeting. One parent created a book in electronic form and e-mailed the book to all of her daughter's prospective teachers in middle school before the term began. It is especially helpful when your child is changing school levels, or when you are moving or redistricted and are changing schools. On the next page are some suggestions of information to include in a Me Book.

One parent of a child with Down syndrome, Molly Mattheis, first designed a porfolio called *The Mac Book* when her son, Mac, was transitioning from preschool to kindergarten. She says, "Reading the IEP before school begins creates an image of the academic challenges the student brings to the classroom. *The Mac Book* creates a vision of the fun and personality he will add.... The IEP is the legal tool for families, but the portfolio shares more valuable information about our son. In fact, we now include a goal on the IEP that *The Mac Book* be made available to all school staff prior to working with him" (Mattheis, 1996, p. 4-5). In Mac's book, she also included sections for teachers and therapists to write about their experiences with Mac each year, so the book became a living, expanding document.

Another mother, Kim Voss, designed a student portfolio for her daughter, Ashley, when she transitioned to middle school. She used technology, word processing, databases, and painting/drawing software to develop a personal portfolio for Ashley. She even included links to Internet websites that provide resources for information and assistive technology. Since the portfolio was done on the computer, additional copies could be made for key personnel, including regular and special educators, the speech-language pathologist, and other therapists. It could also be e-mailed to their computers.

The IEP/IFSP provides a plan for speech and language services and other academic services and serves as a commitment to provide these services for your child. A personal portfolio can add another dimension. It can provide a picture of your child as a complete person. The more knowledge that you can bring to the IEP meeting, the better. You are an important part of the planning team, and working

Planning a "Me" Book

"Me" Book for _____

Family Information
Name, including nickname (include photo): _____
Birthdate and birthplace: _____
Address: _____
Names and pictures of parents: _____
Names, ages, and pictures of siblings: _____
Names and photos of significant people in your child's life (babysitter, grandparents, etc.):
_____

My Favorite Things to Do
Hobbies and activities (include photos): _____
Favorite toys: _____
Family activities: _____

How I Communicate
Speech (include words used if speech is limited): _____
What I understand (important to explain if child understands more than she can express):
_____
Augmentative & alternative communication (include signs or description of communication system); you can also include photos. Describe how they are used: _____
_____
Situations in which I communicate best: _____
Difficult situations (such as when upset): _____

My Learning Style
Learning strengths: _____
Learning needs: _____
Favorite subjects: _____
Good motivators: _____
Motivators to avoid (e.g., specific foods): _____
Modifications needed for learning: _____
Verbal abilities: _____
Writing skills (may include samples): _____
Transitions (problems with, ways to make them go more smoothly): _____
Routines (used at home; ways to teach routines): _____
Following instructions, how can they best be presented: _____

Medical and Sensory Issues

How Down syndrome affects me: _____

Visual skills (acuity, problems making eye contact, need for preferential seating): _____
_____

Hearing (problems and needed adaptations): _____
_____

Medications: _____

Allergies and dietary restrictions: _____

Sensory issues (sensitivity to loud noises, dislike of being touched on the head, etc.):
_____

Additional diagnoses (AD/HD, autism, epilepsy): _____
_____

Feelings

What makes me happy: _____

What makes me sad: _____

What I am sensitive about: _____

Samples of Schoolwork

Include samples from the previous year.

Resources

Include any reports from specialists that would be helpful.

Include books, articles, and references: _____
_____

People to contact: _____
_____

Child's Hopes and Dreams

My goals for this year: _____

What I want to do when I grow up: _____

Parents' Hopes and Dreams

Parents' goals for me this year: _____

Some of my past achievements: _____

Ways my parents can help (inside the classroom, for special events, and with homework and assignments): _____
_____

My parents' dreams for my future: _____

together with the speech-language pathologist and the other professionals on the team, you can ensure that the services provided will meet the needs of your child.

Conclusion

Your child's IEP should include objectives to master in each area of communication that will be addressed in treatment. A comprehensive plan for treatment should consider whether your child has difficulties and needs to master skills in many different areas of speech, language, and listening skills. It also should consider what language skills are needed to help your child succeed in her educational placement, including the language of the curriculum, instruction, routines, and behavioral considerations. At the ends of chapters and in the Appendix, you will find a variety of forms and resources to help you and your child's IEP team plan for her speech and language treatment.

REFERENCES

ASHA (2001). Guidelines for the roles and responsibilities of the school-based speech-language pathologist. Rockville, MD.

ASHA (1996). Inclusive practices for children and youths with communication disorders: Position statement and technical report. ASHA, 38 (Suppl. 16), 35-44.

Ferguson, M. L. (1991). Collaborative/consultative service delivery: An introduction. *Language, Speech and Hearing Services in Schools, 22,* 147.

A Guide to the Individualized Education Program, Office of Special Education & Rehabilitative Services (OSERS), July, 2000. Available from Editorial Publications Center, U.S. Dept. of Education, P. O. Box 1398, Jessup, MD 20794.

Kumin, L., Goodman, M. & Councill, C. (1999). Comprehensive speech and language intervention for school-aged children with Down syndrome. *Down Syndrome Quarterly, 3,* 1-8.

Mattheis, M. G. The Mac book: Highlighting the person in the I.E.P. *Disability Solutions 1, No. 3:*1-7, 1996. (Can be downloaded from the website: www.disabilitysolutions.org.)

Reynolds, M., Wang, M. & Walberg, H. (1987). The necessary restructuring of special and regular education. *Exceptional Children, 53,* 7-11.

Simon, C. S. (1991). *Communication skills and classroom success.* Eau Claire, WI: Thinking Publications.

Voss, Kim. Designing dynamic student portfolios. www.ashleysmom.com/student_portfolios.htm

CHAPTER 5

Helping Children Learn in Inclusion

One of the results of inclusion has been the realization that children learn in different ways. It is true that children with Down syndrome may share some similarities in learning with one another. For example, visual processing is usually easier than auditory processing for them. However, every child is an individual with his own learning style. Understanding how a child learns best is therefore crucial to helping him learn at school.

Ideally, your child's IEP team will keep his learning strengths and needs in mind when choosing the accommodations, modifications, and learning aids to help him learn. In this chapter, we will discuss a variety of general modifications and techniques involving language that will help children with a variety of learning styles learn. We will also outline how assistive technology can be used to help children with Down syndrome learn. In later chapters, we will discuss language modifications and aids that will help in adapting the curriculum, the language of instruction, testing methods, and classroom routines so that children can succeed.

Discovering Your Child's Learning Style

Each child has strengths and approaches to learning that help him understand the world and the people around him. As mentioned above, understanding your child's unique learning style can help you understand how best to modify the classroom for his success.

The theory of multiple intelligences is one that is often used in discussing learning styles. This theory was first proposed in 1983 by Howard Gardner, in his book *Frames of Mind*. Gardner theorized that there were at least seven different intelligences. Recently, an eighth intelligence has been added to the list. If you know which intelligences are strengths for a child, they can be used to help him master information and concepts. They also help explain why some children find mathematics or geography very easy to learn, while other children excel at dance or music.

The multiple intelligences are:

Linguistic. The ability to use language effectively, and to easily understand the meaning and order of words. Children with linguistic intelligence generally excel in school and do well on standardized intelligence tests. They understand language concepts easily, and are facile at using language for speaking, writing, and comprehending. They do well at word games such as Scrabble and crossword puzzles and enjoy playing with language through jokes, puns, tongue twisters, etc.. Linguistic intelligence is the major emphasis in school at all levels. This intelligence is usually a challenging area for children with Down syndrome.

Logical-mathematical. The ability to devise and to follow a logical chain of reasoning and to recognize patterns and order, numerical and time concepts. This is a skill that is often measured on standardized intelligence tests, and contributes to success in school. Children with logical-mathematical intelligence are good at problem solving and analytical reasoning. They often excel at games of strategy such as chess and Battleship. They ask a lot of questions about how things work. They enjoy organizing knowledge and putting things into categories and hierarchies.

Naturalist. The ability to recognize flora and fauna, to make other distinctions in the natural world, and to use this ability productively. People with naturalist intelligence excel in biological science, farming, and hunting. This skill that would be highly prized in societies where finding food sources on a regular basis is essential.

Musical. Sensitivity to pitch, melody, rhythm, and tone. People with musical intelligence may excel as singers and instrumentalists, as well as composers. They learn well through using music and rhythm, and they often like to study with background music. Children who have musical intelligence often have a rhythmical way of speaking, and may hum to themselves or tap on the desk as they work. Many children with Down syndrome learn well using music. Songs or jingles (such as for the order of the planets) may help your child memorize and retrieve information for school. Likewise, tapping out the number of syllables in a word, or tapping to expand the number of words that they use in a sentence can help.

Bodily-kinesthetic. The ability to use the body and handle objects skillfully and easily. Often people with bodily-kinesthetic intelligence are excellent athletes and dancers. They often learn well when they can move at the same time that they are processing information. Games such as charades and Twister tap into this skill. Some children with strengths in this area also have difficulty sitting still and will fidget or move when asked to sit for long periods of time. Many children enjoy gross motor (sports, dancing), as well as fine motor activities (crafts, painting). Many children with Down syndrome love to dance, and use dance as a form of exercise as well as a source of joy.

Spatial. The ability to perceive the world accurately and to re-create or transform aspects of the physical world. People with spatial intelligence are excellent architects, artists, builders, or movers. Spatial learners learn best through visual presentation using graphics, color coding, and other images. Games such as Pictionary tap into this skill. Visual organizers such as charts and diagrams can help children who have good spatial intelligence learn the curriculum. Movies, videos, slides, and demonstrations also help children who learn well spatially.

Interpersonal. The ability to understand people and relationships. This intelligence often contributes to life success, and to being well-liked by people. People with interpersonal skills are often very understanding, can take different points of view, and are good leaders and mediators. They learn well through cooperative learning, group projects, and partnering. This area is usually a strength for older children and adults with Down syndrome. They may remember personal data such as birthdays, and may sense when others are feeling low or are very happy. Children and adults with interpersonal intelligence enjoy socializing and group activities.

Intrapersonal. The ability to understand oneself and to act on that understanding. This intelligence helps people choose jobs, situations, and relationships that are good "fits" for them. They often work best independently, at their own pace. Older children, adolescents, and adults with Down syndrome may have good intrapersonal skills, but, due to verbal limitations, have difficulty using them in certain situations. For example, although they may know that they are having problems with a peer at school or coworker in a job setting, they may have difficulty expressing their feelings. The individual with Down syndrome will look sad and upset, but it is often difficult for family members, teachers, or counselors to figure out what is at the root of the unhappiness.

The interpersonal and intrapersonal intelligences are often grouped together. They are sometimes referred to as *EQ, the emotional quotient, SQ, the social quotient, EI, emotional intelligence* or *SI, social intelligence.*

When we think in terms of multiple intelligences, it can help us structure learning opportunities to take advantage of each child's strengths and to compensate for their limitations. It can also help us develop cooperative learning groups within the classroom that balance the intelligences of children in the group so that the group strength for learning is greater than the strength of each individual.

The theory of multiple intelligences helps explain the relationship (or lack of relationship) between school performance and life performance. If education prepares us for life, it would seem logical that the children who excel academically in school would grow up to succeed in the workplace and in life. But, studies do not usually bear out this correlation. My opinion is that this is because academic learning focuses on linguistic and mathematical intelligence, whereas in adult life, success can result from excellence in any of the multiple intelligences. As an adult, you can choose a job based on your intelligences, achievements, and interests in a specific area. In adult life, there is also a high correlation between interpersonal and intrapersonal intelligence (emotional quotient) and success. This is why it is sometimes difficult to predict which children will succeed in adult life.

Many parents of young adults with Down syndrome tell wonderful stories of successful jobs in the community, despite the gloomy predictions they may have heard at school conferences. Sociability, behavior, organizational skills, and work habits are often more closely related to job success than scores on standardized tests. At a family workshop I was presenting, the father of an adult son with Down syndrome and an adult daughter who has tested in the gifted range made an interesting observation. His son had fine manners and was friendly and sociable, whereas his daughter had high IQ scores, but was not adept at interacting with people. His son was welcomed in social situations, whereas his daughter had great difficulty. We cannot generalize about the social skills of all people with Down syndrome or all people with high measured IQ. Social skills, however, are important for everyone, and do contribute to success and to quality of life for all people.

At present, job options for adults with Down syndrome are often limited to positions in food service, horticulture, mailing, and office work. But, if the multiple intelligence areas were evaluated for each adolescent, I think we would find many other areas in which adults with Down syndrome could excel. I urge parents to ensure that their child's multiple intelligences, as well as school performance in academic subjects, are considered in lifetime planning. Some suggested readings are included at the end of the chapter.

General Strategies and Supports for Learning

There are many types of supports and assists that can be used in the classroom, for studying, and for homework assignments, especially in later elementary school and middle school. Many supports provide visual cues, diagrams, and frameworks to fill in that can be very helpful for children with Down syndrome, who are often visual learners. By capitalizing on your child's learning strengths and multiple intelligence strengths, these materials can help your child succeed in inclusion.

In the elementary school grades, teachers often use visual supports to help *all* students organize and learn the material (for example, worksheets with fill-in questions or diagrams that aid in categorization). In the later elementary school and middle school years, however, textbook material is often presented in one way. For children who have difficulty learning that way, supports can be individually designed to help them learn the textbook material in the way they can learn it best. For example, if your child is musical, a support might involve setting material he has to memorize to music, or making a jingle to remember the words. If your child is visual, you can color code the material that he needs to learn (red for fruits, green for vegetables), or create visual mental images to help him remember the material (a picture of someone named George carrying a ton of wash to help remember that Washington was the first president).

There are many specific supports and assists that can be used to help individual students with Down syndrome learn in the classroom. General types include:

- **Organizers:** Visual and graphical ways of structuring information to help students learn. Many organizers provide visual cues, diagrams, and charts to fill in. Venn diagrams are a well-known form of organizer. They can be very helpful for children with Down syndrome, who tend to learn best through the visual channel. Organizers can be used in the classroom, and also at home for studying and for homework assignments. Some teachers may use the term *worksheet* to describe fill-in sheets that help children learn.

■ **Cues and Prompts:** Verbal, gestural, written, or other reminders of what the student is to do. These usually require a person assisting the child who can provide the cues or prompts as needed. Cues and prompts may be used regularly, or only when needed. They may also be faded out when they are no longer needed.

■ **Scaffolds:** Frameworks that help students with communication and learning. The term scaffold is used to describe the purpose of the assistance. Just as a window washer relies on a scaffold to support him so that he does not fall and can accomplish his goal, a language scaffold provides a framework that enables the child to accomplish his language goal. Scaffolds may be incomplete sentences that the child fills in. They are often questions that help the child to think through their answer. Scaffolds may be written, but they are often verbal and can be provided by a speech-language pathologist or teacher.

There can be some overlap among organizers and scaffolds. In general, however, *scaffolds* is a term most often used by speech-language pathologists and linguists to refer to frameworks that can change as a child needs less help. They are often more grammatical and language-based than organizers are. Organizers, or graphic organizers (the term favored by most educators) tend to be more visual. Just be aware that although we have categorized the types of supports below as either cues, scaffolds, or organizers, some scaffolds could also be classified as organizers, and vice versa.

SCAFFOLDS This section describes scaffolds that are helpful for elementary school children.

CLOZE PROCEDURES

Cloze Procedures are fill-in frameworks that can help your child with word retrieval or with structuring his answers to questions. They can be either spoken or written. For example, if you want your child to say down, you might say "up and _____." If you want him to say the word milk, you might say, "We eat cookies, and we drink _____."

Although cloze procedures usually use words, they can also involve filling in a sound or an entire phrase. For example, teachers may be working in class with word families such as cat, hat, and bat. To help children remember the final sound, they might use a visual cue for "t" at first. Later they might give children a blank fill-in (ca_. ha_. ba_). This technique is used a great deal in the early elementary school years.

When you read predictable books with children and ask them to fill in the repetitive phrase, you are using a cloze procedure. ("I'll huff and I'll puff, and I'll blow your house in.") Predictable books using cloze procedures help children remember and reproduce what they have heard. Children hear and say the repeated phrase, but they also anticipate when the phrase is coming and can remember and predict what the phrase will be. Children love predictable stories. They get a big kick out of remembering the phrase and being able to shout it out at the right moment. Some predictable books that children enjoy are:

- Brown, M. *The Three Billy Goats Gruff*. New York, NY: Harcourt Brace Jovanovich, 1957.
- Campbell, R. *Dear Zoo*. New York, NY: Four Winds Press, 1982.
- Carle, E. *The Very Hungry Caterpillar*. New York, NY: Philomel Books, 1969.
- Galdone, P. *Henny Penny*. New York, NY: Seabury Press, 1968.
- Hutchins, P. *Good Night, Owl*. New York, NY: Penguin, 1982.
- Martin, B. *Brown Bear, Brown Bear, What Do You See?* New York, NY: Holt, Rinehart & Winston, 1983.
- McGovern, A. *Too Much Noise*. New York, NY: Scholastic, 1967.
- Numeroff, L. J. *If You Give a Mouse a Cookie*. New York, NY: Harper Collins, 1991.
- Peck, M. *Mary Wore Her Red Dress and Henry Wore His Green Sneakers*. New York, NY: Houghton Mifflin, 1985.
- Sendak, M. *Chicken Soup with Rice*. New York, NY: Scholastic, 1962.
- Sendak, M. *Where the Wild Things Are*. New York, NY: Scholastic, 1984.

COMPREHENSION/ELABORATION QUESTIONS

When your child comes home from school each day, the general question, "How was school today," usually doesn't yield too much information. But, if you ask specific questions, such as "What did you do in science today? Did you get to use those lima beans you brought in? How much math homework do you have tonight?," you are more likely to get specific information. These are all examples of comprehension/elaboration questions.

Elaboration questions are often used in language arts and book report assignments in elementary schools. Questions such as "What is the title of the book?" "Who is the author?" "Who are the people in the story?" "What happened in the story?" "What was your favorite part of the book?" help the child elaborate on the story and demonstrate that he comprehends it. These questions can be posed verbally or written down, as on the next page.

CUES AND PROMPTS

PREPARATORY PROMPTS

Preparatory prompts are spoken, gestural, or visual cues that help a child get ready for what is to come. There are centers in the brain that alert the system to be ready to see or to listen. Preparatory prompts help children get ready to respond in the appropriate manner.

Preparatory prompts are used during transition times such as lunch, recess, and assemblies to help children get ready to change to the new activity. Preparatory prompts can also be used to help children get ready to use a specific channel for learning. For example, we sometimes have young children put on Mickey Mouse hats as listening ears, and we say, "Are you wearing your listening ears? Are you ready to listen?" For older children, we may use a prompt such as pointing to the ears or cupping the ears. We may use a pair of glasses or a prompt such as pointing to the eyes and say to a child, "look at this" or "Are you ready to look carefully?" For older children, visual reminders such as a small Post-it note with ears or eyes drawn

Questions to Help You Understand the Story

Setting: Where does the story take place? _____
_____
_____

Characters: Who are the people the story is about? _____
_____
_____
_____

Time: When does the story take place? _____
_____
_____

Events: What happens to the characters? _____
_____
_____
_____

Goals: What are the characters trying to do? _____
_____
_____
_____

Attempts: How will the characters reach their goals? _____
_____
_____
_____

Results: How does everything turn out? _____
_____
_____
_____

End: How does the story end? _____
_____
_____

on it can be used to remind the child as part of class routines that you must always listen and watch.

GESTURES AND PANTOMIME

Gestures or pantomime can provide visual cues to help your child follow directions that the teacher gives in class. For example, when the teacher says, "Line up on this side of the room," and points to the area, she is using gesture to help clarify her message. The examples of preparatory prompts above such as pointing to the eyes and ears are also gestures. Pantomimes might include providing visual models of what the child is supposed to do. For example, the teacher might say, "Hold up your pencil when you have finished writing the sentence," holding up a pencil as she speaks. Or, "Close your book when you have finished reading the paragraph," holding up the language arts book and closing it as a visual model of what children are supposed to do.

PACING BOARDS

The Pacing board is a visual motor cuing system. The pacing board is a visual representation of the units of language in which dots or pictures serve as place markers for the words of speech. See examples below.

Pacing board with dots

Pacing board with pictures

Pacing board with print cues

The pacing board may be used first when your child is beginning to transition from single-word to multiword utterances (for example, to help your child learn to use "big blue car" instead of "car"). As your child gets older, it may be used, in school, to remind your child of how many words he needs to use in the sentence. For example, a pacing board with five dots could promote practice of five-word sentences. It may also be used to visually cue your child for certain word skills, such as verb endings. A pacing board such as the following may help the child who is working on present participle verbs:

●	●	●	●
He	is	____	ing

●	●	●	●
She	is	____	ing

MANIPULATIVES

Manipulatives are various types of objects that can be held and manipulated by the child as cues. Anything that your child can touch and use as a cuing system may be helpful. Using a rosary as you say the words of The Lord's Prayer is an example of using a manipulative.

The *Story Grammar Marker* (listed in References) is a published example of a manipulative cuing system that helps a child organize his retelling of a story. The *Story Grammar Marker* has items you can touch to remind you to include the important parts of the story including characters, setting, initiating event, plan, actions in the plot, and resolution. My opinion is that the *Story Grammar Marker* is too complicated for most children with Down syndrome until at least middle school, but the concept of using a manipulative as a reminder is a good idea.

For an elementary school child with Down syndrome, I created an individually designed manipulative to help with book reports. First, I listed the information that the child needed to include in the book report:

- Title
- Author
- Main Characters
- Setting
- Plot
- Ending

Then I designed the manipulative using:

- A piece of felt as the background
- A small piece of tag board with the word "Title" on it, painted to look like a theater marquee
- A button with a profile of a face as a cue for "author"
- 2 buttons shaped like people as a cue for "main characters"
- The numbers 1, 2, 3 on tag board for three things that happened (the plot).

I glued the buttons and the tag board onto the felt, then glued a second piece of felt to the back to make the manipulative more sturdy. (See next page for finished samples.) The child practiced using this manipulative to tell stories from

books she was reading at home. It was also used in school as a manipulative cuing system, so that when the child touched the buttons, she was reminded of what needed to come next in the book report. (Instead of using felt to mount the manipulatives, tag board or small popsicle sticks could have been used.)

A child in later elementary school would be required to put more detail in a book report. Here is a longer manipulative (example at left) that I designed for an older child that includes:

- Title
- Author
- Characters (who?)
- Setting (where? when?)
- Plot (three things that happened)
- Your feelings about the story
- How did the story end?

AUDITORY AND VISUAL CUES

Auditory and visual cues can assist your child in answering questions, speaking, and following directions for class and home assignments. Some examples of cues that can be used in school by the teacher, aide, or peer buddy are:

- **Initial Phonemic Cues:** Initial phonemic cues provide the first sound of the word. For example, you want the child to say "peach," so you say "p-p-p" as an initial phonemic cue.
- **Initial Sound Placement Cue:** Placing the lips and tongue in position to say the first sound in the word. For instance, the teacher may put her lips together for /b/ for "beach" or put her tongue between her teeth for /th/ for "thumb."
- **Rhyming Word Cue:** You provide a rhyming cue to help the child remember a word. To cue "peach" say, "Not beach but ___."
- **Associated Word Cue:** Associated word cues provide a word connected in some way by meaning. For example, you might say "Pen and _____" to help the child remember "paper." Opposites are often used as cues; for example, "up and ___," "day and ___," "cold and ___."
- **Sequential Word Cue:** Sequential word cues provide a word that would appear in sequence; it may be similar to a fill-in question. To cue phone, say "Talk on the ___" or "the cell ___."
- **Visual Cue:** These can take the form of:
  1. *Written cues* (using the word, part of the word, or the initial consonant sound to provide a print cue);
  2. *Picture cues* (a picture or photo associated with the word, or a picture of the object);
  3. *Icon cues* (a symbol that will provide a cue for the word or concept, such as eyes to remind the child to look at

Book report long manipulative example shown directly above; short manipulative example shown above right

the speaker, or the icons used in *The Story Grammar Marker* to remind the child what needs to be included in retelling a story);

4. *Color code cues* (coloring material to be learned different colors, using colored highlighters or highlighter tape, to assist the child in learning);

5. *Gestural cues* (a hand signal or pointing signal that will cue the word or concept, such as holding up a finger for silence, or holding up two hands when you need to find your buddy).

In the beginning, it may seem awkward or cumbersome to include these cues, but it becomes very natural to use them. Whoever will be assisting your child in school, whether the classroom aide, peer buddy, communication aide, or a classroom volunteer, it is essential that the person(s) be trained to use these cues, and be responsible for using them.

MNEMONICS

Mnemonics are aids to memory and information retrieval which may take several different forms. The mnemonic is a type of shorthand in which you remember simpler cueing sounds, letters, or words to help you retrieve the more complex information that you are trying to remember. You use the mnemonic as a self-cue/prompt to help you remember. Types of mnemonics include:

Acronyms. An acronym is an aid in which you use the first letter of a group of words to form a new word. For example, to remember the great lakes, Huron, Ontario, Michigan, Erie, Superior, you would remember HOMES. To remember the colors of the spectrum, red, orange, yellow, green, blue, indigo, violet, you could use Roy G. Biv as an acronym. SCUBA is an acronym for "self-contained underwater breathing apparatus."

Acrostics. An acrostic uses the first letter of each word that you are trying to remember to make a sentence. For example, when you learn the musical notes, you remember them by using Every Good Boy Does Fine (EGBDF) for the treble notes and Good Boys Do Fine Always (GBDFA) for the bass notes. Likewise, My Dear Aunt Sally helps you to remember the order of mathematical operations, multiply and divide before you add and subtract.

Rhythm, Rhymes, and Songs. These can all can aid memory. Preschool and early school concepts are often taught using songs. An example is when children learn the letters of the alphabet to the tune of "Twinkle Twinkle Little Star." Some rhymes that are used in elementary school are:

- "When two vowels go walking, the first one does the talking."
- "I before e except after c, or when sounded like a as in neighbor and way; either, neither, leisure, seize are 4 exceptions if you please."

For children with Down syndrome, these rhymes can be used or specially designed rhymes and songs can be created. For example, "Use plus for addition and minus for subtraction" sung as a chant.

To practice identifying initial sounds in words, a skill that is taught in reading, the following jump rope chant may be used: "A, my name is Alice and my husband's name is Allan, we come from Alabama and we sell apples." This is fairly advanced, but it can be used with cue cards, or done with a buddy. We can also create original songs and lyrics to teach initial letter sounds, such as (sung to "The Farmer in the Dell"):

"Soup starts with S

Soap starts with S

Sandwich, snake, and spaghetti all start with S."

Rhythm and cheers can be used to help children with Down syndrome learn their spelling words. Use pom poms or streamers and a team hat to make the spelling practice more fun. Divide the spelling words into sounds. You might begin by giving your child the correct spelling in the form: "Give me a C, give me an A, give me a K, give me an E, C-A-K-E and what have you got . . . CAKE." Then your child can lead the cheer, "C-A-K-E, CAKE CAKE CAKE. Starts with C, but rhymes with rake."

There are other aids to memory including:

Chunking. This is an effective device when you need to remember lists of words or categories of information. Telephone numbers and social security numbers are divided into chunks to aid in memory. For example, when we are trying to remember a phone number, we remember it in 3 chunks, 555-234-5678. When we are trying to remember a list, we often use chunking. If you are asked to go to the store to buy milk, orange juice, soda, apples, and oranges, you will usually remember the list by grouping it into category chunks such as beverages (milk, orange juice, and soda) and fruits (apples and oranges). Children with Down syndrome often have difficulty remembering lists, and chunking the information into smaller units can be helpful.

Rehearsal. This is an aid to memory in which you use practice to help in short-term memory. In rehearsal, you say the words that you need to remember over and over. For example, if someone gives you a phone number and you don't have a pen nearby, you say the number over and over until you are ready to dial that number. For chunking and rehearsal, rhythm can be used, so that you are making the words almost song-like. Rhythm and song help children remember. That is why television commercials are so successful. Children remember the jingle and remember the name of the product.

ORGANIZERS Since children with Down syndrome often learn best visually, organizers can often help them learn. In this chapter, we will look at examples of how these visual organizers can be used to help children in class and with homework assignments. Chapter 10 offers some suggestions for using organizers to help children understand and follow routines.

Use the suggestions in this section to let your creativity and organizational skills soar. You can make an unlimited number of visual organizers. Visual organizers are often used for all elementary school children, but even when they are not used for all children in the class, their use can be written into the IEP. It is important that the IEP specify who will be responsible for creating these sheets on a daily basis. This requires time and effort and will not just happen if someone is not responsible for their development and use.

VENN DIAGRAMS

A Venn diagram consists of intersecting circles that have separate as well as overlapping sections. The Venn diagram is used to visually document the similarities and differences between two concepts or events. It can be used for simple or complex concepts, for objects, animals, people, or events. For example, in science, a Venn diagram can be used to diagram the similarities and differences between dogs and cats, or mammals and reptiles, or broadleaf and tropical trees. For early reading, a Venn diagram can be used to compare the experiences of the characters in the book with the experiences of the child. For example, compare the child's sleepover to Ira's experience in *Ira Sleeps Over*.

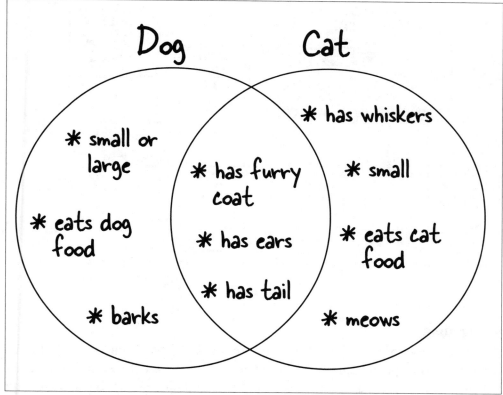

Dog | Cat

* small or large
* eats dog food
* barks

* has furry coat
* has ears
* has tail

* has whiskers
* small
* eats cat food
* meows

Venn diagram example

To teach children to use Venn diagrams, first use a simple example such as the comparison of a cat and dog. Take a picture of a cat and a picture of a dog. Paint the entire page of the cat picture blue. Paint the entire page of the dog picture yellow. Now, on the Venn diagram that you give to the child, one circle should be blue, one should be yellow, and the common overlap space should be green. Discuss the concepts of same and different and what things have in common and how they are different. Then, make a list with the child of the things that he knows about cats and the things that he knows about dogs. For example,

Cats have ears	Dogs have ears
Cats have a tail	Dogs have a tail
Cats say meow	Dogs bark
Cats have a long tongue	Dogs have a long tongue
Cats eat cat food	Dogs eat dog food
Cats have whiskers	Dogs bark when they see a stranger

Now, color code the information using highlighters. Everything that refers to a dog is yellow (e.g., barks). Everything that refers to a cat is blue (e.g., whiskers).

Find the items that refer to both (e.g., dogs and cats have long tongues) and put them on a separate list. On the list that refers to both dogs and cats, use the yellow highlighter and then the blue highlighter. Those items will now be green. If the child can write the characteristics, have him write or word process the information on the Venn diagram. Or the aide or peer tutor can write the characteristics on the diagram. Or the child can paste pictures that have been prepared beforehand that show the characteristics. Here is an example of a Venn diagram comparing spiders and insects that was completed by a boy with Down syndrome using pictures that he glued on.

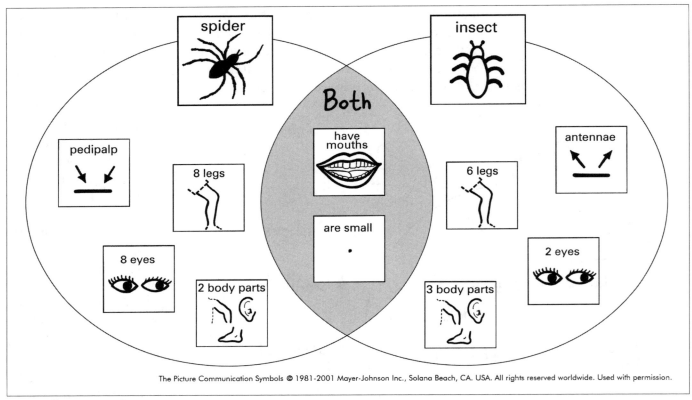

The Picture Communication Symbols © 1981-2001 Mayer-Johnson Inc., Solana Beach, CA. USA. All rights reserved worldwide. Used with permission.

Venn diagram example

ATTRIBUTE WEBS

An attribute web can be used to help a child learn the vocabulary that goes with a specific concept. It visually "lists" or organizes the attributes that go with a concept. For example, in a second grade science unit on the earth's surface, the child is asked to learn ten words related to the unit. Early in the unit, an attribute web filled in by the teacher or by a group in class can help him make sense of the words by grouping them, and at the end of the unit, his ability to fill in the attribute web can show that he has learned more about these terms.

canyon	dam
delta	deposition
erosion	stream
surface	volcano
weathering	wind

Attribute webs, such as the example at right, help organize attributes of concepts

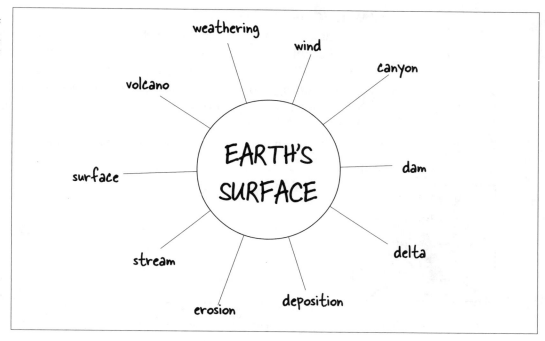

A more advanced attribute web might describe the concepts related to government. The attribute web can help the child learn those vocabulary words. It also can help the child write a paragraph or a report because it presents the concepts that relate to the main word or idea.

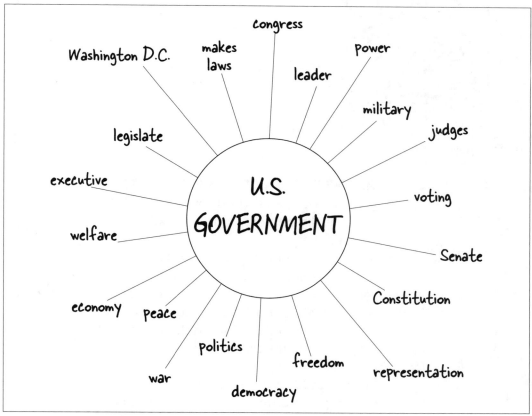

A more complex attribute web example

SEMANTIC WEBS

Semantic webs or vocabulary webs enable the child to see the concepts that go with a vocabulary word by visually surrounding the word with the associated terms. For example, if the vocabulary word is *apple*, the circles on the web may have the terms *fruit, red, crunchy, grows on trees, tastes good*, etc. Here is an example of a vocabulary web for seasons using picture symbols for the child who cannot write the answers in the boxes. This type of assignment could also be completed by having the child dictate the answers to an aide or peer buddy who would write them in the boxes.

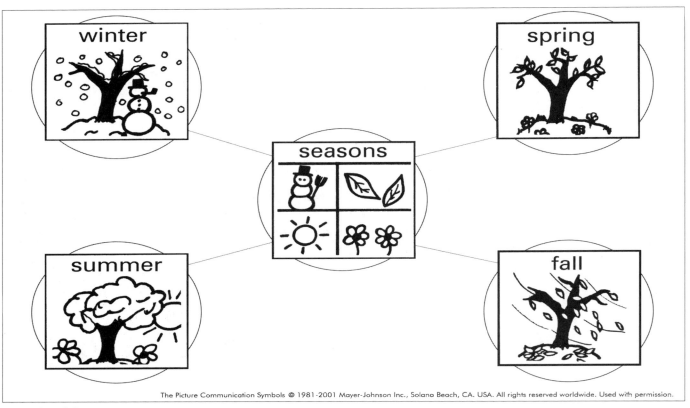

Semantic web for seasons

ASSOCIATED WORDS PRACTICE LISTS

An associated words practice list helps the child learn vocabulary in a different way, by helping to define the characteristics of the word. Associated words may include:

- synonyms (big-large)
- antonyms (up-down)
- part/whole relationship (A *finger* is part of a *hand*)
- superordinate/subordinate (An *apple* is a type of *fruit*)
- function (You drink from a cup)
- temporal (breakfast-morning)
- spatial and other relationships (caboose-end)

For the child, simpler terms would be used to specify these concepts. For example, you might use the words "category" and "example" to talk about superordinate/subordinate relationships, or the word "opposites" to talk about antonyms.

Associated Words Practice Sheet

Note: words in parentheses are for teachers' use

Key Word: _____

Similar meaning (synonym): _____

Opposite meaning (antonym): _____

Part/whole: _____

Larger category (superordinate): _____

Example or smaller category (subordinate): _____

Function: _____

When something occurs (temporal): _____

Where something occurs (spatial): _____

Rhyming word: _____

ORGANIZERS FOR COMPLEX CONCEPTS

A variety of graphic organizers can be used to help children with Down syndrome learn words and concepts related to particular units at school. There are many ways in which organizers can be used, and their specific use for a unit will depend on the nature of the material and on the learning styles of the students. Some of the more common are described below.

Fishbone Maps. A *fishbone map* allows you to graph information about a complex concept, showing how categories and subcategories are related. For fifth grade science, students may study a unit on fossil fuels. A fishbone map can visually organize the information in the textbook on the making of fossil fuel. Usually, the completed fishbone map would be given to the child or the map would be completed as a cooperative group activity. The child with Down syndrome would not be expected to fill in the map on his own. (See example on the next page.)

Sequence Maps. A *sequence map* can be used to map out a sequence of events that lead to the development of fossil fuel. This may be filled out beforehand, filled in with the assistance of an aide, or completed as a cooperative group activity. The sequence map could be filled in with sentences or with pictures representing the concepts. These organizers are designed to help children learn about the development of fossil fuels from the following text discussion:

Fossil fuels (coal, natural gas, oil) are remains of plants and animal life that lived on Earth many millions of years ago. The plants and animals died, decayed, and then were buried under soil or mud. The buildup of soil, mud, and rocks created tons of pressure

Fossil fuels fishbone map

on the plant and animal remains. Over time, this pressure caused the remains to become coal, natural gas, or oil. Peat is the result of the same kinds of conditions but without the extreme pressure. It is found in bogs on the surface of the earth. Because of the long period of time it took for coal, oil, and natural gas to form (millions and millions of years) they can't be replaced quickly by man.

Coal is the result of plants that grew, lived, then died in swamps. Because of the lack of oxygen, they did not decay completely. In time the plant remains turned into a brownish-black material called peat. More and more layers of soil and rock built up over the peat as the millions of years passed. This buildup placed more and more pressure on the peat and eventually the peat became the very hard material called coal.

Oil was formed a lot like coal except that instead of being plant remains, oil came from the remains of plants and animals that lived in the shallow seas and that washed into the seas from the land.

Natural gas is found near oil deposits, for it is made of the same thing that oil is. The difference is that the natural gas is found much deeper in the earth. The higher temperatures deeper in the earth have changed the oil into natural gas.

Spider Maps and Network Trees. In the early grades, a social studies unit is often devoted to studying the local community, services needed in the community, workers in the community, and a discussion of careers. One teacher divided the class unit into sub-units on utilities, protection and law, schools, and health as needed services, and discussed the jobs workers might do in each of the four areas. Two types of visual organizers could be used to help children learn these concepts. One is a ***spider map*** in which the four service areas radiate from the overall topic in the center. Under each service area are the jobs that would go with that service. Another visual organizer that could demonstrate the same concept is a ***network tree.*** Here, the overall topic would be at the top. The four areas would arise from that circle, and the jobs would be seen under each area.

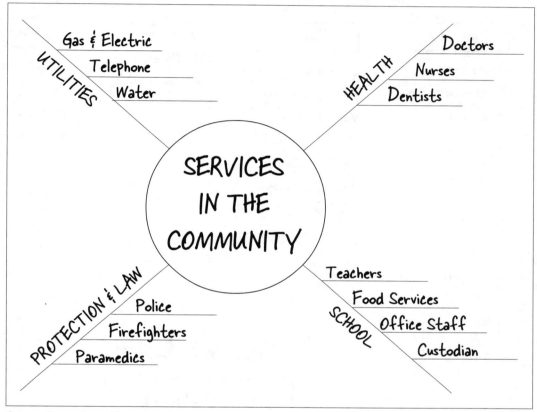

Community services spider map

Structured Overview Maps. In grade 5, a typical social studies unit teaches about the age of exploration. A variety of visual organizers can be used to help children with Down syndrome learn about the explorers. A ***structured overview map*** or a network tree can be used to visually group the explorers (e.g., by the country that supported them) so that the information will be easier for students to learn and remember. An individually designed organizer could be a map that has the countries that sent the explorers and the countries that they explored. As a cooperative group activity, children could paste pictures and then write the names of the explorers on the countries that they were sent by and the countries that they explored.

In social studies, units on exploration, Colonial life, and the revolution often lead to discussions on settling the West and pioneer life. A structured overview may be used to explore and categorize the many ways pioneers used animals. Animals were used as food, for clothing, and as "power" to assist in field and farm work. Rather than reading a textbook and trying to remember the information regarding the many uses of animals, the organizer helps children identify the important points in the textbook chapter, and make sense out of the information that they read. (See examples on the next page.)

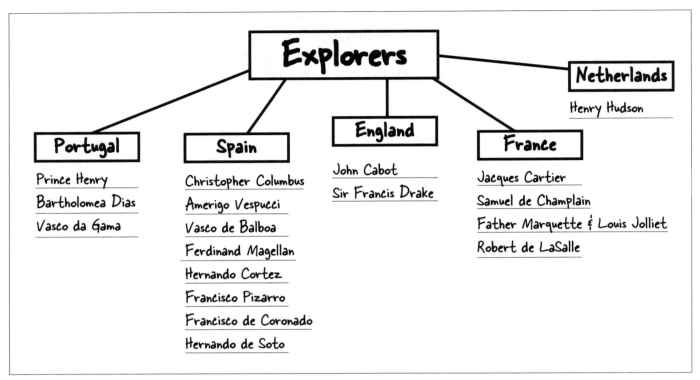

Explorers structured overview map or network tree

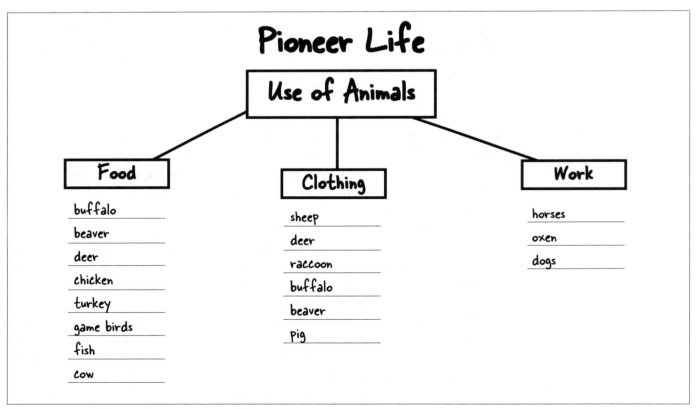

Pioneer life structured overview map or network tree

An organizer can also be used to set up a comparison of pioneer life with life today. For the child who is more advanced, you may just have two columns on a worksheet, Then and Now (see example below). For a child who needs further assistance, the teacher might list all of the areas on which she would like the students to compare life for the pioneers in the West in the 1800s with life today (sample questionaire on the next page). For the child who has some difficulty reading, icons may be used to suggest the areas for comparison, and the child might dictate the information to the classroom aide, who would write the answers on the worksheet, or the child might paste pictures in the appropriate columns on the worksheets.

Name: _____

Title / Topic: Pioneer Life

Then:

1. Family members dependent on each other to meet basic needs.

2. Settlers moved west for resources, excitement, freedom, and in search of riches.

3. People relied on natural resources for energy.

4. Shelter included log cabins, dug outs, and sod houses.

5. To obtain food, people hunted, fished, or farmed.

6. Food was preserved by drying, storing underground, salting, or smoking.

7. Recreational activities included house raising, husking bees, quilting, apple cuttings, corn husking, popping corn, games, and dancing.

Now:

1. Families are more independent.

2. People move for similar reasons. Moving and travelling is much less complex.

3. There are other available resources such as electricity.

4. People live in apartments, townhouses, and individual houses.

5. Today we go to the market and buy food.

6. Food is preserved by storing in the refrigerator or freezer or can be chemically preserved.

7. Recreational activities include sports, computer games, watching TV, board games, and surfing the internet.

Example of an organizer used for comparisons

Name: _____   Title / Topic: **Pioneer Life**

Let's Compare Pioneer Life with Life Today.

Comparison	Pioneer Life	Today
Did families work together?		
Why did people move?		
What sources could people use for energy?		
Where did people live?		
What did they eat?		
What did they do for fun?		

Example of a comparison organizer using questions

SEMANTIC FEATURE ANALYSIS

Organizers can also be used to master vocabulary concepts or to help children learn how to describe objects. A type of organizer called a semantic feature analysis may be used to help older children compare and contrast word meanings. For example, what is the difference between an envelope and a suitcase? Both hold things and both can be carried. They are usually made of different materials, paper vs. leather or canvas. They differ in size. How about an envelope and a carton? They have similar functions, both can be mailed, both can be carried, both hold things, both can be opened and closed. They differ primarily in dimensions and in size, and in the material they are made of.

A semantic feature analysis can also be used to help children learn to describe. If shown a large blue pitcher full of lemonade, the child can use a semantic feature analysis to describe what he sees (color, function, size, etc.). These types of organizers are sometimes called "grids for learning" by teachers. Below and on the next page are examples of two different kinds of organizers for semantic feature analysis.

LEARNING FRAME AND HOMEWORK FRAME ORGANIZERS

Learning frames and homework frames are fill-in types of scaffolds that usually include comprehension questions. They are worksheets that provide a framework that the child can use to fill in the answers. They organize the material for the child. Teachers sometimes refer to them as learning grids.

	Features						
Term (class or example)	drink from it	has handle	made of china	made of glass			
mug	+	+	+	+			
glass	+	–	–	+			
teacup	+	+	+	–			
jar	–	–	–	+			
plate	–	–	+	+			
paper cup	+	–	–	–			
styrofoam cup	+	–	–	–			
briefcase	–	+	–	–			
pitcher	–	+	+	+			

Semantic feature analysis example

Describing Objects

Name: _____   Date: _____

Object to be described: _____
_____

Shape: _____
_____

Size: _____
_____

Color: _____
_____

Material made of: _____
_____

Texture: _____
_____

How is the object used? _____
_____

Example of a semantic feature organizer

Learning frames can be used after your child has completed a reading assignment to help him write a report about the book. They can also be used before your child begins reading to assist in reading comprehension by letting him know what questions he will be required to answer. For example, a learning frame can be used to help students organize facts for fifth grade social studies. When learning about the events leading to the signing of the Declaration of Independence, the important information can be summarized with the use of a learning frame or through a 5 Ws (Who, What, When, Where, Why) visual organizer (example on next page).

The example on page 98 shows a learning frame that could be used to help a fifth grade student write a bibliography. Assuming the student needed to use at least two books, one encyclopedia, and one periodical, this learning frame would ensure he used and listed the right resources. See pages 99 and 100 for examples of learning frames that can be used in different subjects.

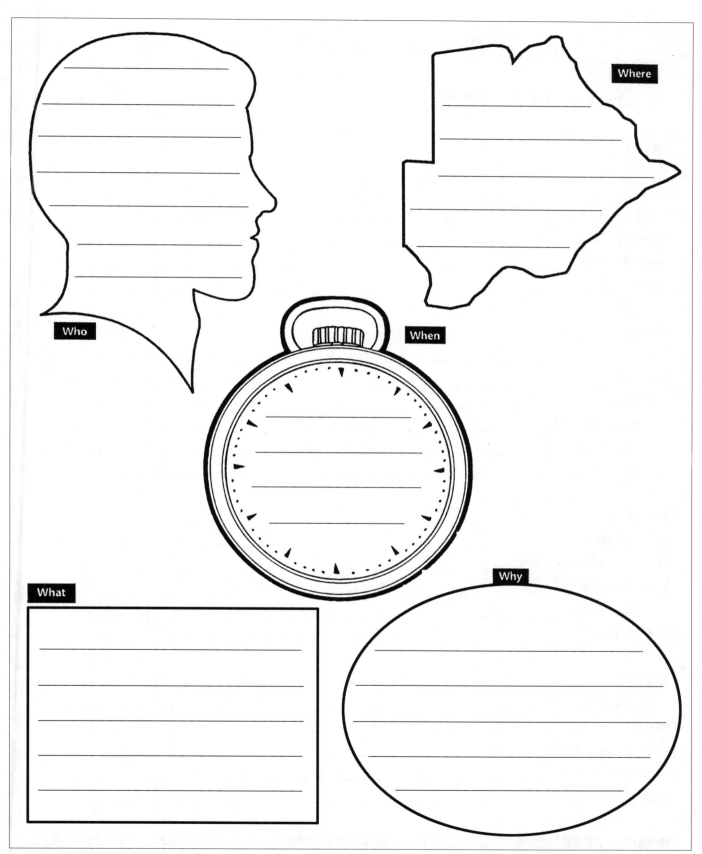

Example of a 5 W's visual organizer

Name: _____   Topic: _____

RESOURCES USED IN MY REPORT

Book 1
Title: _____

Author: _____

Publisher: _____

Where published: _____

Year published: _____

Pages used: _____

Book 2
Title: _____

Author: _____

Publisher: _____

Where published: _____

Year published: _____

Pages used: _____

Encyclopedia
Title of article: _____

Name of encyclopedia: _____

Year published: _____

Volume number: _____

Pages used: _____

Periodical
Title of article: _____

Author: _____

Title of periodical/magazine: _____

Month and date: _____

Pages used: _____

Example of a learning frame used as a guide to write a report bibliography

Learning Frame for Information Synthesis (WWBS)

Name: _____   Date: _____

WHO: _____
_____

WANTS: _____
_____

BUT: _____
_____

SO: _____
_____

Learning Frame for Definitions

Name: _____   Date: _____

SIZE: _____

SHAPE: _____

COLOR: _____

MATERIAL: _____

FUNCTION: _____

WHEN USED: _____

WHERE USED: _____

Homework Frame for Geography Report

Name: _____   Date: _____

What country did you study? _____

Location: _____

Population: _____

Area in miles: _____

Any large mountain ranges? List: _____

Any large bodies of water? List: _____

Any deserts? _____

Capital: _____

Type of government: _____

Name of governing bodies: _____

Name of leader of the country: _____

Money used: _____

Languages used: _____

Major religions: _____

Five main products: _____

STORY MAPS AND STORY LINES

A story map with illustrations may be used to help children sequence the events in a story, and understand the sequential nature of the plot in children's literature. Below you see a story map that was developed for *The Three Little Pigs.* The numbers help teach the concept of sequencing, and the pictures provide cues to help the child remember the events in the story.

After the child has used a story map, the teacher might use a story line (example on next page). This has fewer pictorial clues, and is more of a timeline visual organizer. Story lines are also more detailed than story maps. The story line developed for *The Three Little Pigs* has ten points, representing a more detailed story sequence then developed with the story map. The teacher or aide might provide the first description so that the child knows what is expected. Then, an individual child working with an aide, a group of children working cooperatively, or the entire class working with the teacher could complete the story line. When the child understands the sequence of events and knows the plot, the teacher may ask him to tell what happened in the story, or to write about what happened. A story map that was already filled in or that the child had done previously could be used to cue him to verbally sequence his answer.

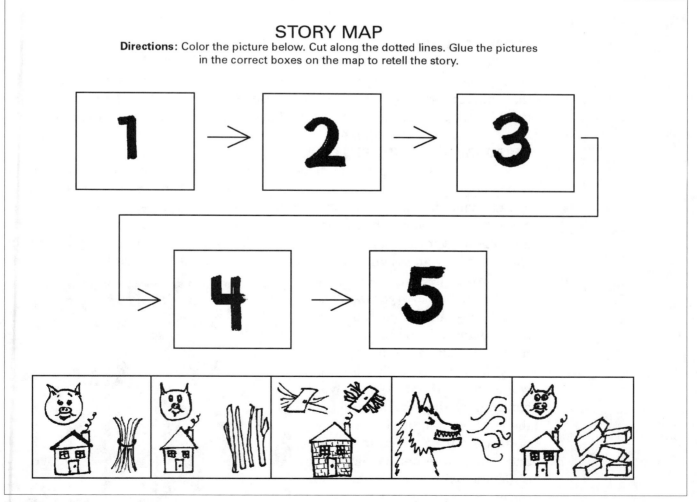

STORY MAP

Directions: Color the picture below. Cut along the dotted lines. Glue the pictures in the correct boxes on the map to retell the story.

Story Map example

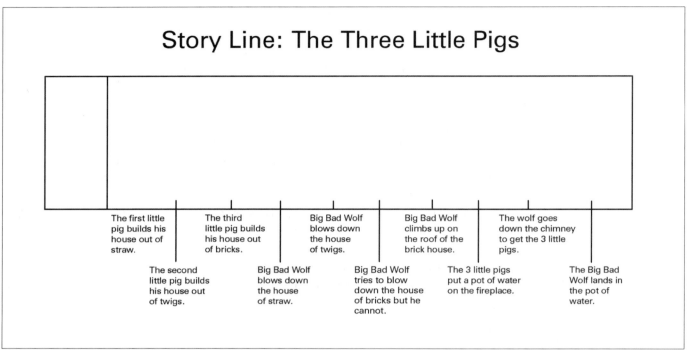

Story Line: The Three Little Pigs

The first little pig builds his house out of straw.

The second little pig builds his house out of twigs.

The third little pig builds his house out of bricks.

Big Bad Wolf blows down the house of straw.

Big Bad Wolf blows down the house of twigs.

Big Bad Wolf tries to blow down the house of bricks but he cannot.

Big Bad Wolf climbs up on the roof of the brick house.

The 3 little pigs put a pot of water on the fireplace.

The wolf goes down the chimney to get the 3 little pigs.

The Big Bad Wolf lands in the pot of water.

Story line example

STORY STARTERS

Story starters are words and frameworks that help children get started telling stories. They are opening phrases (such as "The best thing I did this weekend was…) that children can add to. They are often used for compositions. Here is an example in which the story starter is "At recess, I like to..." (See example on the next page.)

PERSONAL WORD BANKS

A word bank is a personal dictionary that lists and defines the words that the child knows. Usually, each word is placed on an index card and the words are kept close at hand, in a small file box. They may also be kept in loose leaf notebooks, so pages can be organized by categories—for example, you could have a tab for nouns and one for verbs, or tabs for social studies words vs. science words. When the child is writing an assignment, he can look through the word bank to help remind him of words he knows how to use. Word banks are organizers, although they can be used by the child as a prompt to help him remember the words that he can use.

Word banks can be used on worksheets and tests. When a word bank is used, the child has to choose the right answer, but has a "bank" of answers from which to choose, and is therefore not penalized for difficulties with word retrieval. See the example on page 104.

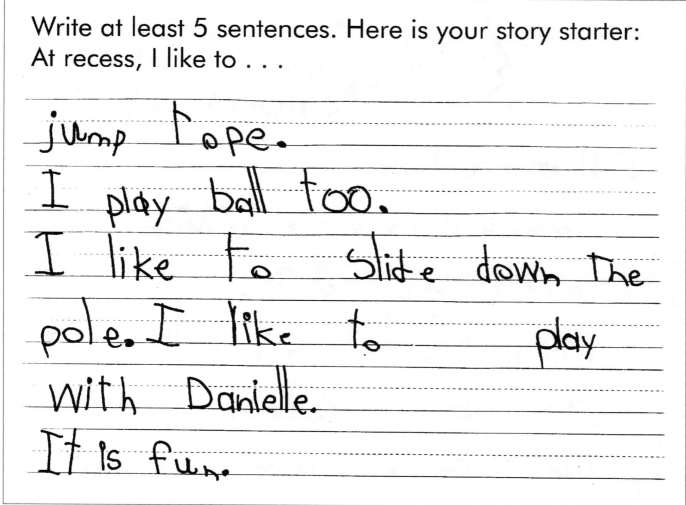

Write at least 5 sentences. Here is your story starter:
At recess, I like to . . .

jump rope.
I play ball too.
I like to slide down the
pole. I like to   play
with Danielle.
It is fun.

Story starter example

Assistive Technology

Like the general supports and strategies described above, assistive technology can also be very important in helping students with Down syndrome succeed in school.

IDEA 97 defines assistive technology (AT) as *any tool or item that increases, maintains, or improves functional capabilities of individuals with disabilities.* The specific type of assistive technology that speech language pathologists are usually associated with is augmentative and alternative communication devices—systems that are used to replace or supplement speech. These systems will be discussed in Chapter 11.

Under the federal definition, augmentative communication is just one type of assistive technology. Assistive technology also includes many other types of aids, such as: a pencil grip that helps the child hold the pencil, an enlarged push switch for a tape recorder so that the child can turn it on and off independently, a computer program that will help the child write a story, a picture symbol system that

SPELLING HOMEWORK

Fill in the blank.

1. I plant a flower in the SOIL.

2. There is a loud NOISE.

3. Will you JOIN the group?

4. The water will BOIL.

5. Use OIL and vinegar for the salad.

6. A quarter is a type of COIN.

Word Bank

~~boil~~   ~~noise~~   ~~coin~~

~~soil~~   ~~join~~   ~~oil~~

Word bank worksheet example

can be used to adapt and develop worksheets based on the curriculum, a hearing aid, or a classroom amplification system. Abledata, a national database of assistive technology information, lists over 23,000 items that could be considered assistive technology.

Some AT is just common sense and can be implemented without any formalities. For example, if your child needs triangular pencils or paper with more widely spaced lines to write well, there is no need for an evaluation. With more "high tech" types of AT, however, you will need to locate the specialist in your school responsible for planning and implementation of assistive technology. In some school systems, assistive technology is the domain of occupational therapists. In other school systems, it is the domain of the special education teacher, or the special educator working in collaboration with the regular education teacher and the SLP. The evaluation for and treatment with augmentative communication is usually done by speech-language pathologists who have specialized training.

This section will discuss technological-based assistive devices, including computers, that can help many students with Down syndrome learn in the classroom. Chapter 12 discusses using augmentative and alternative communication devices with students who cannot communicate adequately using speech alone.

USING COMPUTERS TO ASSIST LANGUAGE LEARNING

Computers can help children learn vocabulary and curricular material, improve their ability to follow directions, and continue to develop language. The growing area of literacy for children with disabilities, including Down syndrome, has increasingly demonstrated the important role of computers in creating accessible, understandable literacy activities for students.

Computers can be especially suited to help children with Down syndrome learn because:

- *Computers provide a visual display and visual reinforcement,* which capitalizes on the visual strengths in children with Down syndrome.
- *Computer graphics provide visual cues* that can reinforce the visual message and help teach a concept.
- *As inclusion focuses us on individualized and customized learning opportunities for each and every child, computers can play an important role* in providing these opportunities.
- *Computers can provide information in a multisensory mode.* Children are not just seeing a picture of a zebra; they are seeing the movements of the zebra in its natural habitat. Some software is more similar to taking a field trip than to reading a book description.
- *Computers can provide instant feedback* so that the child knows whether he has correctly answered the question. If he is incorrect, the computer can be programmed to provide the correct response, and then re-ask the question, providing an additional opportunity to learn. Errors can be handled in a positive manner, and this can help self-esteem.

- *Computer work can be highly individualized.* Many programs can be modified for learner differences.
- *Computers with speech synthesizers can provide verbal stimulation and verbal reinforcement that is slower than typical speaking rate, reliable (e.g., volume will not vary), and can be repeated.* Regular speech is fleeting, and may not be exactly the same when it is repeated each time. Synthesized speech will be the same and can be repeated over and over. Often children with Down syndrome will imitate the words being "said" by the computer, although they will not imitate words in class or in therapy.
- *Reading, writing, understanding, and speaking are all language skills. Computer software can help practice these skills.* For children who are not yet reading, software can help them learn concepts using picture symbols. For children who cannot write and have difficulty spelling, they can compose and write their own sentences and stories using picture symbols.
- *Your child feels in control on the computer.* On the computer, he usually can control which activity he chooses and the number of repetitions for an item or a program. Control can help develop feelings of mastery and self-esteem.
- *Most children love computers,* talk about them, and compare and trade software. Computers have high interest for children and they view their time on the computer as fun, rather than work.

SOFTWARE

There is a vast array of educational and language software available. Software packages need to be appropriate for your child's learning needs and capable of engaging your child's interest. Speech-language pathologists, educators, and parents can suggest programs that they have found work well.

Electronic books such as the Living Books (Broderbund software), can be motivating to beginning readers. Each CD has lively graphics, the capability to read text aloud while highlighting the words being read, and an accompanying book. Commercial software such as the Stickybears series (Weekly Reader software), the Jumpstart series, and the Reader Rabbit series (The Learning Company) are inexpensive, widely available, and provide practice for a variety of language concepts, such as opposites and early reading skills. Laureate and Edmark are companies that provide software that addresses language concepts specifically for children with special needs. (See the Resources at the end of the book.) They are companies with a strong tradition of customer service, and have technical representatives who can be of assistance to families and professionals.

Your child or the professionals working with him may also benefit from software that provides picture symbols. The symbols can be used to create worksheets, develop communication systems, for help in developing receptive understanding of concepts, or to augment or substitute for spoken language. It can be used with communication partners as a 2-way communication system. The pictures can enable the child to be both a listener and a speaker, both a decoder and encoder of language.

AT in Action

Last quarter at school, Alex and his Dad worked together to adapt an assignment from his health class about sexual harassment. They chose a few main points and re-worded them to a more appropriate reading level for him. Then Alex and his Dad made a one-page poster on the computer (see below). Alex chose fonts, size, colors, and did most of the keyboarding. They printed it, laminated it, and Alex took it to school. A few days later, the family received a note from Alex's paraprofessional. She told them how well Alex did giving a presentation in front of his general education eighth grade health class. He was able to read the information from his poster and explain what it meant to his class. The family hadn't even known there'd be a presentation.

Sexual Harassment

Is:

1. Someone touches your body, and you don't want them to.

2. Someone touches you, you say stop, and they don't.

3. Someone calls you bad names.

What to do:

1. Tell your teacher.

2. Tell your principal.

3. Tell your parents.

4. Tell a friend you trust.

Boardmaker™ software (Mayer-Johnson Company) provides the most extensive picture library. Other software available includes *Picturebase Pictogram* (Zygo Industries), as well as programs available from Don Johnston Software, Mayer-Johnson Software, and IntelliTalk©2. In the Resource Guide, there is a list of companies that have picture symbol books and software. (See below for an example of an adapted worksheet for a science unit on measuring temperature made with the Picture Communication Symbols© from Boardmaker.)

SCIENCE WORKSHEET

In lab we are learning about thermometers.
Read the statements below with a helper.
Fill in the correct circle.

1. The thermometer measures temperature.

2. Look at the thermometers below. Do they show a hot or cold temperature?

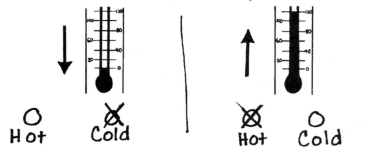

3. Draw a thermometer showing your favorite temperature.

Example of a worksheet adapted using the Picture Communication Symbols© (Mayer-Johnson)

For children who need help with spelling, or find the physical act of typing difficult, there are two general types of software that reduce the number of key-strokes needed:

- Word prediction programs, in which the computer lists several possible words to choose from after the student types in the first one or two letters of the word;
- Abbreviation expansion software, in which the computer substitutes a whole correctly spelled word after the student types in a previously programmed abbreviation for that word (for example, every time the student types in "gov," the software would automatically insert "government" in its place).

KEYBOARDS

Many children with Down syndrome are eventually able to use a standard computer keyboard, but there are also a variety of alternatives and adaptations:

- Touch screens: Screens that fit over the computer monitor that the user touches in specific locations to communicate with the computer (instead of using a keyboard).
- Nonstandard keyboards: Keyboards with larger keys, smaller keys, fewer keys, different colored keys, keys that are arranged in a different order than on a standard keyboard.
- Customized keyboards: Keyboards with varying numbers of keys that can be customized with pictures, symbols, or words on the keys. The IntelliKeys® keyboard by IntelliTools, for example, offers a picture multiple choice keyboard with a limited number of choices, based on the child's needs and abilities. The choices can be increased as the child is able to handle a larger number of vocabulary or access words.
- Adaptations to standard keyboards: Stickers (alphabet, colored) can be applied to keys to aid in discrimination or you can purchase "keyguards" to make it easier to find and depress the right key. In addition, most operating systems such as Windows come with "accessibility features" that users can program in, such as shortcut keys, larger buttons on toolbars, and the ability to use arrow keys instead of a mouse.

ADVICE ON COMPUTER OPTIONS

There are centers dedicated specifically to the use of computers to enhance learning. Some centers are linked to a comprehensive Down Syndrome Center. For example, the center at Hope Haven in Jacksonville, Florida, is in the same facility as the Down Syndrome Center. These centers have a high level of expertise and knowledge concerning technology and software, and the learning needs of children with Down syndrome. Other centers are part of a national network of centers that specialize in computers and learning and computers and communication. One example is the LINC center in Baltimore, Maryland, which is part of the Alliance for Technology Access network. (See Resources at the end of the book.)

These centers typically have a variety of computer-based communication devices, and can provide evaluation services. Some of the technology assistance centers will evaluate software, as well as hardware that would be appropriate for your child. Some centers will serve as a lending library for software, while others will work with your child at the center to evaluate the appropriateness of the software, but then you are responsible for purchasing software. More information on how to locate these centers is included in Chapter 12.

Computers can be powerful learning tools. With early exposure to computers, many children feel comfortable and are advanced in using computers. What seems awkward to us as adults seems natural to children who are familiar with computers. Computers can assist learning for children and adults with Down syndrome and serve as an information resource and communication tool for adults. Computers can't replace hands-on situational learning, but they can serve as a strong support to learning.

OTHER ASSISTIVE DEVICES

Besides computers, some other types of assistive technology that can be used to help children with Down syndrome with language skills include:

- Card reader devices: cards with magnetic strips; when run through the accompanying scanner, the voice output reads the card. They can be used for vocabulary practice, for auditory memory practice, and for increasing mean length of utterance. The teacher or aide can "tape" words, sentences, and phrases onto the cards.
- Different types of voice output devices: hand-held or laptop devices that "speak" for the child. They may be talking word processors or reading devices: they could be used to help children with sound-letter correspondence and other phonological awareness activities (e.g., you press down a key with a letter and the equipment makes the sound of the letter). (See Chapter 12 for more information.)
- Low technology assistive devices: Almost anything that you do not plug in or use with batteries can be considered low tech AT if it helps a child learn. Paper with raised or colored lines, for instance, can be useful AT for children learning to print. Magnetic

boards or sentence builders using magnet or index card symbols can help children learn to create sentences. And picture symbols can be used to design early readers for children. Picture symbols can be used to help a child organize a language activity, and can be used to assist a speaking child in retelling a story or relating an experience. Picture boards or symbol boards can also be designed to help children participate in class. On the next two pages are examples of category practice boards that were designed with Picture Communication Symbols© (Mayer-Johnson).

Using a Category Dictionary

animal

Aa	Bb	Cc	Dd	Ee	Ff	Gg	Hh
alligator	bear	camel	deer	eagle	fish	giraffe	hippo
	bee	cat	dinosaur	elephant	fly	goat	horse
	bird	caterpillar	dog		frog	goose	hamster
	butterfly	chick	duck		fox·	gorilla	

Example of a category practice board designed with Picture Communication Symbols© (Mayer-Johnson)

Databases such as Abledata can help you learn more about the types of assistive technology that are available. Dr. Penny Reed, of the Wisconsin Assistive Technology Initiative, has developed several excellent resources that include assessment guidelines, and information on the wide variety of devices available. (See the Resource Guide.)

Conclusion

Language is an integral part of learning and living in the school environment. There are many levels of assistance that we can provide to help children succeed in school. Through collaboration between families, classroom teachers, special educators, speech-language pathologists, administrators, and school-aged children, highly individualized learning materials can be developed, success can be maximized, and children with Down syndrome can be active, contributing members of the community of learners at school and in the community.

Using The Verb Category

C	D	D	D	E	F	F	F
count	dance	do	drive	eat	fall	file	fix
crawl	decorate	draw	drop	enter	feed	find	fly
cry	deliver	dress, wear	dry	exercise	feel	finish	fold
cut	dig	drink	dust	exit	fight	fish	follow

Example of a category practice board designed with Picture Communication Symbols© (Mayer-Johnson)

REFERENCES

Blenk, K. (1995). *Making school inclusion work: A guide to everyday practice.* Cambridge, MA: Brookline Books.

Chisler, J. & Oaks, R. (1995).*The collaboration companion.* Moline, IL: Lingui-Systems.

Christensen, S. L., & Cleary, M. (1990). Consultation and the parent-educator partnership: A perspective. *Journal of Educational and Psychological Consultation, 1,* 219-242.

Coufal, K. L. (1993). Collaborative consultation for speech-language pathologists. *Topics in Language Disorders, 14,* 1-14.

Creaghead, N. A. (1990). Mutual empowerment through collaboration: A new script for an old problem. *Best Practices in School Speech-Language Pathology, 1,* 109-116.

Ferguson, M. L. (1992). Implementing collaborative consultation: An introduction. *Language, Speech and Hearing Services in Schools, 23,* 361-362.

Filbin, J., Rogers-Connolly, T. & Brewer, R. (1996). *Individualized learner outcomes: Infusing student needs into the regular education curriculum.* Colorado Springs, CO: PEAK Parent Center.

Gardner, H. (1983). *Frames of mind: The theory of multiple intelligences.* New York: Basic Books.

Hasselbring, T.S. & Glaser, C.H. (2000). Use of computer technology to help students with special needs. *The Future of Children, 10,* 102-122.

McCormick, L., Loeb, D. F. & Schiefelbusch, R. L. (1997). Supporting children with communication difficulties in inclusive settings: School-based language intervention. Boston, MA: Allyn and Bacon.

Miller, L. (1989). Classroom-based language intervention. *Language, Speech and Hearing Services in the Schools, 20,* 153-170.

Moreau, M.R. & Fidrych-Puzzo, H. (1994). *Story grammar marker kit.* East Hampton, MA: Discourse Skills Productions.

Nelson, N. (1989). Curriculum-based language assessment and intervention. *Language, Speech and Hearing Services in the Schools, 20,* 170-184.

Pehrsson, R.S. & Denner, P.R. (1994). Semantic organizers: Implications for reading and writing. In Butler, K.G. *Best Practices II: The classroom as an intervention context.* Gaithersburg, MD: Aspen Publishers.

Prelock, P. A., Miller, B. L. & Reed, N. L. (1995) Collaborative partnerships in a language in the classroom program. *Language, Speech and Hearing Services in Schools, 26,* 286-292.

Roschelle, J.M., Pea, R.D., Hoadley, C.M., Gordin, D.N. & Means, B.M. (2000). Changing how and what children learn in school with computer-based technologies. *The Future of Children, 10,* 76-101.

Rynders, J., Abery, B., Spiker, D., Olive, M., Sheran, C. & Zajac, R. (1997). Improving educational programming for individuals with Down syndrome: Engaging the fuller competence. *Down Syndrome Quarterly, 2,* 1-11.

Schaffner, B. & Buswell, B. E. (1992). *Opening doors: Strategies for including all students in regular education.* Colorado Springs, CO: PEAK Parent Center.

Simon, C. (Ed.) (1991). *Communication skills and classroom success: Assessment and therapy methodologies for language and learning disabled students.* Eau Claire, WI: Thinking Publications.

Stainback, S. & Stainback, W. (1992). *Curriculum considerations in inclusive classrooms: Facilitating learning for all students.* Baltimore, MD: Paul Brookes.

Udvari-Solner, A. (1995). Curricular adaptations: Reconfiguring teaching practice to support students with disabilities in general education classrooms. In Nadel, Rosenthal, D. (Eds.) *Down syndrome: Living and learning in the community.* New York: Wiley-Liss, 170-181.

Wiig, E. & Wilson, C. (2000). *Map it out: Visual tools for thinking, organizing and communicating.* Eau Claire, WI: Thinking Publications.

Wisconsin Assistive Technology Institute has developed: *Assessing students' needs for Assistive technology* and *Designing environments for successful kids.* Order from: WATI: Wisconsin Assistive Technology Initiative, 57 North Main Street, Amherst, WI 54406, (800) 5-65-8135.

CHAPTER 6

The Language of the Curriculum

Curriculum is the basic content of what is being taught. The curriculum specifies the information that each child is expected to learn in a specific subject during the academic year. All school systems have curricula for each subject in each grade, such as third grade language arts or second grade social studies. The curriculum is taught through a combination of classroom instruction, class and home assignments, and projects. To determine whether students have learned the material and mastered the skills in the curriculum, tests are usually administered.

Every classroom teacher is expected to follow the curriculum of the local school system. Special educators, however, can work with classroom teachers to adapt material to meet a student's special needs. Speech-language pathologists can help too, by analyzing the language level and language requirements of a task, and suggesting adaptations and modifications.

In fact, in many schools SLPs are taking a very active role in making the regular classroom curriculum accessible to students with disabilities. Thanks to inclusion, there is a movement away from pulling students out of class for therapy to

work on goals that are not related to the curriculum. Instead, speech therapy increasingly emphasizes the child's requirements and experiences in the classroom. Under IDEA, treatment must be justified based on whether it helps the child progress in the general curriculum, and eligibility is determined based on whether speech and language problems affect the child's educational progress. Both special education and speech-language pathology treatment are supposed to be focused on helping the child achieve success in the classroom with the regular educational curriculum.

Not every school has adopted this curricular focus for therapy yet. In some schools, all students are still pulled out of class for speech therapy. In others, SLPs use a combination of pull-out and push-in (therapy within the child's classroom) therapy. Whatever model your child's SLP uses, it makes sense that the material used in therapy relate to the curriculum. This is what your child needs to learn to succeed. If your child is working on a unit about Africa, but in speech therapy, she is working on learning the names of communication devices such as telephone and television, this does not make sense. Instead of getting help in learning what she is required to know, she is getting extra work on another topic, thus increasing her workload. So, it makes sense for the material used in treatment to be the material that the child needs to learn to progress in the regular educational curriculum.

How Well Does the Curriculum Match Your Child's Needs?

The first step in helping your child with Down syndrome learn the information included in the curriculum is to analyze that curriculum. This should preferably be done in the spring when the IEP is written for the next school year. If this is not possible, the curricular material should be evaluated before the school year starts. In some schools, classroom assignments are not made until sometime during the summer or even the week before school starts. In that case, evaluation of curricular material would need to occur soon after school began.

When the curriculum is analyzed early enough, you will ideally be able to use summer vacation to help your child become familiar with some of the concepts and vocabulary that she will need for the next school year. For example, if she will be working on a unit on Deserts, you can plan a family trip to a natural history museum, see videos on desert habitats, and perhaps even visit a desert climate. If your child will be studying colonial America, you can visit a history museum, or a restored colonial village. You can play colonial games, read books about children who lived during that time, discuss what events occurred during that period, and use cookbooks and research to cook a colonial dinner. Since children with Down syndrome often learn best through the visual channel and through real life experiences, summer is a valuable time to help your child experience some of the knowledge base that she will need to master the curriculum during the following year.

Some of the questions that might be helpful to ask include:

1. What is being taught? Consider the content and the information.
2. Why is it being taught? What skills are being targeted?
3. What is the child expected to learn and retain?
4. How can the knowledge be used? How will the knowledge be used?
5. How will the knowledge be tested?
6. How can the knowledge be reinforced and practiced?
7. Will this knowledge contribute to success in adult life?

The second step is to describe your child's learning style and learning patterns, and to determine how your child can best learn the required material. Some questions that might be asked include:

- Can your child learn the content and the information as it is being taught to the rest of the class? If not, through what channels and through what experiences can she learn the material? Can she learn the material with assistance and using adaptations such as modified worksheets or tests or the help of an aide? (See below for information on these and other curricular adaptations.) If not, what are alternative goals for your child to master?

- What skills are being targeted in the lessons? Can your child master these skills in the same way as other students, or does a different approach need to be used to help her master those skills?
- What is your child expected to learn and retain? Are these realistic goals for her? If not, what goals may be substituted?
- What methods will be used to teach the material to your child? How will materials be adapted, and what materials will be used? Are the planned methods a good match for your child's learning style?
- How can the knowledge be used? How will the knowledge be used by your child currently and in the future?
- How will the knowledge be tested? How can your child demonstrate that she has learned the material? Are her strengths being used to test her knowledge of the curriculum?
- How can the knowledge be reinforced and practiced? How will your child best retain the information?
- Will this knowledge contribute to success in adult life? for employment? for daily living? for recreation?

The third step is to develop an individualized plan for assisting your child in learning the material in the curriculum. This plan should result in IEP goals and benchmarks (see Chapter 3). The IEP plan must specify who will be responsible for implementing the goals. Who will make up worksheets? Who will monitor the level of participation and whether the plan is working for your child? How often will the team meet to check on whether the plan is working? How will the parents and school communicate? Some questions that might be asked include:

- Can your child participate in the activity just like the typical student?
- Can your child participate in this activity, but with adapted materials or expectations? (See below for suggestions for adaptations.)
- Can your child participate in this activity, but concentrate on working on embedded skills in the areas of motor, social, or communication skills? For example, the group is working on a report on Ghana. To work on her fine motor skills, your child cuts out pictures of the major export products of Ghana to mount on the project poster. She is also learning the names of the products, which she will present during the oral report.
- Can your child be with the group, but work on an activity that fulfills a very different purpose? For example, your child might assemble the materials for a science group using a written list, so her goal would be a reading goal, rather than a science goal.

Multiple Intelligences and the Curriculum

Some schools are using multiple intelligences to develop the school curriculum, especially focusing on the intrapersonal and interpersonal intelligences. When multiple intelligences are the basis for classroom learning, children learn to perceive themselves as individuals who have strengths and weaknesses, and they learn to use their strengths to help compensate for their weaknesses. Children will say, "I'm strong at math and sports, but I have difficulty with writing and with getting angry." In fact, knowing yourself and understanding your strengths and limitations, and how you learn is one of the intelligences—intrapersonal intelligence.

Even if your child's school is not basing the school curriculum on multiple intelligences, the information can be used to help adapt the language of the curriculum to help your child learn. For example, if your child has strength in the musical intelligence area, spelling words can be set to jingles and tunes to help her remember the spelling. If your child has strength in the bodily-kinesthetic area, she can use dances or even tapping her leg or desk to help her remember spelling words.

The information can also help families, at home, to help guide children to learn more about themselves and to help children achieve success. Many children with Down syndrome are involved in Special Olympics or music and theater groups. Some children in our community are active in Little League and in community basketball. These activities tap into different talents and skills than are needed in school. Bodily/kinesthetic intelligence helps children with Down syndrome excel in dance or in sports. In local recitals and at national conferences, we have watched dazzling displays of dancing by adolescents with Down syndrome. I have talked with parents whose children demonstrate musical intelligence. They are involved in choruses and orchestras. Sometimes, they even conduct a local orchestra, a dream come true. Children, adolescents, and adults with Down syndrome often have excellent understanding of other people and interact well with others. Sports, teams, groups, and community events enable them to use this interpersonal skill.

- Can your child participate in the activity with assistance from a peer or aide?
- Can your child participate in a parallel activity that addresses the curriculum theme? For example, she will collect information on the major waterways of a country, but will not be responsible for identifying the capital of the country or finding it on a map.
- If most students are involved in an activity that isn't relevant for your child, can she work on a task in another part of the room that is related to her educational priorities?
- Can your child do an out-of-class activity, such as a speech therapy pull-out session or resource help, during times when the regular class material isn't relevant to her needs?

Another consideration is how independently your child can work. Some questions that might be asked include:

- Can your child participate in the activity independently?
- Will your child be successful in structured cooperative groups (e.g., a group of four students working on a report for geography)? If there is a group activity, what role will your child play? How can her skills help the group and how can the group help her?
- Can your child participate independently with adapted materials and devices designed to facilitate full or partial participation?
- Will your child need the assistance of adult supports such as a classroom aide or a communication aide? If so, when will they be needed?

Many children with Down syndrome require the assistance of a classroom aide or peer tutor at times during the day, or possibly full-time. The aide can assist in:

- simplifying or explaining instructions for assignments,
- modifying worksheets,
- helping the child with classroom rules and routines,
- helping the child stay focused on her work,
- helping with written assignments or writing the answers as the child dictates,
- helping the child finish the work in the designated time period,
- providing individual help with reading or other academic skills.

Modifying the Curriculum

The curriculum can be modified in a variety of ways to help students with Down syndrome be more successful in an inclusive classroom. To be effective, modifications must always be made based on the needs and learning patterns of the individual child. This chapter will provide many examples of the integral role of language in mastering the curriculum and many examples of how to modify the language. Some curricular areas that may be modified include:

- textbooks
- daily assignments
- written language assignments
- spelling assignments/tests
- study skills/organizational skills
- testing (discussed in Chapter 9)
- classroom behavior (discussed in Chapter 10)

Table 1 on the next page shows some of the general ways in which materials can be adapted. The sections below explain how to apply these adaptations to particular areas of the curriculum.

Table 1: Classroom Adaptations

Possible adaptations include changes in:

Size:	Reduce the number of items to be learned or for task completion. For example, the child needs to write sentences for 5 spelling words instead of 10. Or, break the task down into smaller units to be mastered.
Layout:	Reduce the number of items on a sheet or change the physical layout to match the child's visual needs. For example, items may be arranged in a row rather than four pictures on a page in four quadrants. Items may be increased in size, darkened, or simplified. Color-coding may be used. You may block part of the sheet, so that only the items the child is working on can be seen. NOTE: As far as possible, adapted materials should not draw attention to the child as different. If your child is completing a worksheet with picture cues, it can be handed out with the other sheets and can be placed in her portfolio or folder the same as the assignments that the other children are completing.
Time:	Adapt the time requirement for learning and/or the task completion limit. The child may be given extra time to complete the assignment, or may be given unlimited time to complete a test.
Level of Support:	Increase the amount of assistance available for completing a task. An aide may help the child make sense of the task and complete the assignment.
Additional Practice:	Provide additional worksheets to help the child practice and reinforce the learned skills.
Input:	Adapt the way instruction is given to the learner. For example, in addition to the verbal instructions given by the teacher, each worksheet for the child with Down syndrome could have two examples at the top.
Difficulty:	Adapt the skill level or the type of problem. Examine the difficulty of the actual task, as well as the language level of the instructions and the desired response. For example, the addition sheet for the class may use pictures of coins in addition to number sentences such as $5+1+10=$ to provide variety. For the child with Down syndrome, this may increase the difficulty of the task because children with Down syndrome often have difficulty recognizing and distinguishing between coins. So, the child with Down syndrome can be given only the mathematical problem, or next to each coin, the numerical value can be written.

Implementation Plans

Anybody on your child's IEP team, including parents and professionals, can suggest modifications to try in the classroom. Any modifications that are suggested by the IEP planning team should be included in the IEP document. The IEP team

Output:	Adapt how the student can respond to instruction. For example, she can glue pictures or a written answer to the sheet if she cannot write the answer independently. Or, she can answer in a multiple-choice format rather than fill-in format.
Participation:	Adapt the participation activity. For example, use a cooperative group rather than an individual assignment.
Alternate Goals:	Adapt the goals or outcome expectation. For example, a student with Down syndrome could be working on sharing materials during a group project or audiotaping the sounds we hear at school rather than learning the parts of the ear.
Grading and Feedback:	Mark the number of correct items, and provide feedback on the error items, or create performance goals rather than grades that will help the child increase her level of performance. Some teachers use a check sheet so that the child can monitor her own progress, such as: Spelling Homework _____I have included the heading. _____I have spelled each word 3 times . _____I have written a sentence for each word.
Substitute Curriculum:	At times when the class is doing an activity that the child cannot participate in, she works on individualized goals. For example, she might work on the computer during a language test or go to a pull-out speech-language pathology session.
Physical Environment:	Provide preferential seating, adapt a desk to help the child's posture and stability, or ensure that the child can hear the instructions well.
Tools and Materials:	Adapted tools and materials may be needed to help the child complete the task (e.g., thicker pencil grips, adapted scissors, paper with larger lines or extra lines). The special educator and occupational therapist can provide analysis and feedback for these adaptations.

should then discuss and agree on a plan to implement the modifications. The following issues should be covered in writing:

- A general statement that modifications of curricular materials will be used
- Who will take the responsibility for making these modifications? (One or more persons must be listed on the IEP as responsible for the daily task of making modifications.)

- Who will monitor the use of the modifications and how? (The benchmarks in the IEP must include criteria for determining whether the plan is working and when progress will be measured.)
- How will the family be kept informed about their child's progress (home-to-school communication program)?
- The implementation plan should also specify the kinds of adaptations to materials, physical environment, and participation that are needed for each subject area.

Adaptations to Classwork

Later chapters discuss adaptations to instruction, testing, and classroom routines that can be written into the IEP. This section discusses adaptations to materials used in helping children learn the curriculum.

In general, specific materials that can be adapted include:

- reading assignments,
- class worksheets,
- projects and reports.

Reading Assignments

Reading assignments may involve reading stories (fiction or non-fiction such as biographies) or reading textbook material. Learning material from textbooks is usually more difficult for children with Down syndrome than reading stories and writing book reports.

Around third grade, there are important changes in reading instruction. Up until third grade, children are learning to read. Reading assignments and worksheets focus on identifying initial sounds and word families, sound blending or how you combine letters into words, counting the number of syllables in words, and other skills that children need to be a successful readers. After third grade, children are expected to know how to read, and they are now asked to read to learn. So, textbooks become more difficult, and the emphasis is on comprehension and memory rather than on the techniques of reading.

This is often a difficult leap for children with Down syndrome. Even though a child with Down syndrome may read on a third grade level, she may not understand and be able to remember all of the details of the science, social studies, or other concepts that are judged to be at a third grade level. At this point, memory and retrieval skills gain greater importance. In all grades, but especially

Personalized Books

In the early grades, a language experience approach can be used to help children with Down syndrome learn to read. After a school event such as a holiday party, field day, or picnic, have the child dictate her story about the event. Write a personalized book about the event for her to read. Include photographs, if possible, to help cue her as she is retelling the event. She can then take the book home to share the experience with her family.

after third grade, reading is not only an individual subject, but it is the vehicle through which you learn all subjects. You not only need to read your reading text, but read, understand, and remember the information in your science and social studies textbooks.

Some children with Down syndrome learn to read with little or no problem using the same method used to teach other children in the class. Others need a more specialized or individualized approach such as the one outlined in *Teaching Reading to Children with Down Syndrome* by Patricia Logan Oelwein (Woodbine House, 1995). It is beyond the scope of this chapter to explain how instruction in reading *per se* can be modified for children with Down syndrome. Instead, we will look at ways to modify reading assignments for children who need adaptations for whatever reason—whether it is because they are not reading on grade level, not reading at all, cannot sustain their attention long enough to finish an assignment, can read the words in an assignment but cannot understand all the concepts, etc.

THE WHOLE LANGUAGE APPROACH TO READING

Whole language is a current approach in which reading, understanding, writing, and expressive language are taught as a whole. Activities designed to strengthen reading and writing skills are done throughout the day, incorporated into *all* subjects in the curriculum. The whole language approach often is based on children's literature and thematic activities accompanying the books. For example, as students are learning to read a book about weather, they might also learn some weather reporting skills, build a weather station, draw pictures or take photographs of different weather conditions, etc.

The overall approach is good for children with Down syndrome because it provides many different experiences with the concepts to be learned. However, whole language does not teach in discrete linguistic units, such as focusing on plurals or verb tenses. Rather, it teaches in larger themes using meaningful multi-sensory experiences to teach concepts. So, if your child needs help with grammar, such as with word order or verb tenses, this may need to be done as part of speech-language therapy, or through using supplemental workbook practice.

Grammar-related goals might include:

- The child will be able to write the plurals of words.
- The child will be able to use plurals in conversation.
- The child will be able to understand the regular verb tenses for past and present.

■ The child will be able to use the regular verb tenses for past and present in speech.

MODIFYING READING ASSIGNMENTS

Reading passages can be modified in a variety of ways, for a variety of reasons.

1. The reading assignment can be **shortened** by:
   ■ telling the child how far to read,
   ■ just photocopying a small portion for her,
   ■ marking how far she's supposed to read with a visual cue such as a STOP sign or a colored paper clip,
   ■ summarizing the story's main points.

A child might be asked to read just the first few sentences or paragraphs of a longer assignment if: a) the goal is for her to practice reading, and she just reads more slowly than the other children; b) she is only responsible for learning the information at the beginning of the passage; the main idea of the paragraph is stated in the first sentence and subsequent sentences elaborate on the concept, but don't necessarily provide new information.

2. The reading assignment can be **simplified** by:
   ■ using pictures under the words so that the child always has a picture cue for the words,
   ■ combining pictures with a few words the child knows, rebus style,
   ■ rewriting the assignment with shorter sentences and simpler words on a computer.

There are software packages including *Picture Communication Symbols© for Boardmaker* (Mayer-Johnson) that make it easy to design picture-based or picture-assisted stories. There are also published picture-assisted versions of children's stories, such as *Old McDonald had a Farm, The Three Little Pigs,* and *A Cold and Snowy Day* from the Mayer-Johnson Company (see the Resources at the end of this book) that are very helpful for language arts assignments such as book reports. A child might be given a simplified version of the entire assignment if: a) she needs just the reading level modified, but can master the information; b) she needs both the reading level and information modified; c) her memory and retrieval skills make long reading assignments difficult (she forgets what the story was about if the reading is too long).

3. The reading assignment can be **adapted to a child's individual needs.** For instance, some children may only be able to read words written in certain fonts; may be confused by passages written in two columns, newspaper style; may need larger print; may need fewer words on a page.

4. The reading assignment can be **adapted for a child who can't read** by:
   ■ having an aide or peer read it to her,
   ■ taping it for her so she can listen to it,
   ■ providing the information in picture form. Picture adapted material is available commercially (see Resource Guide) or can be custom designed for the individual child.

There are also a variety of ways to modify the way a child responds to a reading assignment.

- One strategy is for the child, if possible, or the teacher or aide to read the questions first so the child knows what she is looking for in the paragraph.
- Highlight the answers within the passage.
- Highlight important words in the instructions.
- Provide a written example of a question and the answer.
- Provide picture symbols; child then chooses the correct picture answer and glues it to the answer sheet.
- Have the child draw a picture of her answer.
- Provide multiple choices and have her circle the right answer rather than write answers in complete sentences.

Modifying every reading assignment throughout the day takes a lot of preparation on either the teacher's or aide's part. The IEP must specify who will be responsible for adapting materials and that person must be provided with the time to do this on a daily or weekly basis. In practice, even when the need for adaptations is written into the IEP, it often does not happen. That is not acceptable, and violates the IEP contract. By default, parents often become responsible for making these modifications. If you have the time and feel comfortable designing the worksheets for your child, that is acceptable. But, you should not feel compelled to take on this responsibility. If the need for adapted materials is written in the IEP as necessary to help your child progress in the regular educational curriculum, it is the school's responsibility to provide personnel to accomplish the goal.

Here are some examples of reading assignments completed by children with Down syndrome, with comments about how they were or were not successfully adapted:
1. A comprehension paragraph followed by questions.

"See the boats! They float on water. Some boats have sails. The wind moves the sails. It makes the boats go. Many people name their sailboats. They paint the name on the side of the boat."

The instructions state: "Read about boats. Then **answer** the questions." The word "answer" was bold in the regular education text. No modifications were needed for the girl with Down syndrome answering the questions with the rest of her class. The only suggested strategy was that, after reading the questions, she reread the paragraph and underline the answers. Then, to answer the questions, she simply needed to copy the words that she had underlined. The questions were:

1. What makes sailboats move? wind
2. Where do sailboats float? water
3. What would you name a sailboat? Easter

2. A cause and effect worksheet assignment. See the next page for an example.

The instructions state: "Read each cause sentence. Write an effect sentence." The child with Down syndrome completing the assignment understood cause and effect, but answered in phrases rather than sentences for all but one of the items. Simply highlighting "Write an effect **sentence**" would probably have helped, as would an example or two provided at the beginning. An aide or teacher could also

What Might Happen?

A **cause** is the reason something happens.
An **effect** is the thing that happens.
Read each cause sentence. Write an effect sentence.

Cause: A big wave hit Alma's sand castle.

Effect: <u>go away</u>

Cause: Three feet of snow fell in a snowstorm last night.

Effect: <u>Snow flakes</u> <u>and no school</u>

Cause: Friendship School has a new computer lab.

Effect: <u>more time to</u> <u>play on the computer</u>

Cause: Tony practices the piano 20 minutes every day.

Effect: <u>he will get</u> <u>better at music</u>

©Frank Schaffer Publications, Inc., FS-11005 *Second Grade Activities.*

A cause and effect worksheet assignment

have asked, "Is *go away* a sentence? What do you need to do to make it a sentence?" An organizer could have been used to help the child develop a complete sentence.

3. A longer reading from a third grade science text for a unit on tornadoes.

> *A tornado is a windstorm that contains very strong swirls of air. The wind twirls around in an area that is usually about 100 meters wide. Sometimes the wind inside a tornado is blowing 100 miles an hour but usually 60 to 70 miles an hour.*
>
> *A tornado cloud is shaped like a funnel. When the end of the funnel touches the ground, it causes lots of damage because the wind is blowing so fast.*
>
> *The blowing wind crashes into buildings and breaks the wood, metal, and glass. The wind also pulls up trees and other plants.*
>
> *A tornado cloud is easy to see in daylight because it is so dark. The dark color comes from all the dirt and other materials it picks up. It is also easy to hear a tornado coming because the wind makes so much noise. Some people say it sounds like a train.*
>
> *When a tornado forms over water it is called a "waterspout." A waterspout picks up water and makes it swirl around."*

The language in this passage may be complex for a child with Down syndrome in third grade. One way to assist the child is to provide a version using simpler language and sentence constructions. We can also divide the reading into separate paragraphs with each paragraph followed by questions. A further level of assistance would be to italicize the answers to the questions within the paragraph. A slightly reduced level of assistance would be to have the answers in only the first paragraph or to have the questions and answers written out to the first paragraph only. The amount of assistance could be varied as needed by the individual child. One child might only need the text divided into smaller sections in order to answer the questions. Another child might need to dictate the answers rather than write them. As the child progresses, some of the assistance can be faded out. That is why it is important to monitor your child's progress.

Here is the simplified version:

> A tornado is *a strong windstorm*. The wind usually blows at about *60 to 70 miles an hour*. The wind twirls in an area *about 100 meters wide*.
>
> **Questions:**
> *What is a tornado?* a strong windstorm
> *What is the speed of the wind in a tornado?* 60 to 70 miles an hour
> *How wide is the area that the wind twirls in?* about 100 meters wide

> A tornado cloud is *shaped like a funnel*. When the end of the funnel touches the ground, it causes lots of damage *because the wind is blowing so* fast. The blowing wind *crashes into buildings and breaks the wood, metal, and glass*. The wind also *pulls up trees and other plants*
>
> **Questions:**
> *What is the shape of a tornado?* a funnel

Why does the tornado cause damage? The wind blows fast.
What does the tornado damage? buildings, trees, and plants

A tornado cloud is easy to see in daylight because *it is so dark*.
The tornado is dark because *it picks up dirt*. The wind from the
tornado makes a very loud sound. It sounds like *a train*.
Questions:
Why is it easy to see a tornado? It is a dark color.
Why is the tornado dark? It picks up dirt.
What does a tornado sound like? a train

A *waterspout* is a tornado that forms over water. A waterspout
picks up water and makes it swirl around.
Question:
What do you call a tornado that forms over water? a waterspout

Another approach is to teach the information not only through the textbook reading, but through a multimedia experience. For example, learning centers relating to tornadoes could be set up around the room. Many visual organizers can be used at these learning stations and in home assignments to help the child learn the material of the science curriculum. At the learning station for tornadoes, the child could listen to an audio tape of information on tornadoes. While she listened, she could look at a bulletin board posted with pictures of tornadoes. An attribute web could visually organize the information and concepts (see example at right). Or a Venn diagram could be used to visually describe the similarities and differences between tornadoes and hurricanes.

Class Worksheets

In elementary school, worksheets are frequently used to help children learn concepts and skills, to practice the skills, and to reinforce and maintain the skills.

Worksheets can be adapted in many different ways to meet the needs of children with Down syndrome. As described above, the number of items, physical layout, instructions, output, and expectations can be modified. Vocabulary and grammar may be simplified to help the child understand the task. Symbols and visual cues such as arrows, smile faces, and numbers may be used to organize the material. Cloze procedures (fill-ins) may be used to guide the child in providing the desired information. Learning frames (story frames, information frames, homework frames) may be used to help structure and organize the information that the child has to find or retrieve. Review Chapter 5 for information on these general types of adaptations.

ADAPTING THE LANGUAGE ON WORKSHEETS

The level of language used on a worksheet can greatly influence a child's ability to respond. This makes it important for the teacher, aide, or SLP to examine the language and, if necessary, modify it to help your child learn. The language on worksheets often closely resembles the language of instruction, so you can find additional helpful information on these types of modifications in Chapter 7.

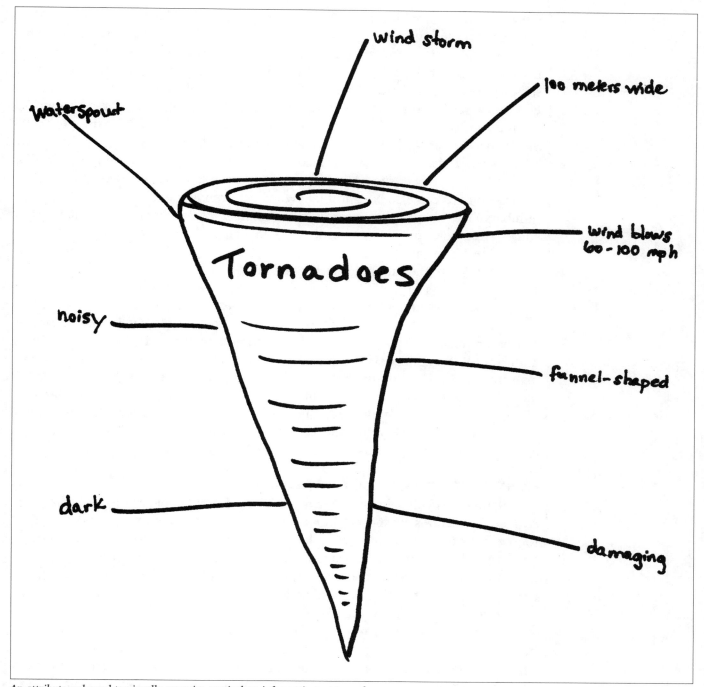

An attribute web used to visually organize curriculum information on tornadoes

SYNONYMS

One problem that children with Down syndrome often face is that there are many ways of expressing the same concept in the English language. Your child may understand a concept, and know how to express it one way, but worksheets may express the concept in another way that is unfamiliar to her. For example, many worksheets use the verb *to circle*, and children learn to do that. But, here are instructions from a text used in the primary grades: "Anansi is the spider. It is a hero in many Ashanti stories. Find and *ring* Anansi and some of his animal friends." *Ring* is an unusual instruction, but it is used here without first teaching what it means.

Using too many terms or expressions or different terms to express the same concept is especially a problem on math worksheets. For example, your child may know how to subtract, and may understand the words "minus" and "take away." But if a worksheet uses the words "subtract," "what is the difference," "how many more (or less) than," or "regroup and subtract" in the instructions, it may confuse your child. Likewise, your child may know how to add, and may know that the words "add" or "plus" mean to use addition. But if she encounters instructions such as "find the sum," "what is the total," or "how many altogether," she may not realize that she is supposed to add.

Synonyms can also be a problem when children are learning how to sequence numbers. The simplest question is what number comes before or what number comes after, but worksheets to practice sequencing use all of the following:

- Write the missing numbers.
- Write the number that is one less.
- Write the number that comes between the numbers.
- Write the numbers in the correct order.

It is very important for the teacher and aide to be made aware that synonyms can be confusing to your child, and that sometimes what looks like a problem understanding a concept is really a problem understanding the specific words used in instructions. The language of instruction can interfere with her learning the material in the curriculum and demonstrating that she has learned the material. The instructions may be modified and rewritten on the worksheet. Or the aide or teacher may simply tell your child verbally that "what is the total" means the same as "add." The language of instruction will be discussed in detail in the next chapter.

MULTI-STEP OR CONFUSING DIRECTIONS

Sometimes children with Down syndrome are only able to follow one-step or two-step directions in speech, but classroom worksheets may demand that they follow three or more steps to complete them. Or worksheets may be written using language and vocabulary that is not even clear to parents or other adults. Clearly, these types of directions need to be modified for children with Down syndrome. Ideally, written instructions should be clear and short: "Capitalize the first word"; "Write the correct word in the blank space."

When it is necessary to give multistage instructions, it is best to break them into their smallest components and perhaps number them. For example, in the capitalization practice sheet on the next page, the child is asked to "Choose a word from the word box to begin each sentence. Write the word using a capital letter." An example is given. It might help the child with Down syndrome to break these commands down further. For example:

1. Choose a word from the word box to begin each sentence.
2. Use a capital letter to start the word.
3. Write the word in the space.

The second set of instructions on the worksheet could be broken down as follows:

1. Circle the first letter of the sentence.
2. Rewrite the sentence.
3. Use a capital letter for the first letter in the sentence.

Name _____ **First Word in a Sentence**

> **Use a capital letter at the beginning of every sentence.**
> The class is learning to tell time.

Choose a word from the word box to begin each sentence. Write the word using a capital letter.

how	this	he	the	we	let

1. **He** is going to the store.

2. **The** children played all day.

3. **We** are going to the library.

4. **How** are you today?

5. **Let** me tell you a story.

6. **This** pie tastes great!

Circle the first letter of each sentence and rewrite the sentence using a capital letter.

7. do you like to skate?

Do you like to skate ?

8. jumping rope is fun.

Jumping rope is fun .

9. he has a new watch.

He has a new watch .

BONUS Choose one word from the word box at the top of the page. Write your own sentence using the word at the beginning of your sentence.

An example of multi-step directions on a worksheet

Another language arts worksheet (on the next page) focuses on plurals, but the instructions are more difficult than the task, and would be confusing for a child with Down syndrome. The first instruction asks the child to copy seven words from the newspaper that mean **more than one.** Then the child is asked to: "Use CAPITAL LETTERS for the **more than one** letters." This is especially confusing because the letters used to make words plural are not supposed to be capitalized. For this child with Down syndrome, the aide gave a handwritten example, even though there were three printed examples. A better adaptation for *all* of the children in the class would have been to use color instead of capitalization. The instructions could say:

1. Find seven words from the newspaper that mean more than one.
2. Write the words on the sheet.
3. Underline the letters that mean more than one with red crayon.

Using Visual Organizers. When your child needs to follow complex instructions to complete a worksheet, visual organizers can help her understand what to do. For example, on the worksheet on page 134, there are six small pictures in boxes. The teacher gives verbal instructions to cut out the pictures. Then, the child is asked to follow written instructions on the sheet. These instructions would be difficult for many children with Down syndrome. The visual organizer below could help. It includes a grid to divide the instructions into understandable chunks. (This is similar to the word definition organizer discussed in Chapter 5.) The child could then organize the information so that she can choose which picture to paste and determine where to paste the picture.

Paste	Which Picture	Where
Paste	the snake	in the crate
Paste		
Paste		
Paste		
Paste		
Paste		

On page 135 is another worksheet that could be made more understandable with a visual organizer. This worksheet gives clues and asks the child to make inferences and deductions. There are pictures of five children carrying balloons. The clues relate to the children's hair and the varying numbers of balloons they are carrying. The child completing the worksheet is asked to color the balloons specific colors. For example, Bennie has curly hair. He is holding 3 red balloons. For step 1, the child needs to identify the balloons and determine how to color them. Step 2 involves identifying the pictures of the children by name and writing their names. A visual organizer with the information below could help the child complete this worksheet:

Child's name	Hair	Number of balloons	Color
Bennie	curly	3	red
Alice	straight	5	green

more than ONE

flowerS

bunnIES

dressES

ACTIVITY

Copy seven words from the newspaper that mean **more than one.**

Use CAPITAL LETTERS for the **more than one** letters.

flowerS   bunnIES   dressES

1. <u>Nurser IES</u> example
2. <u>part IES</u> ✗
3. <u>Day S</u> ✗
4. <u>CiTIES</u> ✗
5. <u>BoxES</u> ✗
6. <u>RescuES</u> Rescue S ☺
7. <u>RulES</u> ✗

An example of a potentially confusing multi-step wortksheet

Name: Date:

Paste the snake in the crate.

Paste the fish under the crate.

Paste the chicken on top of the crate.

Paste the daffodil to the left of the crate.

Paste the lizard on the side of the crate.

Paste the horse next to the daffodil.

An example of a potentially confusing multi-step worksheet which could be improved by the child's use of a visual organizer

Read the clues below. Write each child's name under the correct picture. Color the balloons by following the clues.

RaY Alice BennieTom   Janine

Bennie has curly hair. He is holding 3 red balloons.

Alice has long, straight hair. She is holding 5 green balloons.

Ray has straight hair. He is holding 3 purple balloons.

Janine has long, curly hair. She is holding 5 blue balloons.

Tom has light-colored hair. He is holding 4 yellow balloons.

How many balloons can you count on the page?

An example of a potentially confusing multi-step worksheet which could be improved by the child's use of a visual organizer

Using Visual Cues and Color. Sometimes visual cues or color can be used to help a child with Down syndrome understand the instructions. See, for example, the worksheet on the next page. The instructions ask the child to color in a certain number of pairs of boots. First, the aide drew two boot outlines right above the word *pairs* and underlined the word. Then she circled the number of pairs that needed to be colored in with each separate color. As the child colored in the boots, the aide counted out the number of boots with the child. The next instruction asked the child to complete a bar graph about the number of boots. In the instructions, the aide highlighted the words "1 square for each boot" to emphasize that the child should stop looking at the boots as pairs, but instead count each boot individually.

The child was able to correctly complete the graph with only one error, filling in 8 instead of 6 squares for the 3 pairs of boots. The final question asks which bar on the graph is the longest, but the answer they want is not which bar, but how many squares is this longest bar? This child, an eleven-year-old with Down syndrome, was able to answer the question correctly, but many children would probably have responded with *purple*, the color of the longest bar, or may not have been able to answer the question at all.

Sometimes instead of adapting an existing worksheet with color or visual cues, the teacher or aide may want to create a new one. Software such as Writing with Symbols, PixWriter, PixReader, WYNN, Access Pac, Boardmaker, and Print 'n Learn Thematic Units for Boardmaker can help professionals, paraprofessionals, and parents develop adaptive materials for children with Down syndrome. (See the Resources at the end of the book.)

Math Worksheets. We tend to think of reading and math as two very different subjects. But, in reality, math worksheets are often very confusing to children because of the way the instructions are written. On page 138 is a math worksheet with complicated instructions. First, the child must determine which are addition problems and which are subtraction problems. Then, she must draw a red stop sign (octagon) around the addition problems and a yellow yield sign (triangle) around the subtraction problems. Then, she must solve the problems. The girl with Down syndrome who completed this worksheet was able to solve the math problems, but she was not able to draw the stop signs and yield signs. This worksheet could have been made much more user-friendly by breaking down the multistage instructions and by reducing the fine motor demands. For example:

1. Look for the - sign. This means to subtract.
2. Draw a yellow circle around all subtraction problems.

An example of a worksheet that is well designed for a child with Down syndrome appears on page 139. This example uses rebus pictures and short phrases. The instructions simply state: "Solve each problem." The language in the word problem is also short and straightforward.

On page 140 is a very similar math addition exercise. These problems are easier mathematically than those on the previous worksheet. But this exercise is made much more complicated because of the language of the instructions. "Listen to the story. Act it out. Write the number sentences." Many children with Down syndrome would not know what "number sentences" are. Also, the only picture on the worksheet refers to the example and shows four boys. But the other word

Look at the long line of boots. Use the clues to color them all in.

(3) pairs of boots are red.
(2) pairs of boots are green.
(4) pairs of boots are purple.
(1) pair of boots is yellow.
(2) pairs of boots are orange.

Cool !!

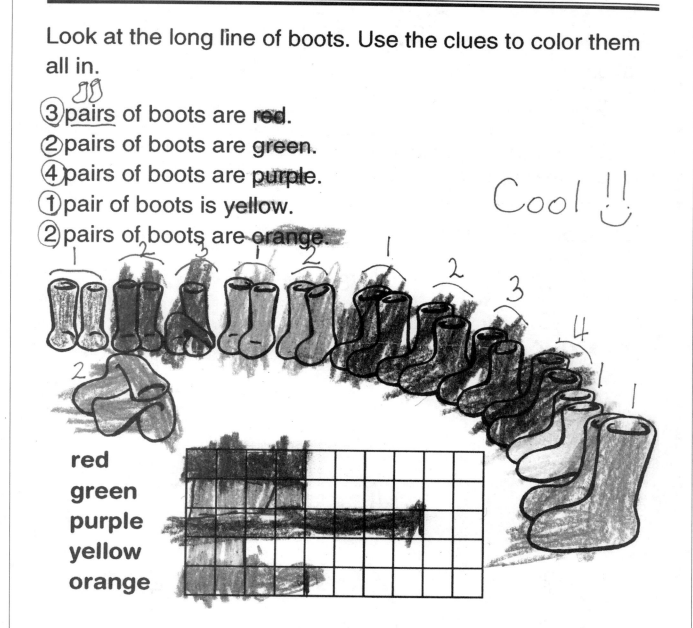

red
green
purple
yellow
orange

Now color in the bar graph. Use the clues to color 1 square for **each** boot in every color. Think carefully!

Which bar is the longest? How many colored squares does it have? ___8___

Example of a worksheet which uses visual cues

Obey the Sign!

STOP and draw a red around the problem if you must add.

YIELD and draw a yellow around the problem if you must subtract.

Solve each problem.

26	78	66
+ 72	− 45	− 14
98	**33**	**52**

82	75	66
− 41	− 34	+ 22
41	**41**	**88**

38	81	46
+ 21	+ 18	− 14
59	**99**	**32**

71	26	46
+ 15	+ 63	+ 42
96	**89**	**88**

Example of a complicated math worksheet for a child with Down syndrome

NAME: _____

PROBLEM SOLVING

Solve each problem.

Vince sees 25 🐦 .

Fred sees 34 🐦 .

How many 🐦 in all?

$$\begin{array}{r} 25 \\ + 34 \\ \hline 59 \end{array}$$

2 3 4

Corey bought 14 📓 .

Cody bought 12 📓 .

How many 📓 in all?

$$\begin{array}{r} 14 \\ + 12 \\ \hline 2\ 6 \end{array}$$

Louis drinks 21 🥛 a week.

Dan drinks 28 🥛 a week.

How many 🥛 do they drink in 1 week?

$$\begin{array}{r} 21 \\ + 28 \\ \hline 49 \end{array}$$

Kristie has 31 💄 .

Melodie has 24 💄 .

How many 💄 in all?

$$\begin{array}{r} 3\ 1 \\ + 2\ 4 \\ \hline 5\ 5 \end{array}$$

Meredith peeled 41 .

Heather peeled 37 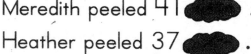 .

How many did the girls peel?

$$\begin{array}{r} 41 \\ + 37 \\ \hline 78 \end{array}$$

Example of math worksheet which uses short and straightforward instructions

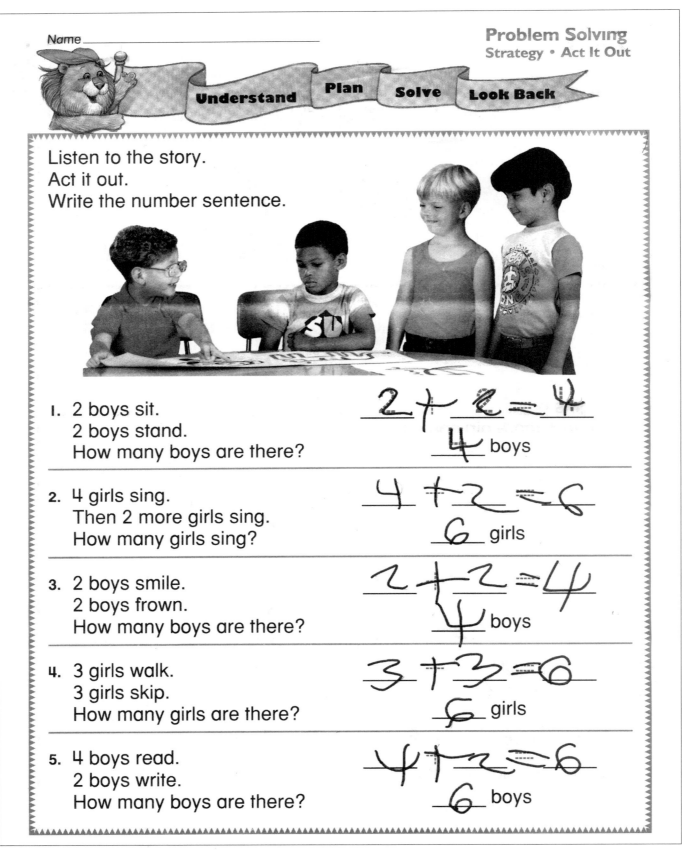

Name _____

Problem Solving
Strategy • Act It Out

Understand | Plan | Solve | Look Back

Listen to the story.
Act it out.
Write the number sentence.

1. 2 boys sit.
   2 boys stand.
   How many boys are there?

   $2 + 2 = 4$
   ___4___ boys

2. 4 girls sing.
   Then 2 more girls sing.
   How many girls sing?

   $4 + 2 = 6$
   ___6___ girls

3. 2 boys smile.
   2 boys frown.
   How many boys are there?

   $2 + 2 = 4$
   ___4___ boys

4. 3 girls walk.
   3 girls skip.
   How many girls are there?

   $3 + 3 = 6$
   ___6___ girls

5. 4 boys read.
   2 boys write.
   How many boys are there?

   $4 + 2 = 6$
   ___6___ boys

Example of a simple math worksheet complicated by confusing wording

problems refer to boys and girls or to girls only. This would probably be confusing for a child with Down syndrome who is trying to finish this worksheet. The good part of the worksheet is that there is a sample problem that uses dotted lines that can be traced to correctly answer the problem. For the remaining five problems, there is an addition sign, equals sign, and the word "boys." So, it becomes a cloze procedure or fill-in question.

> 4 boys jump
>
> 2 boys walk
>
> How many boys are there?
>
> ____+____=_____boys

The child with Down syndrome who completed this exercise did not require any assistance. Some types of modifications that could have been used are drawing or using picture symbols to show 4 boys jumping and 2 boys walking, or circling or highlighting the numbers 4 and 2 and then writing the numbers in the spaces at the right of the page. An aide or peer buddy could have written in the numbers if the child could not write numbers.

VOCABULARY

Just as the vocabulary in reading assignments may need simplification, so does the vocabulary on worksheets. This may especially be the case in science, where most of the vocabulary used may be unfamiliar to your child. If the class were studying seeds or tornadoes, children might have some general familiarity with the vocabulary, but many of the terms would be new.

Some general ways to help your child learn vocabulary of the curriculum include:

- The SLP can get lists of important vocabulary words the class is studying from the teacher. The SLP can then work these words into speech therapy (such as using words like "sphere" or "cylinder" to work on /s/ sounds).
- Flash cards of pictures alone, words alone, or pictures and words together can be used at home or school.
- New words on worksheets can be accompanied by pictures or definitions.
- Include word banks with new vocabulary words at the top of worksheets (or provide them on a separate page).
- Families can help by taking their child to museums, watching educational videos or television programs, or involving their child in experiences related to vocabulary being learned. For example, watching a program on tornadoes will enable children to see what a tornado looks and sounds like, and get some idea of the force of the tornado and the wind tunnel effect.
- Use role play (or actual experiences) to help your child understand common vocabulary words that appear on worksheets. For example, students are often asked to underline or circle the "best choice" on worksheets. If your child doesn't understand the concept of "best choice," you could ask her to choose between mustard and ketchup to dip French fries in, or a warm or cold water in the bathtub and talk about which is the

best choice. Or you could role play waiting your turn at the busstop as compared to pushing to the front of the line to teach "best choice, " or grabbing another child's pencil away instead of asking to use it politely. Only after the child had mastered that concept would I use a worksheet to practice it.

On the next page is an example of a math worksheet that would place formidable demands on many children's vocabulary skills. The child is asked to estimate the length and then measure with a centimeter ruler. Many children with Down syndrome would need help in understanding the concept of estimate. Both measure and estimate are terms that should be flagged. That is, they should be defined and discussed, put into the child's word bank, and the child should have some additional experience with measuring objects.

If there is a good home-to-school communication plan, estimating and measuring would be a perfect activity for home practice. Your child could use a one centimeter square of cardboard to help her estimate length and then use the regular centimeter ruler to help her measure accurately.

You could measure spaghetti, cereal boxes, furniture, trays, place mats, picture frames, and rooms. To help the child learn to follow the instructions on the worksheet, you could practice:

- counting units (squares, paper clips)
- using a ruler measured in inches
- using a ruler measured in centimeters
- measuring to the nearest inch
- estimating measurements in centimeters

Experience is probably the best assistance that can be provided for this type of worksheet. Many children with Down syndrome, however, would probably need a simplified worksheet that would not require the child to use estimates and rounding up, but just learn to measure in units, inches, and centimeters.

METALINGUISTIC SKILLS

Many worksheets for language arts tap into skills known as metalinguistic skills—that is, the ability to analyze and talk about language units such as words, sentences, and sounds. For example, to understand the instruction "Capitalize the first word in each sentence," a child needs to have a general understanding of what words and sentences are. Or to know how to count the number of syllables in each word, a child needs to understand what a syllable is.

Here are some terms and concepts children need to learn to participate in the language arts curriculum:

- sound,
- letter,
- word,
- syllable,
- sentence,
- question,
- statement,
- parts of speech (noun, verb, adverb, adjective), and

MEASURING OBJECTS

About how many centimeters long is each one of the objects? First estimate the length. Then measure with a centimeter ruler.

OBJECT	ESTIMATE	MEASURE
pencil		
pen		
spoon		

Example of a math worksheet complicated by difficult vocabulary

■ the verb "to mean" (so kids can ask "What does that word mean?" and can answer questions about what words mean).

This is a natural subject area for collaboration between the classroom teacher and the speech-language pathologist. If the teacher gives the worksheets to the SLP in advance, the SLP can work with your child on the concepts she needs to understand in order to understand the terms used in the unit and on the worksheets.

Many early language arts activities focus on phonological awareness skills—that is, being able to analyze the sounds in a word. These include being able to identify the first sound in a word, rhyming words, blending sounds into words, and breaking down words into individual sounds.

When working with children on phonological awareness, graphic worksheets work well. For example, in the worksheet on the next page, the child is asked to name the picture, listen to the first sound, and then circle the picture that makes the same sound. On the worksheet on page 146, the child is asked to circle the letter corresponding to the beginning sound. A first grade worksheet on page 147 asks the child to find things in your home that begin with /a/—which is good because it involves the movement and visual senses.

Another early language skill is the ability to count the number of syllables in a word. This helps the child spell and write a word, as well as say it correctly. On the worksheet on page 148 the child is asked to count the number of syllables. She may be told to tap out the syllables to help her count them.

Rhyming skills are yet another important area for children to master in language arts. The worksheets that your child is asked to complete may have instructions at very different language levels. The simplest might involve matching pictures of words that rhyme, as in the example on page 149. Worksheets that ask the child to recognize and circle words that rhyme and all have the same ending can be a good activity for students who are beginning to read, as in the example on page 150. Cloze or fill-in activities, such as on page 151 can work well for children with a wide range of activities. An initial phonemic cue (e.g., "c-c-c") can cue the child to write the first letter. If necessary, the child can also be given a written model of writing in the rhyming part (the "word family"). If the child cannot write "c" or "-ake," she can choose and then glue on answers that have been written or typed by an aide.

A phonological awareness worksheet from fifth grade asks the child to finish a poem by writing a line that ends with a spelling word that will rhyme with the line above. (See page 152.)

An even more advanced phonological awareness sheet asks the child: "Which word begins with a vowel?" and "Which word ends with a vowel?" (See page 153.) "In which word does the /ou/ sound like or (yours) and in which word like move (soup)?" This is more difficult and the instructions use more difficult language, yet the child with Down syndrome was able to complete the worksheet correctly. If assistance had been needed, some things that could have helped include:

■ writing a list of vowels at the top of the worksheet;
■ having the teacher, aide, or a peer partner say the word aloud so that it would be easier to figure out which is the rhyming word;
■ creating an easier worksheet that deals with the /ou/ sound (e.g., a worksheet where all the words with /ou/ rhyme).

LEARN TO READ

Say the name of the first picture in each row.
Listen to the beginning sound.
Then name the other pictures in the row.
Circle the picture that has the same beginning sound as the first picture.

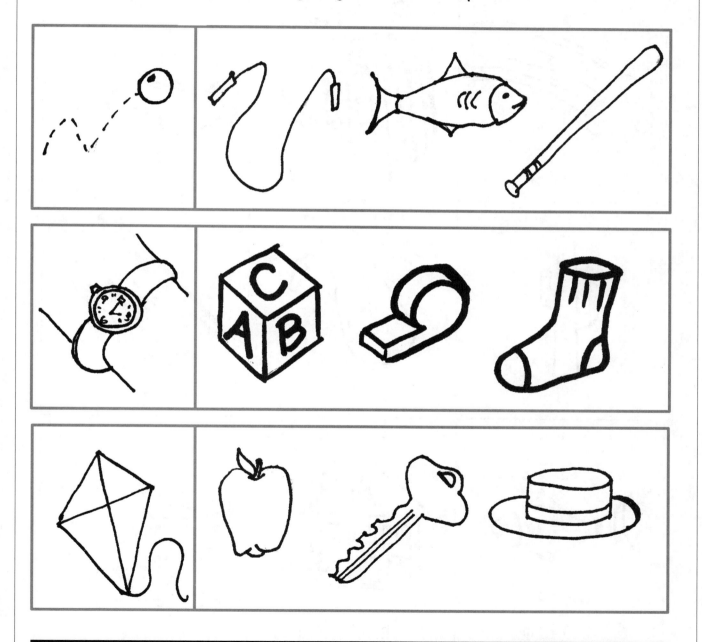

Skills: Recognizing beginning consonant sounds; Building vocabulary

Example of an early language arts activity which focuses on the phonological awareness skill of identifying initial consonant sounds

LEARN TO READ

Say the name of each picture.
Listen to the first sound.
Then circle the letter that makes that sound.

p r k	t p g	w l d
n j c	j d x	m v c
t f m	h t r	d f b

Skills: Recognizing beginning sounds and their symbols; Auditory discrimination

Example of an early language arts activity which focuses on the phonological awareness skill of recognizing beginning consonant sounds and their corresponding letters

Directions: Find things in your home that begin with <u>Aa</u>.

1. <u>Animals</u>
2. <u>Attic</u>
3. <u>Airplane</u>
4. <u>Apple</u>

Pick 2 things from above and draw a picture of them.

Example of a first grade early language arts activity which focuses on the phonological awareness skill of recognizing beginning consonant sounds while involving movement and the visual senses

Counting Syllables

birthday cake ____

railroad train ____

pencil ____

airplane ____

helicopter ____

pen ____

spaghetti ____

balloon ____

Example of an early language skill worksheet which focuses on the ability to count the number of syllables in a word

LEARN TO READ

Look at the pictures on the left.
Look at the pictures on the right.
Draw a line to match the pairs that **rhyme**.

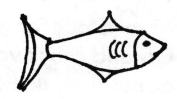

Skills: Recognizing rhyming words; Auditory discrimination

Example of an early language skill worksheet which focuses on rhyming skills

Example of a woksheet reinforcing rhyming skills, completed by a beginning reader

Look at the picture. Add one letter to the first line to make a word. The word tells what the picture is. Then add letters to the other lines to make words that rhyme.

Cake
r ake
b ake
t ake

Cat
b at
r at
s at

hen
p en
t en
m en

ball
f all
t all
c all

Can
f an
m an
r an

book
t ook
l ook
c ook

Example of a completed cloze (fill-in) activity; cloze worksheets can be used for a wide range of activities

Spelling Words	struck turned turning	bushes finding returned	bull tire	fool wild	mind push	tools truck

F. **Spelling Poems.** Finish each poem by writing a line that ends with a rhyming spelling word.

Sound the same

1. When I fell into the pool,

   I felt like a fool.

2. Although the dragon looked very mild,

   He was wild.

3. After my car ran over the wire,

   I got a flat tire.

4. I'm sure that you will find,

   Life is easier if you mind.

5. Because his car was stuck,

   He pulled it out with a truck.

6. The workers who repair our schools,

   Use many tools.

7. I don't think you should pull,

   when the rope is tied to a ball.

Example of a phonological awareness worksheet using a word bank and focusing on rhyming skills

Words with "ou" Vowels

Part G   Fill in the missing word for each sentence.

about
cloud
cound
group
loud
mouse
soup
yours

1. The **l o u d** noise scared the baby.

2. A large **g r o u p** of people came to the party.

3. This is my ball. Where is **y o u r s** ?

4. My mom made chicken **S o u p** .

5. The **c l o u d** in the sky was moving east.

6. Tell me **a b o u t** your vacation.

7. We caught a **m o u s e** in the trap.

8. Close your eyes and **c o u n t** to ten.

Part H Answer each question.

Vowels
(A E I O U)

1. Which word begins with a vowel? **about**

2. Which word ends with a vowel? **mouse**

3. Which words have the "ou" sound you hear in "out?" **loud about cloud count mouse**

4. In which word does the "ou" sound like "or?" **yours**

5. In which word does the "ou" sound like "move?" **soup**

6. Which word is pictured on this page? **cloud**

Example of a more advanced phonological awareness worksheet focusing on specific vowel sounds. Note the used of a word bank.

SPECIFIC TYPES OF WORKSHEETS

Many of the worksheets described above call for some version of "fill in the blanks" or cloze procedures to complete. Once a child with Down syndrome has completed a few of these worksheets, she usually understands the concept of fill in the blank. Your child may also encounter the following types of worksheets, which may be more difficult for her to understand initially.

Negative Practice. When your child understands punctuation, capitalization, and use of period rules, a "negative practice" type of exercise may be used. This means that the child is given examples that are incorrect and asked to correct them. On the worksheet on the next page the number of mistakes that are in each sentence are given. This makes the instructions more complex, but it allows the child to check whether she has found all of the errors. This child was able to complete the sheet without difficulty, but if she hadn't, she could have been given a checklist of every error to look for.

On page 156 is another example of negative practice in which the instructions were too vague. "Please rewrite the following sentences on your notebook paper, so they look right to you." The child with Down syndrome worked on the sentences and they looked right to her, but they were incorrect. She could have used a sheet with cues such as:

- Begin every sentence with a capital letter.
- Put a period or question mark at the end of every sentence.
- Begin names with a capital letter.
- Check for missing commas.

Codes. Another activity used in language arts and sometimes math is teaching children to use codes. This is really a following directions task. In preschool and kindergarten workbooks, for example, children are asked to find a hidden picture by coloring in numbered sections. For example, use green to color all of the parts with the number 1. Use brown to color all of the parts with the number 2. After the child has colored in the sections, she finds a picture of a tree. If a child doesn't know colors or numbers, these worksheets would not be appropriate. The prerequisite skills (learning the colors and numbers) would need to precede using a worksheet that practices those skills.

On pages 157 and 158 are two more advanced examples. In the first example, shapes are used to correspond to six alphabet letters. The child would need to be able to understand the correspondence and then write the letters in the correct spaces. This child was able to solve the riddle correctly. If she had difficulty, a simpler worksheet to teach the concept could be used. For example, assuming that the child can recognize squares and circles, make a square correspond to b and a circle correspond to e. Solve the riddle, what was buzzing around the flower?

The next example uses the same kind of task, but with eighteen number and letter correspondences. Although this is a longer task, there are visual cues. The words that the child is writing are the spelling words with which she is familiar, and the words are listed in the box at the top of the page. So, once she has solved the /a/, the word could be air, army, or alive, but no other word. She would still need to complete the word puzzle, but would be able to self-monitor and check her accuracy at the end.

FORMATTING WORKSHEETS

Children with Down syndrome frequently need modifications made to the formatting of class worksheets. They may, for example, need a larger space in which to record their answers or to have the fewer items on a page so as to reduce "busy-

Find the mistakes. Rewrite each sentence correctly. The number of mistakes in each sentence is written in each block.

mike wants to help (2)	Mike wants to help.
who wants to run (2)	Who wants to run?
i can't get a ball (3)	I can't get a ball.
i rides a bike (3)	I ride a bike.

Example of a negative practice worksheet which uses incorrect examples needing to be corrected

ness." They may need to be able to scan the items from left to right, or to scan from top to bottom.

The computer has made it much easier to adapt worksheets. The size of the print and the physical layout can be easily changed. Picture cues on worksheets can be added through the use of various clip art programs. At the end of this chapter, there is a resource list of companies that provide picture cues and materials (such as pocket boards and books) that can be used to adapt materials. The program that is most widely used to adapt materials is *Boardmaker*™. It is available from:

Mayer-Johnson Company
P.O. Box 1579
Solano Beach, CA 92075
800-588-4548
www.mayer-johnson.com

DAILY WRITTEN LANGUAGE

Please rewrite the following sentences on your notebook paper, so they look right to you.

2/3   1. lad wants to eat

2/3   2. daddy he comes here

2/3   3. bill didn't want to play   *did not*

4/6   4. mother, daddy, and lad will come

2/2   5. did mother get a ladder ?

+ 12/17 = 71%

Example of a negative practice worksheet with instructions that are too vague

Use the secret code to answer the riddle.

Where does a sheep get a haircut?

at the

b a a - b a a
Y ☆ ☆   Y ☆ ☆

s h o p
□ ⬠ ✪ △

Secret Code

□ = s   Y = b   ⬠ = h   ☆ = a

△ = p   ✪ = o

Example of a simple code exercise used for a language arts worksheet

Spelling Words	baking	hardly	air	army	grain	hello
	thread	taking	trail	alive	rake	stairs
	while	football				

H. Complete the Story. Choose the best words from your spelling list to complete the story.

3/7

My parents are __taking__ me to a __football__ game.

We will walk up the __trail__ to get to our seats. The

__air__ will be cold __while__ we are watching the

game. I may get to say, " __hello__ " to the players. I can

__hardly__ wait to go!

I. Break the Code. Use the code to write your spelling words.

| 1 = a | 3 = d | 5 = f | 7 = h | 9 = k | 11 = m | 13 = o | 15 = s | 17 = v | 19 = y |
| 2 = b | 4 = e | 6 = g | 8 = i | 10 = l | 12 = n | 14 = r | 16 = t | 18 = w | |

army hello cake
1 14 11 9   7 4 10 10 13   14 1 9 4

100%

trail air while
16 14 1 8 10   1 8 14   18 7 8 10 4

baking stairs
2 1 9 8 12 6   15 16 1 8 14 15

alive grain
1 10 8 17 4   6 14 1 8 12

thread hardly
16 7 14 4 1 3   7 1 14 3 10 19

taking football
16 1 9 8 12 6   5 13 13 16 2 1 10 10

Example of a more complicated code exercise used for a language arts worksheet

Boardmaker software provides a large number of pictures that can be imported into materials to provide cues or for creating pictured instructions. The example on page 160, shows a communication board made with Boardmaker's Picture Communication Symbols©. This sheet was used in a language therapy session during a crafts activity—making a Spring garden plot.

Projects and Reports

When your child has a book report or long-term project to complete, schedules and cloze procedures or learning frames (see Chapter 5) can be very helpful. A picture or written schedule will help your child organize the report, and complete each portion in sequence (see examples of book report learning frames on pages 161-166). Fill-ins and frames will structure the report and help your child to include all of the necessary information. Checksheets such as the one below are often used to help children monitor that they are including all of the material need.

Book Report Checklist

1. I put the title of the book on the cover. ____
2. I put the author's name on the cover. ____
3. I listed 3 characters in the book. ____
4. I described where the story takes place. ____
5. I described what happened in the story. ____
6. I described how the story ends. ____

Homework

The same techniques and adaptations that are used for class work can be used for homework assignments. Whoever is responsible for adapting in-class practice sheets should also adapt or modify worksheets assigned as homework. At home, parents may use various types of organizers such as homework frames or story lines or maps to help their child. You can also provide cues, prompts, and supportive assistance as needed. Through the home-to-school communication plan, parents and teachers/SLPs should be frequently communicating about what types of cues or organizers

Example of a communication board for a crafts activity made with Boardmaker's Picture Communication Symbols ©

Book Report — Fiction

Name: _____ Date: _____

Title: _____

Author: _____

Who were the main characters? _____

_____

_____

Where was it set? _____

When did it take place? _____

What happened?

1. _____

_____

_____

2. _____

_____

_____

continued ▶

3. _____

_____

_____

Did you like the story?(circle one)

Why? _____

_____

_____

How did the story end? _____

_____

_____

The
End

Book Report — Non-Fiction

Name: _____ Date: _____

Title: _____

Author: _____

What is the book about? _____
_____
_____

List 4 new facts you learned from the book.

1. _____
_____
_____

2. _____
_____
_____

3. _____
_____
_____

continued ▶

4. _____ 4. ____

_____

_____

Did you like the story?(circle one)

Why? _____

_____

_____

Book Report — Biography

Name: _____ Date: _____

Title: _____

Author: _____

Who is the book about? _____

When was the person born? _____

Where was the person born? _____

Is the person still living? or When did the person die? R.I.P. _____

What were the person's main accomplishments? _____
_____

List 3 new facts you learned from the book.

1._____

_____

_____

continued ▶

2. _____

_____

_____

3. _____

_____

_____

Did you like the story? (circle one)

Why? _____

_____

_____

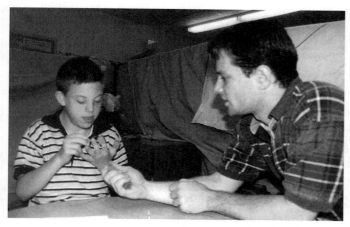

work for the child. Parents should let teachers/SLPs know if an assignment is just too hard for their child, or if she has specific problems with the language.

One of the main differences between class work and homework is in the physical environment. Be sure that your child has a quiet, comfortable work area in which to complete homework assignments. Tools such as adapted pencil grips, special scissors, pencils, pens, eraser, and/or word processor should be available.

It is also important that parents and school staff agree upon a formal system to make sure homework assignments arrive home. A homework sheet listing assignments for the day or week can be sent home or emailed to parents. Or, a fill-in form in which the child copies all of the assignments onto one sheet can be used. It may be helpful to color code homework sheets for each day of the week. For example, the homework sheet for the weekend is always blue, the Monday sheet is green, Tuesday yellow, etc. In higher grades, when an assignment may be due three days later or the next week, rather than the next day, a date book can be used for long-term assignments. The teacher or aide might fill out the date book for your child, or check to see that your child has recorded assignments correctly.

Putting It All Together

Now that we have discussed a number of strategies that can help students with Down syndrome learn, let's look at examples of assignments in elementary school, and discuss how the modifications discussed in this chapter and the preceding one could be used.

For a first grade book report on *Ira Sleeps Over:*

- Modifications and adaptations could be used to shorten the story, or to adjust the level of language.
- Adaptations could be made in the channel of response. For example, the child could draw a book cover or trace the title instead of writing the title and author on the cover. If the book report form asked, "Who are the main characters?" the child could glue pictures of the characters, if she cannot write the names.
- The size of the print could be increased by using a copy machine or computer.
- The length of the response could be changed, so that the child would need to list two things the characters did at a sleepover instead of six things.
- Preparatory prompts could be used to help the child learn to predict from the title what is in the story.
- A book checklist could be used as a learning or homework frame (What is the title? Who wrote the book? Name of main character? What is the setting?)

- A web chart could be used to organize events from the story.
- A manipulative such as the story grammar manipulative described in Chapter 5 could be used to aid in retelling the story.
- A story map, story board, or sequence chain (a sequence chart of the events in the story) could be used to help the child retell the story. See below for an example of a sequence chain.
- A pacing board could be used to prompt the child to make each sentence long enough.
- A Venn diagram could be used to compare the child's sleepover experience with that of the main character in the story. This can also assist in discussing how the experiences were the same and how they were different.
- Story starters and learning frames could be used to assist the child in writing or presenting the book report.

For a first grade book report by a child who can't yet read:
- In the school library, the librarian, speech-language pathologist, or teacher could pre-choose several books that have vocabulary and a story line at the child's language level.

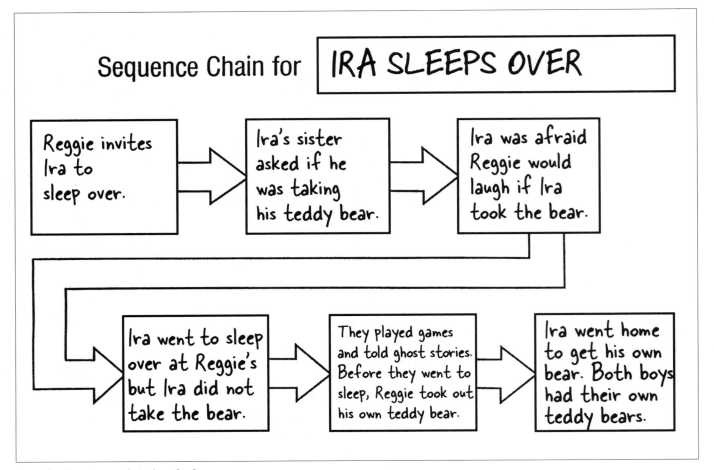

Example of a sequence chain for a book report

A book such as *The Three Little Pigs* or *Chicken Soup with Rice*, which have predictable repetitive phrases, might be chosen.

- *The Three Little Pigs* might also be a good choice because the child could listen to an audiotape and watch a videotape of the story.
- Adaptations could be made in the channel of response. For example, the child could draw a book cover instead of writing the title and author on the cover.
- Preparatory prompts could be used to help the child learn to predict from the title what is in the story.
- A Venn diagram could be used to compare the pigs' houses with the child's house. This could also assist in discussing how the experiences were the same and how they were different.
- A manipulative could be used to help the child retell the story. The child and a peer partner or the aide might draw pictures of the pigs, the wolf, and the houses, or they might instead color in the pictures in a coloring book. The pictures could then be laminated (or use plastic Contac paper) and mounted on tongue depressors. When the child is telling the story, she could move the pictures on sticks around very much like puppets (e.g., the wolf comes to the first pig's house and huffs and puffs and tries to blow the house in). A more general book report manipulative might also be used, as described on page 82. Here, picture buttons represent the characters, setting, etc., to help the child retell the story.

For a second grade social studies unit on community helpers:

- The text material could be shortened and the vocabulary and language level could be simplified.

- If the family were provided with a list of the community helpers (policeman, fireman, school crossing guard, teacher, librarian, car repair man, sanitation truck driver, etc.) that will be included in the unit, they could walk or drive around the neighborhood and find real examples of people working in the community. The parents might even offer to photograph the community helpers that will be studied or create a slide show for the class. This would give the child with Down syndrome extra experience with the names of the community helpers and real-life examples that would make the concepts more meaningful.

- Visual organizers can be used to clarify material in the unit. For example, a chart could be created dividing the workers into categories for safety, food service, etc.
- Some work could be done in cooperative learning groups, and participation could be designed to allow the child to work hard and to experience success. For example, one child may look for information on the Internet, another child may interview a community worker, another may cut out pictures of different workers.
- Test questions and responses can be modified so that a multiple choice question with two possible responses is given, instead of a matching question which has ten possible answer choices. See Chapter 9 for more information on Testing Modifications.

For a third grade science unit on plants and growth:
- The text material could be shortened and the vocabulary and language level could be simplified.
- The SLP could get a list of the words used for the unit and teach the child all of the vocabulary words that are part of the plants and growth unit before or at the same time as the unit is being taught in class.
- Parent involvement and collaboration could be sought through a letter sent home explaining the content of the unit.
- Experiments and scientific observation could be done in cooperative learning groups, and participation could be designed to allow the child to work hard and to experience success.
- Test questions and responses could be modified so that a multiple choice with two possible responses is given, instead of a matching question which has ten possible answer choices. (See Chapter 9 for more information on modifying tests.)

For a fifth grade unit on Colonial America:
- A Venn diagram could be used to compare daily life then and now.
- The vocabulary involved in the unit could be taught by the SLP or the classroom aide before or at the same time the unit is being taught.
- A learning frame could be used to help the child organize all of the information on taxes and the events leading to the American revolution.
- A timeline and learning frames could be used to help organize and learn the material about Colonial America.
- A word bank could be used to help the child come up with the vocabulary she needs for classwork and tests.

How do you choose which organizers, adaptations, or modifications you will use? You choose based on the nature of the material and on your child's learning styles. For example, if she has difficulty memorizing and retrieving information, you might use a mnemonic device to help her remember. Or you might chunk the material into smaller segments that she could remember. (See Chapter 5.) But, for that same child, a worksheet asking her to circle all of the proper nouns would not lend itself to mnemonic devices or chunking. Here, you might want to use her word bank from the unit, and write at the top of the worksheet what a proper noun is. Then give her some examples. That should help her understand and remember what is required. The worksheet on pages 172-173 can help you figure out what kinds of supports your child needs in each subject.

Ensuring Needs Are Addressed through the IEP

Speech-language therapy will probably be crucial to helping your child deal with the language demands of the curriculum. Your child's therapy might focus on:

- *Linguistic skills*—that is, on specific problems with semantics (meaning), morphology and syntax (grammar), pragmatics (social use of language), and phonology (sound production).
- *Different channels*—that is, on your child's abilities to understand and use auditory (hearing), speech, and visual skills to communicate. One channel, such as reading, may be used to assist another channel such as expressive language or written language.

Therapy may also be approached through the needs of the curriculum. This is known as curriculum-based therapy and is definitely worth advocating for. In this approach, vocabulary would be taught based on the vocabulary that your child needs for success in science, social studies, or other subjects. The therapy may be *proactive,* teaching in advance the language skills that your child will need for the official curriculum, formal and informal classroom interactions, following directions in class and learning the rules and routines, and skills for interacting with peers. Curriculum-based therapy may also be *reactive,* targeting areas of difficulty as they occur and providing assistance with study skills and strategies to meet classroom expectations or to overcome difficulties when they occur.

Conclusion

There are many ways in which we can help children learn the material that they need to master for their grade, age, and functional level. Some involve modifying the texts or worksheets that are being used. Other approaches include demonstrations and multimedia. With some subject matter, we can be proactive. The speech-language pathologist can work with your child on creating a word bank

Curriculum Adaptation Worksheet

Name: _____

Subject: _____

Type of Material: *(check all that apply)*
- ❑ Reading assignment
- ❑ Worksheet
- ❑ Book report
- ❑ Project
- ❑ Homework assignment

Type of Adaptations Needed: *(check all that apply; list specifics)*
- ❑ Size: _____
- ❑ Layout: _____
- ❑ Time: _____

Level of Support: *(check all that apply)*
- ❑ Aide
- ❑ Peer tutor
- ❑ Other _____

Additional Practice needed: _____

_____

Input: _____

_____

Difficulty: _____

_____

continued ▶

Output: _____
_____

Participation: _____
_____

Alternate Goals: _____
_____

Grading and Feedback: _____
_____

Substitute Curriculum: _____
_____

Materials Used: *(check all that apply; list specifics)*

❏ Visual organizers _____
❏ Cues & prompts _____
❏ Mnemonics and memory devices _____
❏ Assistive Technology _____
❏ Other _____

with the vocabulary words for the next science unit. The family can plan a trip to Jamestown and Williamsburg, Virginia, during the summer before your child will be studying Colonial America. For other subjects (such as spelling), you and school staff can help your child as she is learning the material. When your child, classroom teacher, speech-language pathologist, and family collaborate, it will maximize the opportunities for your child to succeed.

REFERENCES

Blenk, K. (1995). *Making school inclusion work: A guide to everyday practice.* Cambridge, MA: Brookline Books.

Chisler, J. & Oaks, R. (1995). *The collaboration companion.* Moline, IL: Lingui-Systems.

Filbin, J., Rogers-Connolly, T. & Brewer, R. (1996). *Individualized learner outcomes: Infusing student needs into the regular education curriculum.* Colorado Springs, CO: PEAK Parent Center.

Goodman, G. (1994). *Inclusive classrooms from A to Z: A handbook for educators.* Columbus, OH: Teacher's Publishing Group.

Hammeken, P. A. (1995). *Inclusion: 450 strategies for success.* Minnetonka, MN: Peytral Publications.

Moore, L. O. (1995). *Inclusion: A practical guide for parents - Tools to enhance your child's learning.* Minnetonka, MN: Peytral Publications.

Rief, S. F. & Heimburge, J. A. (1996). *How to reach & teach all students in the inclusive classroom.* West Nyack, NY: The Center for Applied Research in Education.

Schaffner, B. & Buswell, B. E. (1992). *Opening doors: Strategies for including all students in regular education.* Colorado Springs, CO: PEAK Parent Center.

Simon, C. (Ed.) (1991). *Communication skills and classroom success: Assessment and therapy methodologies for language and learning disabled students.* Eau Claire, WI: Thinking Publications.

Stainback, S. & Stainback, W. (1992). *Curriculum considerations in inclusive classrooms: Facilitating learning for all students.* Baltimore, MD: Paul Brookes.

Stainback, W., Stainback, S. & Forest, M. (1989). *Educating all students in the mainstream of regular education.* Baltimore, MD: Paul Brookes.

Tien, B., ed. (1999). *Effective teaching strategies for successful inclusion: A focus on Down syndrome.* Calgary, Alberta, Canada: PREP Program.

Udvari-Solner, A. (1995). Curricular adaptations: Reconfiguring teaching practice to support students with disabilities in general education classrooms. In Nadel, L. & Rosenthal, D., eds. *Down syndrome: Living and learning in the community.* New York: Wiley-Liss, 170-181.

Villa, R., Thousand, J., Stainback, W. & Stainback, S. (1992). *Restructuring for caring and effective education.* Baltimore, MD: Paul Brookes.

CHAPTER 7

The Language of Instruction

The language of instruction is the language used to teach and learn within the classroom. The language of instruction includes:

- ***The channels used for instruction:*** For example, does the teacher provide oral instructions? written instructions? pictured or diagramed instructions? Children with Down syndrome learn well through pictures, reading, watching, and modeling. If the teacher does not provide visual cues, it is harder for children with Down syndrome to follow instructions. When written instructions are used, it is especially important to provide examples.

- ***The length of instructions:*** Does the teacher give long strings of instructions? Or break the instructions into several parts? If instructions are long and complex, children with Down syndrome have difficulty following the instructions.

- ***The vocabulary of instruction:*** What terms are used in teaching and in learning in that classroom? In the primary grades, terms used for instruction might include *underline, circle,* and *draw a line.* In later elementary school, terms might include *cause and effect, factors that influence, action and response.*

- ***The consistency of language used:*** Are the terms that are used to give instructions used consistently? Children with Down syndrome respond best to consistent instructions that they understand and can follow. Teachers often change the language used in giving instructions without even realizing that they are doing this. Workbook and worksheet instructions also tend to be varied without explaining what the changed instructions mean. For example, teachers may phrase the same addition or subtraction problem a variety of ways, such as:

    For *"Add 2 and 3"*
    —How much is 2 plus 3?
    —What does 2 plus 3 make?
    —What is the sum of 2 and 3?

For *"Subtract 5 from 10"*
—Take 5 away from 10
—How much is 10 minus 5?
—How much is left if you take 5 away from 10?
—What do you have if you subtract 5 from 10?
—What is the remainder if you take 5 from 10?
—Find the difference between 10 and 5.

To complicate the subtraction task further, the teacher may give out a worksheet that has a picture of a dime (10 cents), take away a nickel (5 cents). The child with Down syndrome may be able to solve the math problem, 10-5=5, but may not be able to solve the same problem when coin names (nickel, dime) are used rather than numbers. This is a good example of a situation in which the child knows how to perform the addition or subtraction task (the math curriculum) but has difficulty with the language of instruction.

■ ***Differences between subject areas in instructional methods:*** Are there differences between the way that different subjects are taught? For example, science and physical education are usually more hands-on and provide many more contextual cues during instruction. Social studies and language arts generally involve more lecture, fewer visual cues and models, and more use of decontextualized language for teaching. In science, when the teacher is talking about a plant, the child is likely to be looking at or holding various types of plants. When he labels the parts of the flowers or studies the onion skin under a microscope, he is using the real objects. In social studies, when the teacher is talking about the unrest in the Middle East, there are many fewer cues in the environment related to the topic. The teacher may show slides or a video, but the topic is much more abstract.

■ ***The match between your child's needs and the instructions given:*** Can your child follow the teacher's instruction? If not, what is interfering with his ability to follow the instructions? Can he hear the instructions adequately? Your child may need to use an individual or classroom-based amplifications system. Is the language level of the instruction appropriate for your child? The teacher may be giving a long string of instructions too long for your child to process. Or, the vocabulary used may be too difficult or too varied for your child to understand.

Observing the Language of Instruction

In order to develop adaptations in the area of instruction, intensive observation needs to be done in the classroom. Your child's learning style needs to be identi-

fied, and the language of instruction in class must be analyzed. The speech-language pathologist and the special education teacher, working in collaboration with the classroom teacher, are the professionals who are best trained to do these observations. Parents can also provide valuable insight.

The collaborative team can suggest modifications and assistance to help your child understand and follow the instructions given in class. The SLP can suggest language adaptations in the way that instructions are provided, and in the ways your child is expected to respond. At the same time, therapy and a home program can target the specific concepts that your child needs to master in order to succeed in class. The worksheet at the end of the chapter will help in the planning process.

Changes can be made in several areas that can be helpful to your child. These areas include:

- instructional methods,
- instructional expectations,
- physical environment, and
- social environment.

Each of these areas will be discussed in the next section. If the classroom teacher, speech-language pathologist, and special educator have collaborated in the past, they will already have information about the typical instructional methods and language within the classroom. Then, they will need to collaborate with your family and your child to assess your child's needs. If they have not worked collaboratively in the past, an extensive analysis of the language of instruction in the classroom, as well as your child's individual patterns of learning, will need to be done. The questions below can help guide this observation.

CHECKLIST FOR ANALYZING THE LANGUAGE OF INSTRUCTION

These questions should be answered separately for each subject area

INSTRUCTIONAL METHODS

- ***How is instruction being provided, and at what language level?*** Does the teacher give verbal instructions or written instructions? Is the material taught through lecture with note taking or are children working together in teams on projects?
- ***Where is instruction occurring?*** Is the lesson in the classroom? In a resource room? Is it taking place in a small group, such as for reading instruction?
- ***With whom is instruction occurring?*** Is the teacher giving the lesson? Is the information being interpreted for your child by an aide? by a peer tutor?
- ***When is instruction taking place?*** Is it first thing in the morning? After lunch? You will want to consider this

information in light of the next section on your child's learning style. Does your child learn best early in the day? later in the day? Is this affecting your child's performance in the subject?

- ***What teaching style is being used? How does this match the child's learning style?*** Does your child learn best when he can read the instructions and when there are lots of picture cues? Does the teacher write assignments on the board or does he dictate them? Can your child learn in the way that he is being taught? If not, modifications and adaptations can be used to help him learn.

INSTRUCTIONAL EXPECTATIONS

- ***How is your child's knowledge of the subject tested?*** What kinds of tests or worksheets are used?
- ***What does the teacher expect your child to be able to learn?*** Do they match the family's expectations? Do they match the IEP goals?

ANALYSIS OF THE CHILD'S INSTRUCTIONAL NEEDS

- ***What is the child's learning style?***
  Learns best from demonstrations and examples ____
  Learns best by hearing the instructions____
  Learns best by having the instructions in visual form ____
      written ____pictures____
  Learns best when cues are provided, e.g. if the answer is
      Pennsylvania, his worksheet has a /P/ or the teacher gives
      the sound /p/ ___
  Learns best with assistance from another person___
  Other:
- ***What adaptations are currently being used?*** Why were those adaptations chosen?
- ***Do the methods of instruction currently being used match the child's learning styles?*** Do they maximize learning while compensating for his disability? In short, are they effective?

PHYSICAL ENVIRONMENT

- ***Can the physical environment be modified to help the child learn?*** Some possible modifications include:
  - preferential seating so that the child can see the board well and hear the instructions;
  - study carrel for reading and studying;
  - more work space to help the child organize his papers;
  - checklists or other organizers taped to the desk;
  - more or less light in the classroom;
  - background music to help learning and concentration.

SOCIAL ENVIRONMENT

- *Can the social environment be changed?* Changing the participation level may be helpful. For example, cooperative groups, peer partners, or a classroom aide may be used.
  - In cooperative groups, a small group of students from the class work together on completing a project or assignment. This is a good model for children with Down syndrome and for many other children because within the group, each child can play a different role. For example, one child can find pictures, a second child can cut them out, and a third child can paste them on a worksheet. Or for older children, one child can look up census data, a second child can record the information, and a third child can analyze the trends and patterns.
  - In peer partner arrangements, one child usually serves as a tutor and practice partner for another child. The tutor may help the child complete a science worksheet on plants or practice his spelling words. Research has shown that the "tutor" usually increases his skills also. For example, while he is helping a child practice spelling words, he is learning to say the words more clearly himself.
  - A classroom aide is an adult who may be a paraprofessional or may be a volunteer or parent assistant. The aide can help adapt worksheets, interpret instructions, or help your child write the answers on a worksheet.

In short, your child's teachers and SLP need to determine:

- Do the methods of instruction currently being used match the child's learning styles?
- Do they maximize learning while compensating for your child's disability?

MODIFYING THE LANGUAGE OF INSTRUCTION

Once the instructional methods are identified, and your child's learning needs are assessed, what kinds of adaptations can be made to the instructional methods?

ADAPTATIONS TO SPOKEN INSTRUCTION

Many children with Down syndrome have difficulty with long, complex instructions that are given verbally. If the instructions can be shortened, made less complex, or supplemented with picture or written instructions, the child can often do the task. Some possible adaptations in instructional methods include:

- *Keep verbal instructions short.* Use shorter phrases and sentences when giving instructions to complete a task. For example, instead of saying "Take out your language arts homework from last night and pass it to the left of your row," have a routine way that papers are passed in, and just say, "Hand in your language arts homework now."
- *Present the information in several different chunks rather than one long instruction.* For example, instead of

saying, "It's time for math. Take out your mathematics book, turn to page 65, and complete exercises A and B," the information can be presented in three chunks. "Take out your math books." When everyone has the books out, the teacher would say, "Turn to page 65." When everyone has the book opened, the teacher would say, "Do exercises A and B."

- **Provide many visual cues.** In the above example, the assignment could be given in writing, and could be color coded to provide another visual cue. For example, the math assignment is always put on the board using yellow chalk. On the board, it would say: Math: page 65, exercises A and B. If the child needs further help in getting the math book out, we might cover the math book with yellow paper, or have a yellow dot on the side of the book where he can easily see it. Pictographs can be used to help children follow instructions. Boardmaker software, which was discussed in Chapter 5, can be used to create customized visual cues for assignments using Picture Communication Symbols©.

- **Provide demonstrations and sample items.** If possible, use a transparency or pass out a sheet with sample items so that the child has a model available when he is completing the task. This ensures that the child sees a correct model of how he is expected to respond. For example, if he is answering questions on a worksheet that involves matching, is he supposed to put the letter of the correct response, or draw lines from one column to the other? If you have sample items, students can see how to answer the questions. For children with Down syndrome, who learn best visually, this is important. If the worksheet, for example, matches the explorers with the countries that they discovered, you want to be sure that the worksheet is testing whether your child knows the explorers, not whether he knows how to answer the questions by putting in letters or drawing lines.

- **Present the instructions slowly.** The instructor should talk slowly, and ask students for feedback to be sure that they understand the assignment. Children with Down syndrome have difficulty with auditory processing and may need slower verbal instructions given in chunks to enable them to correctly process the information.

- **Introduce a small number of new concepts at a time.** Relate the concepts to what the child already knows. Families can be active in introducing the child to the concepts in daily life. The teacher can send home a note so that you know what is being worked on. For example, if your child's class is going to study the different food groups, you could discuss what your child ate that day. Make a list of the foods. Then introduce the concepts of vegetables, fruits, meat, grains, and dairy as a way of grouping the types of foods that your child eats. Perhaps only introduce one category, such as vegetables, to start. A trip to the supermarket produce section, discussion of foods eaten at dinner, and pictures of vegetables cut out of a magazine or supermarket circular would all reinforce the concept of vegetables. It would be ideal if the teacher sent this information home the week before the class was to discuss the food groups, so that you could introduce one new food group concept every day, and your child would have some familiarity with the information when the material was presented in class.

- ***Give students an overview of the information before beginning the lesson.*** This is the "Here is what we are going to do" approach. This helps children focus on the purpose of the lesson. For example, "Today, we are going to learn about how children live in China."

- ***Give students study questions before they read the material.*** Discuss what they need to look for in the textbook. For example, if students are reading a chapter on the solar system, it helps if they know what information they need to look for. By going over the study questions first, they will be able to find the information in the textbook more easily (e.g., which planet is closest to earth?) If they do not know the questions ahead of time, they need to remember all of the information as equally important and try to retrieve all of the information. Children with Down syndrome may not be able to remember all of the information but may be able to answer the questions and remember the important information.

- ***Highlight important points to be learned.*** For example, use color-coded index cards when your child is writing a book report. Have him put the names of the characters on a pink card. Put what happened, the plot, on a blue card. When your child is learning about how children live in France, use a pink card to describe their homes, a blue card for their food, a white card for what they learn in school, etc. If the teacher can photocopy pages of the textbook or you can purchase a copy of the textbook, your child can actually use colored highlighters or colored highlighter tape to organize the material. Using graphic organizers is another instructional adaptation. Organizers are discussed in detail in Chapter 5.

- ***Talk with the child individually at short intervals to check whether he is understanding the material and understanding the instructions.*** This can be done with a peer partner or a classroom aide. Many children with Down syndrome who are not following the lesson or are having difficulty will not ask for help. So checking regularly to see that he is on task and understands the assignment is helpful.

Understanding Basic Concepts

Sometimes children with Down syndrome have difficulty with the language of instruction because they do not understand basic concepts such as: opposite, same/different, rhyme, before/after. Such words are often used in spoken and written instructions, but if a child does not understand them, obviously he cannot follow instructions without adaptations.

If your child doesn't understand basic concepts, IEP goals should be written so that the special educator, teacher, and/or SLP will work on them with your child. You can also ask the SLP for home activities so that you can help your child work on concepts at home. For example, there are mathematical concepts that you can work on with your child at home that will help him understand mathematical concepts in school. Mathematical language concepts include:

- **Quantitative values:** more/less, few/many, some/none, one/more than one
- **Comparison words:** big/little, tall/short, same/different, empty/full, light/heavy, slow/fast, greater than/less than, small/large, fast/slow
- **Volume:** full/empty
- **Time:** before/during/after, morning/afternoon/night, yesterday/today/tomorrow, past/present/future.
- **Distance:** near/far, next to/far away, here/there
- **Sequences:** counting, ordering, and sequencing

Home activities that can help develop mathematical concepts are:

- **Food shopping:** Check the number of items, weight, and/or volume of certain foods. e.g., talk about how a container holds a gallon or 12 ounces, or that a package contains 6 cupcakes.
- **Clothing shopping:** Look at sizes, prices, amounts. e.g., socks might cost $2.99 each, but be 2 for $4.00.
- **Using a calendar:** Note special days and celebrations on the calendar, teach concepts of beginning and end, count the days until vacation.

- ***Use technology to assist the child.*** Audiotape recorders, videotape recorders, and computers may help the child follow directions and respond to questions and assignments. (See Chapter 5 for more information on assistive technology.)
- ***Allow extra time to complete the assignment.*** Let the child finish the assignment at home, or during a free period. Or, he may be given fewer items to complete (5 instead of 10 items) on a spelling word sentences sheet, but then may be expected to complete the shorter sheet in the same time that other students will be completing the 10 item worksheet.

- **Using a daily schedule:** Begin with picture schedules and work on concepts such as next, before, last.
- **Playing games:** Concepts of first and next, counting number of spaces, sequencing, and ordering can be taught.
- **Cooking:** measuring and sequencing are part of most recipes; full and empty, and concepts of number and time can be practiced while cooking.
- **Measuring activities:** You can measure a room, a floor, your child's height.
- **Using money for purchases:** This can be role played while playing store or playing restaurant. It can be practiced on a trip to the ice cream store, to a housewares store, while using a vending machine, or while driving through a toll booth.
- **Gardening:** You can measure the amount of water and the size of the plant as it grows. You can count the number of seeds that you use, and the number of blossoms that bloom, or the number of tomatoes on a plant each day and compare the number from day to day. You can also make charts of the yield of the plant.
- **Arts and crafts projects:** You can measure for crafts projects such as woodworking or sewing; make greeting cards or gift paper.
- **Computer/video games:** There are many software packages that teach number concepts, or opposites such as few and many or full and empty.
- **Comparing prices in ads from the Sunday newspaper:** The newspaper ads are an inexpensive, renewable practice source. They are perfect because the format is similar from week to week but the items change. You can discuss items from one ad or compare prices in the ads from several different stores, such as supermarkets.
- **TV guide/Sunday TV magazine:** You can make a chart of the programs that you want to watch or look up all the programs that are in a specific time slot.

- *Divide the assignment into segments or shorter or simpler tasks.* If the class has a 30-question worksheet on verb endings, the sheet can be divided into 3 worksheets of 10 items each. Your child may complete the first 10 items with a peer partner or with a classroom aide assisting, complete the next 10 items independently, and the last 10 items for homework. The worksheet can be recopied so that it is now 3 worksheets. Sometimes, it is also helpful to enlarge the type on the worksheets; it makes the worksheets easier to use.

- *Vary the output measures.* Use projects and reports in addition to tests. Children who cannot use speech to respond may be able to use an augmentative communication system, a communication board, or a computer. Children who can read, but cannot speak, may be able to use multiple choice responses to a question, or may be able to write the response. Children who cannot write but can read may be able to respond using sentences that they cut out and arrange for a report. Children who physically cannot write may be able to use the word processor to write. Children who cannot read or write may be able to respond using multiple choice picture cards.

- *Provide feedback in a timely manner to help the child continue to progress.* The child may need feedback after he has completed the first three items, so that he knows that he is on the right track. Checklists may help him provide his own feedback as to whether he completed the assignment correctly. For example, when he is writing in his daily journal, he can have a check-off sheet as follows:

    1. I put the date in the top right hand corner _____
    2. I started writing on the first line of the page _____
    3. I wrote at least 3 sentences _____
    4. I ended each sentence with a period _____
    5. I used my word bank to check my spelling when I was done _____

- *Provide incentives for the child to master the curriculum.* This is important for all children. For example, when everyone learns ten facts about Washington, D.C., they will get an achievement coin. When everyone learns five facts about the president, they will get an achievement coin. When the class collects a total of fifty coins, we will have a pizza party.

- *Cue students in to what is really important in the lesson.* The teacher might say, "This is really important. Are you listening?"

- *Use visual aids (picture, charts, graphs) to supplement verbal information.*

ADAPTATIONS TO CLASSROOM MATERIALS

Some specific adaptations to classroom materials that will help children with Down syndrome include:

- *Allow plenty of space for the child to respond.* Fold the worksheet into eight parts and have one question in each box. It is difficult for many children with Down syndrome to write in a small space, and to complete worksheets that are visually busy. See Chapter 6 for more worksheet adaptations.

- *Make sure that the language of instruction is not interfering with the child's ability to master the language of the curriculum.* When we ask a child to

complete a worksheet for a specific subject, the language considerations relate to both the subject matter and the instructions. Vocabulary such as throat, stomach, intestines, leaves, petals, stems, pioneers, explorers, are all words that relate to the subject matter in science and social studies. The directions for a worksheet, however, might state: "On the diagram, draw a line to the stomach," or "Choose the best adjective to describe the picture." If the child does not know what "diagram" or "adjective" means, he will not be able to show that he knows the subject matter.

- *Help the child with Down syndrome show what he knows by using language consistently.* For example, word problems in math are often confusing because there is so much complex language used. An example of a test that uses simpler, consistent language is shown on page 186. The problems use consistent wording: "How much change will you get back if you buy something for ____. You gave the cashier ____." This is a fair test of math subtraction skills, rather than a language test. In contrast, the end of unit test on page 187 would be much harder for a student with Down syndrome. Its questions use complex and varied language, including sequential terms such as first and second, and terms related to patterns, graphs, and telling time. Not only would a child need to know the wide variety of skills being tested, but he would also need to be able to figure out how to follow the instructions. It is possible that a student could know how to do the math to get the correct answers, but not be able to answer the questions because the instructions are too confusing. Analyzing the language of written class work is discussed further in chapter 6.

- *Reduce the number of responses required.* For example, ask the child to find two cities in a country, instead of five cities.

- *Use visual organizers such as flowcharts, timelines, and webs.* Children with Down syndrome learn very well through the visual channel. (See Chapter 5.)

- *Provide a copy of notes so that the child does not have to copy the notes from the board.*

- *Give written or pictured directions in addition to verbal directions.* Verbal directions are rapid and fleeting. The ability to complete the task is affected by the child's auditory memory ability when instructions are given verbally.

- *Have the student state in his own words what he is to do.* For example, the child tells his peer partner or the classroom

Name: _____ Date: _____

HOW MUCH CHANGE WILL YOU GET BACK IF . . .

1. you buy something for 87 cents. You gave the cashier $1.00.

   • 13

2. you buy something for 24 cents. You gave the cashier 75 cents.

   •.51 ¢

3. you buy something for $4.88. You gave the cashier $5.00.

   • 12

4. you buy something for $1.30. You gave the cashier $2.00.

   •.70¢

5. you buy something for $3.66. You gave the cashier $5.00.

   $ 1·34

6. you buy something for $2.03. You gave the cashier $2.50.

   ‛47

7. you buy something for $7.30. You gave the cashier $10.00

   $ 2,70

Word problems in math are often confusing because there is so much complex language used. Simpler, consistent language, as in the example above, helps the child with Down syndrome show what he knows.

Name: _____ Date: _____

MATH UNIT TEST

1. Steven is first in line. Beverly is at the end of the line. Sean is second in line. How many children are in line?

2. Harry has 6 pennies. Jennifer has 2 nickels. Who has more money?

3. Fill in the missing number.

        3   4   5   ____   7

4. Fill in the numbers for the repeating pattern.

        66   77   __ __   99

5. Joel does not know what time it is because the hands are missing on the clock. Can you help him? Draw a clock. Then draw in the hands on the clock so that it is 3:30.

6. The class is having a bake sale. Nancy brought 1 cupcake. Sheila has 4 cupcakes. Diane brought 6 cupcakes. Tom has 4 cupcakes. Draw a graph to show how many cupcakes each child is contributing to the bake sale. How many cupcakes are there in total?

The test above would be difficult for a child with Down syndrome because of the complex and varied language, including sequential terms such as first and second, and terms related to patterns, graphs, and telling time.

aide what he needs to do to complete the assignment. This is a way to check that the child understands the instructions.

- ***Help the child learn any new vocabulary before it is used in the lesson, so that unfamiliar words don't stop him from moving ahead.*** Create a word bank for new vocabulary when it is mastered. (See Chapter 6.)
- ***Keep a list of "Assignments to complete—things to do" on a Post-It note on the corner of the child's desk.*** If the child can't read, this might consist of picture cues for each subject.

ADAPTATIONS TO THE METHOD OF RESPONSE

Instruction in class involves the teacher asking questions and calling on students to answer those questions. Answering direct requests for specific information in class may be difficult for children with Down syndrome. Your child may need

more time to process the question, and the teacher may assume that he does not know the answer, when he is, in reality, still processing the question. Speech difficulties and word finding difficulties may also affect your child's ability to answer a question rapidly in class.

Children with Down syndrome often respond better to open-ended questioning techniques—that is, to questions in which there is more than one "right" answer. Subjects such as reading or language arts lend themselves well to open-ended questioning techniques, but other subjects such as mathematics and geography do not. Questions that teachers ask may be *divergent* ("Tell me the names of fruits that are red." Or "Name animals that are active during the night."). Or they may be *convergent* ("I am thinking of a fruit that is yellow, turns brown when it is ripe, and is eaten by monkeys."). When a divergent question is asked, there are many possible correct answers and associated words will come to mind. To a convergent question, there is usually one correct answer. For many questions in class or on tests, the questions are convergent and there is only one correct answer. For children with Down syndrome who have word finding problems, convergent questions are very difficult.

Good adaptations to responses for children with Down syndrome include:

- ***Provide more time for the child to answer a spoken question.*** You remain silent and wait for a number of seconds, rather than asking him repeatedly. If he still cannot answer, you might provide auditory or visual cues as suggested in Chapter 5.
- ***Ask the group as a whole to respond.*** For example, the students respond by holding up a yes or no card, or thumbs up or thumbs down. Answers can be given in unison, the teacher counts 1-2-3, and then the class shouts the answer.
- ***Choice questions may be given in which the child is given several choices, one of which is correct.*** (Is Brazil in North America, South America, or Europe?)

- ***Once a unit has been taught and learned, a game show format such as Jeopardy, Who Wants to Be a Millionaire, or Wheel of Fortune can also be used to help children practice and remember the information.***
- ***If the child uses a method other than speech to communicate, it is important for the teacher to be a responsive partner.*** Direct questions to the child and give him time to respond using his method of communication.

In addition, to these strategies that can be used during classroom instruction, your child can work on improving his ability to respond while in therapy with the SLP. Expressive language therapy could focus on:

- vocabulary,
- similarities and differences (being able to express what is the same or different about two things)
- morphology (word parts such as the verb endings -ed and -ing)
- syntax (word order in a sentence such as "The bird flies high in the sky")
- increasing the length of speech utterances (For example, your child might use 2-3 word phrases, and a goal might be to increase the MLU to 4 word phrases and sentences. To help your child lengthen his responses, the SLP might have him use a pacing board, as discussed in Chapter 5. The SLP might also have him use rehearsal (saying subvocally or quietly the sentence that he is trying to express, before saying it aloud); scaffolds, such as a list of word cues to help your child describe an object (see Chapter 5); and scripts (see Chapter 11).

Following Spoken Directions

In order to demonstrate that they know the work, children need to be able to understand and follow the instructions given in class. The language of instruction is different for different subjects. Spelling, for example, is a subject area that usually has a weekly cycle with the same instructions being repeated each week. Some instructions used might include:

- "Write your spelling words three times."
- "Fill in the sentence blanks with your spelling words."
- "Write a sentence using each spelling word."

There are also specific instructions used for a pretest and post test each week.

Your child's ability to follow spoken directions in the classroom is dependent on many factors, including:

- ***Receptive language abilities***—that is, the child's ability to decode the language message that he has heard or read. Usually, children with Down syndrome have relatively strong receptive language abilities compared to their expressive language abilities. This does not mean, however, that your child's receptive language skills will necessarily be on grade level, or on the level at which the teacher is giving instructions. For example, your child may be able to follow an instruction that is given in three short steps, but unable to understand and follow the same instructions when the teacher strings them into one long instruction. Auditory memory and auditory processing abilities affect receptive language abilities.

- ***Auditory processing skills***—that is, receiving and making sense out of what a child has heard. Usually this is an area of relative weakness for children with Down syndrome. Visual processing is an area of relative strength. That is why children with Down syndrome will often understand the task better when written or pictured instructions or models are provided. It is also why children with Down syndrome will perform better in the real environment than they do in class. Children with Down syndrome respond well to visual cues in the environment. In role playing situations in speech-language treatment, we usually try to use many props to make the situation as real as possible. Although it may not be possible to be in natural environments to teach speech and language skills when you are in a school setting, practice in the real world in real communication situations is best once the child has learned a skill.

- ***Short-term memory and recall***—that is, the ability to retain and retrieve recent information. This is often a problem for children with Down syndrome.

This book describes many strategies for adapting spoken instructions, such as having the teacher speak in short, clear sentences, or provide lots of visual cues. But your child should also be working to improve his ability to follow complex spoken instructions. Your child's speech-language pathologist can work on problem areas in therapy. For example, to boost your child's receptive language skills, the therapist might work on:

- following directions with multiple parts, similar to the instructions given in school,
- comprehension exercises,
- reading and experiential activities (role playing what you have just read about, or writing a story based on a field trip),

- phonological awareness (the relationship between letters and sounds, rhyming, and other sound relationship skills),
- specific comprehension of vocabulary, morphology (word parts such as plurals), and syntax (grammatical rules).

Skills needed for direction-following can also be practiced through play. One type of play that provides practice is games that involve giving and following directions, such as *Simon Says,* "The Hokey Pokey Song," and *Twister.*

Other suggested activities are:

- *Barrier games:* See the next section and Chapter 11.
- *Body tracing:* Children can take turns tracing around specified parts of each other's bodies, then follow directions such as "Point to the head."
- *Cooking:* Recipes involve following directions. You might rephrase the instructions for each step, or point out and identify the important words in the instructions, such as "mix" and "pour."
- *Dressing:* Your child can dress a paper doll or a large size doll in clothing appropriate for a season, in response to "Dress the buddy doll for rainy weather," or follow directions for zipping up, etc.
- *You're getting warmer-colder:* Hide a prize in the room. When the child is nearing the hidden prize, the leader will say, "You're getting warmer" and when he is getting farther away, the leader will say, "You're getting colder."
- *Crafts activities:* For example, if you are using rubber stamps, you first need to learn how to use the stamp and ink pad colors. Then a project may involve stamping once or stamping multiple times. Making a braided bracelet or a leather coin purse or belt, or a wooden car are crafts projects that involve following instructions. Crafts may be practiced at home or in community activities such as Girl or Boy Scouts.
- *Map or motor mat activities:* using a map is a good activity for following directions. You might make a map of the neighborhood, and create a pathway for finding a prize. You might map out the way to a bird's nest or to an area where a campfire will be held. A motor mat is a "play map." Motor mats are available in variety stores and dollar closeout stores. They are usually made of plastic, but they are available as rugs too. They have community sites such as the library, firehouse, school, place of worship, movie, and shopping mall. You use toy cars and trucks to move along the roadways. This can be a good following directions activity. You can also make your own motor mat with the specific landmarks in your neighborhood.
- *Music and action songs:* Children with Down syndrome often enjoy music and action songs such as "The Hokey Pokey," which provide opportunities for following directions.

Children's singer Hap Palmer has many recordings of songs for younger children that combine movement with learning.

- ■ *Planting seeds:* Your child can follow directions for planting seeds in pots or in the ground.
- ■ *School:* Playing school with real props helps children practice giving and following instructions.
- ■ *Washing dishes or loading the dishwasher:* These activities involve following instructions, at first to learn the skills. You can practice following instructions by varying the activity. For example, "Let's put all of the big glasses on the left and all of the little glasses on the right," or "Let's dry the big glasses with a blue towel and the little glasses with a yellow towel."
- ■ *Writing skills:* children can follow directions to make circles, x's, underlines, and other worksheet markings with pipe cleaners, Wikki Sticks, playdough "snakes," etc. Circles and x's can also be practiced during games of tic tac toe.

Requesting Assistance or Clarification

When we speak of instruction, we tend to focus on the teacher as provider and the child as recipient. But, part of following instructions is knowing when you do not understand those instructions, and being able to indicate that you do not understand. This is difficult for children with Down syndrome. Often, when children cannot indicate that they don't understand what to do, they fall behind and become frustrated. This can result in behavior problems in the classroom. Behavior concerns are discussed in the chapter on the language of classroom routines, but they may be related to difficulty with the language of instruction as well as the language of routines.

How do we help children learn to recognize that they do not understand the instructions? And, how do we teach them to ask for clarification? One way is to partner the child with a peer buddy. When an assignment is given, the child with Down syndrome and the peer buddy take turns restating the instructions to each other. Each can provide feedback to the other on whether the assignment is correctly understood. For example, the teacher says, "Write down the names of two foods in each food group." If the child with Down syndrome says, "I think we need to write two foods we ate for lunch," the other child can say, "No, it's two foods that are fruits and two foods that are meat." Or "I'm not sure. We better ask the teacher."

A classroom aide could also check regularly with your child to make sure he understands instructions. The teacher could also help out by saying something like,

"If you're not sure what to do, please raise your hand." Or, "Who needs to hear the instructions again?" to get across the idea that it's OK not to understand the first time around. If the teacher prefers that the child raise his hand when he does not understand, a visual cue, such as a Post-It note with "Need help?" and a picture of a child raising his hand, can be placed on the edge of the child's desk.

If your child is able to indicate that he does not understand the instructions, he should then follow up with questions that will enable him to better understand what he is being asked to do. In pragmatics, this is known as a *request for clarification* and *making a repair*. For example, I might say to my daughter, "I saw Ben today and he is working at the library." She may say, "Who's Ben? I don't know him." I might then say, "Oh, that's right, Ben was not in your class. He was in your brother's class." The daughter asks for clarification and the mother makes the repair. An example that might occur in class is:

> *Teacher:* "List your spelling words and write a sentence for each word."
> *Student:* "Which spelling words?" Or, if expressive language is advanced, the child might ask: "Do you mean the spelling words we just had a test on, or the new words that you gave us?" Or the student might point to the two lists, and say, "Do you mean this list or that list?"
> *Teacher:* "I mean the new word list that I just gave you."

GAMES FOR TEACHING CLARIFICATION SKILLS

Children can play games at home and at school aimed at helping them specify what they need to know. One game, for younger children, can be used when the child knows some colors and some shapes. Large and small concepts can be used if the child knows them. Cut out different shapes in different colors (may include large and small shapes). To start, it is best to start with two similar shapes of different colors, or two different shapes that are the same color. For example, cut out one blue circle and one blue square or one blue circle and one red circle. Spread the shapes out on the floor. Ask your child to bring you the blue one. If your child doesn't ask, "Which blue one?" or "The blue circle or the blue square?" cue him (whisper in his ear) or use a sibling as a model, to ask the question. Increase the complexity as your child's skill increases. You are teaching your child how to ask for more information when sufficient information has not been given.

For older children, barrier games are an effective technique for practicing contingent queries and repairs. A physical barrier, such as a portable screen, is put between the two or more communicating partners. One tries to send a message involving instructions and the other tries to follow the message without any visual cues (for example, making a sandwich, decorating cupcakes, or doing a crafts activity). When the activity is completed, the barrier is taken away, the results are checked, and the inaccuracies are discussed. For instance, "Why did she use whole wheat bread and you use white bread?" "She didn't say what kind of bread to use. She just said bread, and I didn't ask 'What kind of bread?'"

Children generally enjoy these games, and they provide very potent demonstrations of the necessity for giving clear directions and asking for information when you don't understand the directions given. More information on requests for clarification (also known as contingent queries) and making repairs is included in Chapter 11.

Ensuring Needs Are Addressed on the IEP

How can you ensure that your child will receive the help that he needs for the language of instruction? Goals, objectives, and benchmarks for the language of instruction should be included in the IEP. The need for modifications and supports should also be included and the responsibility for developing, preparing, and implementing the adaptations should be assigned.

Sample Goals for the Language of Instruction

Goal: To increase vocabulary recall to improve Bruce's verbal responses in class.

Benchmark: Bruce will be able to choose the correct vocabulary word in a multiple choice format 80% of the time by November 15.

Benchmark: Bruce will be able to fill in the correct vocabulary word in a cloze (fill-in) sentence format 80% of the time by February 15.

Benchmark: Bruce will be able to verbalize the correct vocabulary word in a cloze sentence format 80% of the time by May 15.

Goal: To increase the ability to follow instructions in class

Benchmark: Joan will use visual organizers with the support of a classroom aide 90% of the time by midterm.

Benchmark: Joan will use visual organizers independently 90% of the time by the end of the school year. The organizers will be prepared by the special education teacher and will be implemented by the classroom aide.

Goal: To increase the ability to ask for clarification when instructions are not understood

Benchmark: Rachel will ask for help when she does not understand the instructions on worksheets 70% of the time by December 10.

Benchmark: Rachel will hold up a help sign when she does not understand the teacher's verbal instructions 70% of the time by March 15.

Goal: To increase the ability to use assistive technology to ask for help with instructions

Benchmark: Christopher will use his communication board to point to a "please help me" icon and "I do not understand" icon to request help with instructions from the aide 80% of the time by March 1.

Benchmark: Christopher will point to the appropriate "wh" question on his communication board to ask the aide for help with completing his worksheets 70% of the time by May 10.

The worksheet on pages 194-196 can help parents and teachers plan ways to help individual students with Down syndrome manage the language of instruction used in their classrooms. The end result of the process should be an IEP that includes:

- Goals and benchmarks relating to the language of instruction;
- Specifications for the implementation of the plan, including the professionals responsible for preparing and using the adaptations and/or providing the supports;
- A home-to-school communication plan so that you will know on an ongoing basis that the supports needed for the language of instruction are being implemented.

The IEP plan should be examined on at least an annual basis to determine whether the plan is still meeting your child's needs relating to the language of instruction.

Language of Instruction Worksheet

Name: _____ Date: _____

Age: _____ Class Placement: _____

1. What is the child's learning style?

___Learns best from demonstrations and examples.

___Learns best by hearing the instructions.

___Learns best by having the instructions in visual form ____ written ____ pictures_____

___Learns best when cues are given.

___Learns best with assistance from another person.

___other: _____

2. How are instructions provided in class?

This section may need to be more specific based on the classroom situation. Instruction for each subject, and/or for each teacher will need to be described.

_____

_____

_____

_____

3. Are changes needed in the language of instruction?

    A. Format

        ___larger print

        ___fewer items on the page

        ___other: _____

    B. Instructions

        ___repetition needed

        ___written instructions

        ___picture instructions

        ___oral instructions

        ___sign language used for instructions

    C. Engaging student's attention:

        ___make eye contact

        ___touch shoulder

        ___give a sign such as pointing to the child

        ___other: _____

continued ▶

D. Personal assistance

___aide reads the instructions to the child

___aide reads the items on worksheets or the story

___aide rephrases spoken instructions

___aide writes down spoken instructions

___aide creates a sequence of shorter instructions from the longer instructions given by the teacher

___other: _____

E. Specific recommendations: _____

_____

_____

4. Does the child need modifications in timing?

___extra time to respond to spoken questions

___extra time to respond to written questions

___shorter worksheets

___additional worksheets for practice

___breaks needed

___other: _____

_____

5. Does the child need modifications to the physical setting?

___preferential seating so that the child can see the board well and hear the instructions

___seating next to good role models/peer helpers

___study carrel for reading and studying

___more work space to help the child organize his papers

___checklists or other organizers taped to the desk

___more or less light in the classroom

___background music to help learning and concentration

___other: _____

6. Does the child need modifications in the social environment ?

___changes in the participation level

___cooperative groups

___peer partners

___classroom aide

___other: _____

continued ▶

7. Are changes needed in the child's response?
    A. Channel of response
        ___student points to answer on board or worksheet
        ___student glues answers to worksheet
        ___student uses word processor
        ___student uses augmentative communication device
        ___student uses sign language

    B. time for response (from question 4)

    C. personal assistance
        ___student points to answer; aide marks answer sheet
        ___student dictates answer to aide who writes the answer
        ___aide interprets child's signs
        ___teacher cues oral response, as needed

    D. other : _____

    E. specific recommendations:

8. Is home-to-school communication needed to implement modifications to language of instruction?
    ___notify parents about basic concepts to reinforce at home
    ___notify parents about subject vocabulary to work on at home
    ___communicate about health problems (ear infections, changes in medication, etc.) that
        may affect listening, attention

9.   Implementation Plan for IEP:
Summarize the modifications from above, and for each specify who will have the responsibility for implementation. If there are specific instructions that will be modified for written work that are different from modifications for spoken instructions, it may be a good idea to include these in an educational planning matrix (see Chapter 4). For example, when during the day, or during which subjects will clarifications and repairs be addressed? At the beginning when the skills are being learned, they may be addressed solely in therapy. Once they are learned, they may be addressed in a specific subject or throughout all subjects. The educational planning matrix should specific how this will be accomplished.

    _____
    _____
    _____
    _____
    _____

CHAPTER 8

The Language of the Hidden Curriculum

The hidden curriculum is the set of unspoken expectations you need to meet in a specific class with a specific teacher to be a successful student. Originally, the term was used to refer to the expectations instructors have for determining who are the good or problem students in their classrooms (Nelson, 1989). This makes it sound like a very holistic judgment, but I think that the specific expectations for a particular teacher in a particular classroom can be determined.

In this chapter, I have expanded the concept of the hidden curriculum to include expectations for academic performance and success, in addition to the original concept of conforming to teacher's expectations for behavior and self-regulation. For example:

- In Mrs. Brown's third grade class, students need to make their papers look neat. Mrs. Brown does not allow messy erasures, pencil or pen smudges, and ragged edges from paper being torn out of a spiral notebook. If a student turns in messy work, even if she makes good grades on her tests and completes all her homework, she may still get a lower grade.
- Mrs. Johnson, the fourth grade teacher, only likes students who raise their hands.
- In Mr. Black's fifth grade class, students need to write short clear sentences. Mr. Black loves enthusiastic students, so when he asks a question, he wants students to call out the answer. (At the beginning of the year, students who had Mrs. Johnson the previous year are not prepared for Mr. Black's class.)

- Mr. Frank, the sixth grade teacher, gets a scowl on his face when he is angry. He looks right at the student who is causing

the trouble and stares. The student needs to cease that behavior.
(In contrast, Mrs. Brown walks over to the problem student's desk and stands behind her until she ceases the behavior.)

Students who do well in a particular class have mastered the hidden curriculum, but they may not even be able to identify the factors that contributed to their success. It is not purposely hidden; it is largely unconscious. Students must learn how to succeed in school in general, and then must learn what is needed for that particular teacher in that class. Some children can figure out what the teacher wants, even though she has not specified exactly what she wants. They succeed easily in class.

Other children, such as children with Down syndrome and children with learning disabilities, cannot usually figure out the rules of the hidden curriculum. They cannot "intuit" from the language and the facial and vocal cues of the teacher what it takes to succeed. For example, if the teacher emphasizes what is important to know by smiling or by saying it louder, they don't pick up on the nonverbal cues.

They have abilities and skills, and could successfully complete the task, but they don't know exactly what they need to do.

Just as students are different, teachers are different, too. Very rarely do teachers tell students, "Here's what you need to do to succeed in my class." Teachers may act on the hidden curriculum unconsciously, but may not be conscious enough of their hidden curriculum to clearly explain it. Every teacher has some factors that they consider more important than others—when you learn about the hidden curriculum, you are gaining information about what these factors are.

According to a survey study of teachers in the primary grades, the most important skill for children is the ability to understand and follow classroom routines. Teachers also stress the ability to use language for social interaction with peers and teachers. So, how well students follow routines and interact with their peers is probably part of most teachers' hidden curricula. But what happens if a student has a disability that makes it difficult to meet those expectations? For example, how does the teacher react to a child who has difficulty speaking? How does the teacher react to someone who is using an electronic device or signs to communicate? If a child with Down syndrome does not follow the instructions, will the teacher think that she is willfully ignoring the directions, or realize that she is having difficulty understanding the directions? If she takes longer to complete her work, will the teacher penalize her?

Many teachers, even after they have seen the IEP and are aware of their student's difficulties, will assume that the behavior is willful. They will assume that Mary is having behavior problems, even when the basis is a language problem that makes it difficult for her to follow the teacher's instructions. They will assume that Mary does not want to follow the directions.

Academic expectations are sometimes also hidden. When a student writes an essay exam, she may not know what kind of answer will earn her an A, B, C, etc.

For example, a middle school student with Down syndrome was asked the following essay question: Why is it important to know about your roots? This essay was worth 5 points, but students were not told how many reasons they needed to include to earn 5 points, or what constituted a correct answer. The student would only find out what the teacher was looking for when the test papers were graded and returned. Another example of a test question with hidden expectations is: "Give me some reasons why the colonists wanted to break away from Britain." Again, there is no indication of how many reasons the teacher is looking for. Do students need to include five reasons? Three reasons?

Students with Down syndrome (and all students) do much better when academic expectations are stated up front. For example, in a fourth grade class, students were required to write reports on famous Americans. In this class, the teacher handed out a paper that let the students know how their reports would be graded (see page 202). These students could use the guidelines from the teacher as they wrote their reports to ensure that they met the requirements.

Appropriate behaviors, interactive language skills, and organization of assignments and schoolwork can be taught, but the necessary skills must first be identified. Then, the child can experience success in the classroom.

Identifying the Hidden Curriculum

Identifying the hidden curriculum in a class can be crucial to the success of the student with Down syndrome in that class. When should the hidden curriculum be identified? Ideally, it is identified before your child is assigned to a specific teacher, so she won't be placed with a teacher who has a lot of expectations she cannot meet. If the IEP team is able to work with the teachers and the school administrators, your child could be assigned to a teacher with whom she could succeed.

If this is not possible, the next best option is to identify the hidden curriculum in a particular class as soon as your child is assigned to a particular teacher. This may be possible if there has been collaboration between classroom teachers, special educators, and speech-language pathologists over a number of years, because they will know each other well. The IEP team may even set goals that would help your child (through an extended year or home program) work on skills that would enable her to succeed in that teacher's class.

Unfortunately, specific class assignments are often not made until a week or two before school begins. Many teachers and administrators change schools, so there may not be long-term relationships between staff and administrators. Special educators and speech-language pathologists may not know the hidden curriculum of the classroom teacher. To learn about the hidden curriculum, they may need to spend time observing in the classroom. They may not have a good view of the hidden curriculum until they see graded papers and watch as teachers praise and reprimand students in class. Only then can they help children learn how to meet the hidden expectations. Only then can they suggest adaptations to the hidden curriculum that can be made for a particular student. The teacher can be informed of ways in which the student may have trouble meeting expectations, and she may be willing to make modifications for the student.

February Book Report

Name _____

Name of "Famous Person" _____

1. Signed up for "Famous First." _____
2. Completed Biowheel. _____
3. Used some type of visual. _____
4. Completed thank you letter. _____
5. Presented report on time. _____

Grade _____

Comments _____

_____

_____

_____

_____

_____

Because students with Down syndrome do much better when academic expectations are stated up front, handouts giving guidelines, such as above, help ensure that students meet requirements.

If your child's SLP works with the classroom teacher, he or she can talk informally with the teacher about what constitutes success in the class. If your child has more than one teacher (reading teacher, regular classroom teacher, special education teacher, or a team of teachers), the hidden curriculum needs to be determined for each class.

The checklist on the following two pages can help you determine the hidden curriculum for a specific teacher in a specific class. The special educator or speech-language pathologist can observe the teacher in the classroom and may also want to interview her. If a long-term relationship does not exist between the regular classroom teacher, special educator, and speech-language pathologist, the SLP or special educator might tell the teacher that they want to know what the child needs to do to succeed in class so that they can help her learn the skills that she needs.

It is critical to be proactive about the hidden curriculum. You cannot wait until your child has difficulty, because by then, the teacher may have formed a negative impression of her. That will make it more difficult for your child to succeed in that class. So, use the form to determine what constitutes success in the classroom and build partnerships with the classroom teacher, special educator, and SLP to teach your child the skills she needs to achieve success in her class.

Putting It All Together

Now that you have some information that will shine a light on the hidden curriculum, what practical use do you make of this information? Once you know what is expected, you can try to identify the areas of the hidden curriculum that your child will have trouble with (e.g., with making eye contact when she answers in class, speaking up loudly and clearly, writing neatly, making transitions quickly, or whatever). Then there are three possibilities, all of which should be explored:

1. *Help your child (through therapies and a home program) learn the skills that will enable her to succeed.* For example, praise her at home when she makes eye contact, or ask her to repeat a request in a complete sentence, if these are skills that are valued in her classroom.

2. *Talk to the teacher about adjusting expectations (for handwriting neatness or answering in complete sentences, for example), or perhaps ask her to adjust how she grades your child in these areas.* It may also help to ask the SLP or occupational therapist to let the teacher know about reasonable expectations for your child.

3. *Consider adding modifications or goals to the IEP to help your child meet some of these expectations.* For example, if your child's teacher expects students to move in a quiet and orderly fashion during classroom transitions, a modification might be for your child to have a picture schedule of each day's activities so that she knows when to expect a transition. And a goal might be for her to learn to respond to the teacher's verbal instructions to move to a new activity. Or, if your child's teacher expects certain elements in a composition, your child might be provided

The Hidden Curriculum Worksheet

Class: _____

Teacher: _____

1. How should students answer questions verbally in class? Should they raise their hand? How are they called upon? _____
_____
_____

2. What should be included in a good oral answer? A good written answer? _____
_____
_____

3. How should a student ask a question in class? What should she do if she does not understand the assignment? _____
_____
_____

4. How should students answer questions in written assignments? In complete sentences?
_____
_____

5. What counts most with this teacher—complete comprehensive answers, creativity, neatness, being on time with assignments? _____
_____
_____

6. What kinds of testing procedures does the teacher use in class? Is there a weekly test in all subjects? Some subjects? _____
_____
_____

7. Do the testing procedures vary from one subject area to another? (e.g., fill-ins for science and multiple choice for social studies?) Or are there a variety of testing procedures in all subjects?
_____
_____

8. What kinds of homework assignments does the teacher give? What are her expectations for homework assignments? Does she want parents to help? Is homework seen as a work in progress

or a final draft? Should the child leave in any errors as part of her learning process? Should parents correct any errors so that the final result is a perfect paper? Should the child re-copy the paper once she has finished for a neater appearance? Are homework assignments graded or checked off? _

_____

_____

9. What materials are needed to complete the homework assignments?
- What kind of paper should be used? _____
- Is pencil or pen preferable? _____
- What heading should be used (name, date)? _____
- How should papers be organized (skip lines, write on one side of paper)? _____

    _____

- What reference materials are needed? _____

10. How is the classroom set up? Is it part of an open space building or is it enclosed? How are the tables and chairs set up? How does this relate to the teacher's expectations about classroom conduct and behavior? If you are facing other students at a table, are you allowed to talk to them? At specific times only? Under certain circumstances only? _____

_____

_____

11. What is the noise and distractibility level? What are the teacher's expectations related to being noisy or quiet? _____

_____

_____

12. What is a typical day like? How do children move from one activity to another? What are the expectations when transitioning from one activity to another? _____

_____

_____

13. What are the teacher's expectations for behavior? What are the guidelines for behavior that is considered acceptable or unacceptable? What kinds of cues does the teacher give to let the students know she is not pleased with their behavior? _____

_____

_____

14. Can the teacher describe for you her "favorite student"? What determines success in the classroom? What are the criteria used? _____

_____

with a written checklist to help her focus on what needs to be included. For instance:

- Did you write the correct heading on the page (name, date, subject, etc.) ?
- Did you have a title for your composition?
- Did you skip a line after the title?
- Did you write at least three sentences in each paragraph?
- Did you indent the first sentence of each paragraph?
- Did you write at least three paragraphs?
- Did you write a conclusion?

Sample Goals Related to the Hidden Curriculum

Goal: To improve performance on homework assignments
Benchmark: Laura will hand in assignments on time 90% of the time by November 15.
Benchmark: Laura will use a word processor to write sentences for spelling homework. She will have no spelling errors on assignments handed in by May 1.

Goal: To include more detail in written compositions in class.
Benchmark: Steven will identify and describe 3 facts related to the topic of a composition by February 10.
Benchmark: Steven will use at least 5 sentences in each composition assignment by April 15.

Conclusion

Although the staff at your child's school may not be familiar with the term "hidden curriculum," they are undoubtedly familiar with the problems that can arise when students have trouble meeting the demands of the hidden curriculum. You should therefore not hesitate to ask teachers and therapists about classroom expectations, and to join you in brainstorming ways to help your child meet those expectations.

References

Delpit, L. D. (1988). The silenced dialogue: Power and pedagogy in educating other people's children. *Harvard Educational Review, 58,* 280-298.

Nelson, N. (1989). Curriculum based language assessment and intervention. *Language, Speech, and Hearing Services in Schools, 20,* 170-184.

Westby, C. (1997). There's more to passing than knowing the answers. *Language, Speech and Hearing Services in Schools,* 274-287.

Westby, C., Watson, S. & Murphy, M. (1994). The vision of full inclusion: Don't exclude kids by including them. *Journal of Childhood Communication Disorders, 16,* 13-22.

CHAPTER 9

The Language of Educational Testing: Modifications and Adaptations

In this era of educational accountability, testing has grown in importance in most schools. Not only are students tested to show what they have learned in the classroom, but they are also tested to determine whether their school is doing a good job teaching them or whether they are on track to fulfill graduation requirements. Schools are measured and compared based on countywide or statewide test results. Almost all states now have statewide assessment programs, which may target all grades or specific grade levels.

Assessment of Students with Disabilities

In the past, students with disabilities were often excluded from countywide or statewide assessments. Now, IDEA 97, the Americans with Disabilities Act (ADA), and Section 504 of the Rehabilitation Act of 1973 mandate that students with disabilities must be included in state testing programs, with appropriate accommodations.

Needless to say, your child's language skills will affect his ability to complete these tests, just as they affect everything else that goes on in the classroom. And just as with the other areas of classroom learning, there are a variety of accommodations and/or modifications that can be made to the language demands to help your child show what he knows. IDEA 97 requires that a child's IEP specify whether the child needs accommodations or modifications in the administration of district-wide or statewide tests. Testing adaptations may be of various types. In some states, the terms modifications and accommodations are used interchangeably. In other states, they have very specific meanings. In Maryland, for example, the term *accommodations* is used to mean changes in the assessment environment or process that do not affect test reliability or validity (such as responding to a receptive language test by pointing to the correct answer instead of filling in a space on an answer sheet. *Modifications* is used to mean changes in the assessment environment, process, or testing instrument that may affect test reliability and validity (such as repeating the instructions for a test item).

Alternate Assessments

IDEA 97 also provides for states to develop "alternate" assessments for some students to enable them to participate in the statewide testing. Just what these alternate assessments will be has not been clearly spelled out, but every state is mandated to design alternative assessments. For example, in Maryland, students are required to take the Maryland School Performance Assessment Program (MSPAP) testing at specified intervals during their school years. The purpose of the assessment program is to improve school performance and the learning environment for

elementary and middle school. Although individual scores are reported to the schools, the scores are not part of the child's school record. What is being rated is overall school performance, with the target goal being that 70 percent of the children in an individual school should have passing scores. In addition, students in grades 2, 4, and 6 take the Comprehensive Test of Basic Skills. Beginning in sixth grade, students take functional tests in reading, writing, and math. They can retake these tests twice a year until twelfth grade. Achieving a passing grade on these functional tests is a requirement for high school graduation.

If a public school student in Maryland does not currently have the skills needed for the MSPAP, an alternative assessment, Independence Mastery Assessment Program (IMAP), is used. The IMAP is individually developed to allow the child to demonstrate mastery of two functional goals—e.g., potting a plant, navigating around the school, washing his hands independently.

Remember, it is up to the individual states to develop alternate assessments, and the procedures in your state may differ from those in Maryland. The principal at your school or the office of testing in the state department of education should be able to tell you about the procedures for alternate assessments in your state.

Accommodations and Modifications

It is up to the IEP team to determine whether your child should take an alternate test, participate in regular statewide testing, or be excused or exempted from testing. If your child does participate in statewide testing, he will probably be given accommodations to ensure that results are not unduly affected by his disability. Accommodations are meant to be part of the overall learning program for the student. So, any accommodations made for testing should be the same as those used in the classroom for learning.

Accommodations must be based upon *individual* student needs and not based upon a category of disability, level of instruction, or time spent in general education. So, you should never be told, "For children with Down syndrome, we make the following accommodations." The accommodations used should meet your child's needs, and should be documented in your child's IEP.

Accommodations, and modifications may be disallowed or allowed depending not only on the child's needs, but also on whether the change affects the validity of the test. That is, does the change affect the test's ability to measure the targeted skill? For example, if a test involves writing a paragraph, what is the objective of the test? If the test is measuring handwriting ability, using an accommodation in which the student dictated his response to the examiner would affect the validity of the test. If the objective is to measure the student's creative writing ability, his ability to communicate ideas and thoughts effectively, using the accommodation would not affect the validity of the test.

When standardized tests are used, states generally have guidelines that indicate what kinds of modifications can be made. For example, in Maryland, the Comprehensive Tests of Basic Skills, Fifth Edition (CTBS/5) is given to all students in grades 2, 4, and 6. The state testing manual indicates that "Certain accommodations [such as extended time for testing] granted for CTBS/5 invalidate comparisons to national norms. Therefore, the scores for such students will be reported to parents as non-standard administrations that invalidate comparisons to national norms." The scores, therefore, would be reported to parents but would not be counted with the school average, county average, or statewide average scores.

Although testing accommodation and modification decisions are made on an individual basis, some testing adaptations commonly made for children with Down syndrome include:

- changes in timing,
- changes in the physical setting,
- changes in test administration,
- changes in test response,
- changes in test content.

Some states permit students to use the same accommodations for testing that have been agreed upon in the IEP for classroom instruction. Other states have a list of "approved accommodations" that the IEP team can choose from, and only those accommodations can be used for testing. In general, any of the accommodations below that can be made for statewide testing can also be made when your child is taking his weekly spelling, math, or other teacher-made tests.

Types of Testing Accommodations

TIMING OF TESTS

Most classroom tests and standardized district-wide tests are timed. Students are told when to start, how much time they have to complete the test, and when to put their pencils down and stop. For students with special needs, a variety of adaptations to the timing of tests may be allowed. These adaptations to timing may or may not be allowed for a specific test, depending on the scoring systems used. They

Exemptions and Exclusions

Occasionally students with Down syndrome are exempted from state- or district-wide testing. Decisions about exemption from statewide testing can be made on an individual student basis by the IEP team. Students can be excused from testing if they demonstrate frustration or distress before or during testing, or if they disrupt other students and the testing environment. The Local Accountability Coordinator (LAC) and the local supervisor of special education services must approve decisions exempting a student from testing.

Although it is occasionally in a child's best interests for him to be exempted from state-wide testing, this is not a decision to be made lightly. Many parents believe that schools need to be *more* accountable, not less, for what students with disabilities are learning and have advocated strongly for their children to be included in this kind of high stakes testing.

are usually not permitted on standardized tests because those tests specify the time that you have to complete a specific item or a specific section.

Some possible adaptations include:

- Tests may be given to the child as untimed tests, providing as much time as the child needs to complete the test.
- A test may also be administered in shorter segments during the course of the school day. For example, instead of spending two hours straight on a 100-question exam, your child might be allowed to answer the test in four sections of 25 questions each, which will be administered at 9 a.m., 11 a.m., 1 p.m., and 3 p.m.
- Your child may be allowed supervised breaks during the testing session.
- A test may be administered at the time of day when your child is most alert and functions best.
- A test may also be broken down into smaller segments and administered over several days, or even once a week for four weeks.

THE PHYSICAL SETTING FOR TEST ADMINISTRATION

Most tests are given in group settings. If your child has difficulties with testing, or needs special accommodations such as having the directions read aloud to him, the test may need to be administered individually in a separate room. Your child might also need to sit in front of the classroom, or away from the window, door, or fans, or in a study carrel with minimal distractions to help him stay on task. The setting should be a match for your child's needs.

Some possible adaptations to the physical setting include:

- Testing is administered in the regular classroom with special seating.
- Testing is administered in the regular classroom with a support person such as an instructional assistant.

- It may also be administered to a small group of children in a quiet setting away from the classroom. The setting may be chosen because it is quiet, has softer lighting, has fewer distractions, has more comfortable furniture, has computers for typing responses, etc.
- Testing may be administered in a small group setting with the special education teacher as the examiner.
- Testing may be administered individually in a separate room.

CHANGES IN TEST ADMINISTRATION

The physical format of the test may be modified. For example, large print materials can be used. If a child has difficulties when there are many items on a page, the number of items can be reduced. There can be more space left between items, or items can be arranged differently—for example, in a line across the page rather than in four quadrants. Basically, any modification that can be made to worksheets, as discussed in Chapter 5, can also be made to teacher-made tests. Assistance in the form of a reader, or the use of sign language or assistive technology may be used when administering the test.

Although the use of modifications is required in IDEA, some changes may not be allowed on standardized tests. This is because one of the primary tenets of standardized tests is that they have standardized administration. The scores can't be measured in the same way when there are modifications, so standardized tests—especially IQ and aptitude-type tests—are not that adaptable. Some psychologists feel that any changes on standardized test administration are a violation of the standardization and therefore make the scores invalid. On the other hand, criterion-based and achievement tests can usually be modified.

My goal for assessment as a speech-language pathologist is to have information that will enable me to plan better treatment. I look to test results to give me information about the way that a child learns, as well as what skills the child has mastered. But, large scale educational or psychological testing has very different goals. The scores are measures of school performance as well as individual aptitude or achievement. So, although legislation now states that children with disabilities should be included in large-scale testing with accommodations, there is some controversy regarding whether these scores are valid. How (and whether) they should count when school averages are published has not been answered.

Test directions may be modified in several ways:

- The language in the spoken or written directions may be simplified, or may be divided into shorter segments.
- The administrator may be able to provide more examples or more practice with the type of item before your child takes each test section.
- The examiner may be allowed to repeat the directions, or to provide cues to explain the directions. For example, "Circle the picture that is the SAME (say it louder) as the test item."
- The examiner may read the instructions to your child, or provide him with written or pictured instructions.
- The written instructions may have key words highlighted or underlined.
- A sign language interpreter may be used to present the directions or your child may need to use an FM system or hearing aid to amplify the speech.
- An audiotape or an amplified (louder) audiotape may be used to give the instructions.

In general, these modifications can be made as long as the purpose of the test is to determine whether your child has a specific skill and can complete a task, not whether he can follow the directions. If what is being tested *is* the ability to follow directions, modifications may not be possible. For classroom-based, teacher-made tests, most of these adaptations could probably be made. For standardized tests, repeating the instructions, cues, or explanations would not be allowed as they would invalidate the score.

CHANGES IN TEST RESPONSE

If your child has difficulty responding to test items using speech or writing, the channel of communication for responding may need to be changed. Some adaptations that can be made to his method of response:

- An aide can physically write the responses that your child indicates.
- If your child has trouble transferring his responses to a separate answer sheet, he might be allowed to write his answers in the test booklet.
- A larger space can be designed for the student to fill in, or paper with wider lines can be used.
- Rather than hand write the answers, your child could use a word processor.
- Your child could use an augmentative communication device with synthesized speech to respond, or may use sign language.

CHANGES IN CONTENT/ MEMORY LEVEL

Changing the content level is usually not possible on annual or triennial testing, or on statewide standardized tests. Teachers or psychologists who are in charge of testing at the school should find out what adaptations *are* allowed, and work with the local accountability coordinator (LAC) and the student's IEP team to ensure that any adaptations that are allowed for a specific test are used.

Testing Accommodations for Students Who Use AAC Systems

Each local educational agency or state department of education should have guidelines indicating the testing accommodations that are typical and approved. However, accommodations for AAC users so far have been overlooked by most agencies. Parents, teachers, and related service personnel need to discuss the purpose for testing for the student and the accommodations he may need to be successful.

The language of IDEA suggests testing accommodations should include allowing your child to use his typical mode of communication to respond to tests. If your child is using an AAC system, this should be considered a part of his "typical mode of communication" in responding to questions as well as the presentation of the testing material. Some examples of accommodations include:

- Presenting test items through a communication board or with picture symbols,
- Providing written directions rather than verbal,
- Interpreting verbal instructions with sign language,
- Reading test questions aloud to the student,
- Using text-to-speech software to compose answers, and
- Responding with an AAC voice output system.

This accommodation is new with the 1997 amendments to IDEA and is being implemented for the first time. The list of accommodations, alternate testing, and the purpose for them is still developing, even though state departments of education have developed plans and lists of approved accommodations. In addition, for the first time IDEA addresses and requires students with IEPs and IFSPs to participate in school-wide and state-wide assessments. Be prepared to ask questions regarding your child's participation in these assessments regarding accommodations, time spent away from direct instruction to make those accommodations, and the purpose of alternate testing. There may not be a clear answer to your question.

For classroom testing, such as spelling tests or unit tests, however, the content level of the test can and should be changed to reflect whatever IEP goals your child has in that subject. Your child may also have difficulty in memory and retrieval and may need fewer items to remember, or need adaptations that assist memory such as a multiple choice format or a word bank.

Your child might be required to demonstrate mastery of less information than the rest of the class. For example, if the social studies unit is on exploration, your child with Down syndrome might be tested only on which explorers came to America or specifically which men explored the state he lives in, rather than on the full list of explorers. Or he might be tested on five of the ten spelling words assigned to the class for the week.

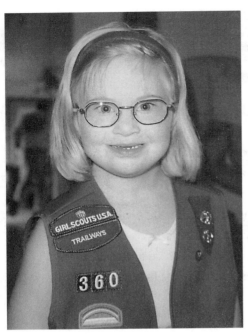

Your child might also be required to demonstrate mastery of different information than the rest of the class. For example, if most of the class is being tested on the content of a novel written on a fifth-grade reading level and your child read a book written on the second-grade reading level, your child's test would be geared to the book that he read. Or if the fifth-grade reading book talked about the plot building to a climax, your child might be able to use a story map to describe the order of the events in the plot in the book that he read.

Changes could also be made to the vocabulary of tests, if necessary to help your child succeed. Difficult terms should be simplified for your child, or he should be given a word bank (see Chapter 5) to help him remember new words.

If your child has difficulty retrieving information to fill-in answers, a multiple choice or matching format could be used to help him demonstrate that he knows the information. Or he may be allowed to have a notecard or "note sheet" with important rules or facts written on it (like spelling or capitalization rules or what the "greater than" and "less than" signs mean). Or he may be allowed to look at a word bank or word book to help him with writing a short essay answer.

On the next page is an example from the fifth grade health curriculum in which *all* of the vocabulary may be new to a student with Down syndrome. This is a quiz that was given at the end of a unit on disease prevention. A word bank was provided at the beginning of the test. This provided the students with the vocabulary to use in the test, but they still needed to recognize and understand the concept represented by the vocabulary. This is an easier task than word retrieval, retrieving the words from memory. The student with Down syndrome understood the concepts and scored 100%.

Another quiz (see page 216) used fill-in questions, and instructed that the answers be given in complete sentences. On this quiz, the same student could only answer one out of seven questions correctly, and did not answer any of the questions in complete sentences. If the language level was changed, I think that the student would have been able to answer more of the questions. For example, instead of "Name one communicable disease you have had," the questions could have used simpler vocabulary words: "Did you ever catch a disease from your sister or friend when they were sick? What disease did you get?"

CHANGES IN GRADING

On a standardized test or a criterion-based formal test, there may be no allowances for adaptations in the scoring system. But, for classroom tests, there can be adaptations to the way in which tests are graded. For example, the IEP team and the teacher may decide that your child will not be marked down for spelling errors on tests in subjects, except on a spelling test. So, if your child spells petal and stem incorrectly on the science test, he will not lose points. Or writing a sentence fragment or a run-on sentence may not be penalized if the content is right on an essay test, but it would count on a composition or book report.

Ideally, the teacher will consult with the SLP for suggestions regarding your child's language abilities and how they might affect her ability to take subject-based

---

Name _____   Health

Disease Prevention Quiz

Word Bank

blood transfusion   bacteria

virus   antibodies

contagious   white blood cells

immunity   bacteria

**Use the word bank to complete these sentences. <u>Be sure you
spell the word correctly.</u>**

1. Two types of germs that cause illnesses are *bacteria*
and *virus* _____.

2. When you are vaccinated for a disease like measles you
develop an *immunity* to that disease.

3. When germs enter our bodies *white blood cells* and
antibodies fight and kill the germs.

4. In our video "AIDS and the Immune System" Kevin got the
AIDS virus from a *blood transfusion* he received when
he was very young.

5. If you have the flu, you are *contagious* and can give
the flu to others.

Example of an appropriate test for a student with Down syndrome. Its use of a word bank gives the vocabulary needed for the exam, but still tests the student's ability to recognize the word and understand its concept.

tests. You could also request that the SLP and teacher consult if you notice that your child seems to be having trouble with the language on classroom tests. The IEP team might discuss any grading accommodations and write them into the IEP.

Responsibility for Test Adaptations

The IEP team should determine what modifications your child needs for testing. The regular education teacher, special educator, parents, and speech-language

Name _____   **Health**

Answer these questions in complete sentences.

1. Name one of the body's defenses and tell how it works to keep you well.

teNS

2. Name one place where germs can be found.

haNds

3. Name one communicable disease you have had.

4. In our video, how did Kevin say the AIDS virus is not transmitted from person to person?

5. When you get sick with the flu, what should you do to help your body fight the germs?

6. Why is it important to wash your hands before eating?

FOOd

7. Why is it important not to touch anyone else's blood directly?

Example of a difficult test for a student with Down syndrome. It tests the student's ability to draw vocabulary from memory and write complete sentences while testing the actual course material.

Controversies in Testing Students with Disabilities

What happens if a child with Down syndrome is not expected to take, or do well on, a state- or district-wide test? Is that a reason for him to be denied an inclusive placement? Could the school keep a child out on the grounds that he would bring the school average down? The answer is a resounding NO! But, could the school try to find other reasons why the child should not be included in the regular educational curriculum so that the child will not bring down the school's test average? Unfortunately, the answer is probably yes. Or, sometimes parents are just told by the teacher or school administrator to keep their child home on testing day.

Amendments to IDEA specify that "aggregate" scores (scores of children with and without disabilities reported together) as well as "disaggregated" scores (separate averages for children with disabilities and children without disabilities) should be reported. It is yet to be seen what impact this practice will have on a school's funding, perceived "excellence," etc. once most students with disabilities are included in district- and statewide testing. It is true, however, that educational reform initiatives such as school choice and vouchers are often tied in to how schools perform on these tests.

Most parents want their children in schools with high test averages. Some educational advocates, however, feel that unless test scores for children with disabilities are included, the services that they need will not be provided in educational budgets—that is, their needs will be overlooked. This presents a difficult problem for parents and educators.

pathologist can all provide helpful input into this decision-making process. The goal is to use modifications that will enable your child to show his true abilities during testing. In some school districts, the IEP form includes a form for checking off types of testing accommodations needed by individual students. If not, testing accommodations can be listed on the same page where other modifications are listed.

The IEP should specify who is responsible for adapting classroom tests, and who is responsible for adapting, administering, and modifying county- or statewide tests. I have talked with many parents who have somehow inherited the responsibility for modifying classroom tests. Teachers have said, "I don't know how to test whether Jessica knows the explorers. Why don't you read over the textbook chapter and write the test?" This is something that should not happen. If parents are frequently asked to make these kinds of adaptations, this is a clue that their child needs more support in the classroom, such as an aide who could be doing this work. Parents are not usually asked for help modifying out-of-class system-wide testing. But, there the problem is to be sure that modifications are used when your child is tested.

Following is a worksheet that can be used to plan for testing modifications. Any modifications and accommodations that are needed by your child should be documented in the IEP. These should include adaptations needed for tests in class, as well as for district-wide and statewide tests and standardized testing. Remember, many states will only allow modifications and accommodations for testing that are already documented in the child's IEP.

Testing Modification Worksheet

Name _____   Age _____

Class Placement _____   Date _____

1. Does the child need modifications in timing?
___untimed
___extra time
___shorter tests
___breaks needed
___test given at specific time of the day
___test given over several days
___other: _____

2. Does the child need modifications to the physical setting?
___different seating
___testing in different room
___testing in smaller group
___individualized testing
___setting with fewer distractions
___other: _____

3. Are changes needed in test administration?
   test format
   ___larger print
   ___fewer items on the page
   ___other: _____

   instructions
   ___repetition needed
   ___written instructions
   ___oral instructions
   ___sign language used for instructions
   ___pictured instructions
   ___other: _____

continued ▶

personal assistance

___aide reads the instructions to the child

___aide reads the test items

___other: _____

specific recommendations: _____

_____

_____

4. Are changes needed in test response?

channel of response

___student points to answer; aide marks answer sheet

___student marks answer in test booklet

___student uses word processor

___student uses augmentative communication device

___answer sheet is modified so that student can better respond

___time for response

personal assistance

___student dictates answer to aide who writes the answer

___student needs person to interpret signed responses

___other: _____

specific recommendations: _____

_____

_____

5. Are changes needed in content/memory?

___changes in number of items

___use of word bank

___notecard with rules/facts as a memory aid

___changes in test format (describe)

___other: _____

6. Are changes needed in grading? _____

_____

7. Who will be responsible for making modifications on a daily basis? _____

_____

CHAPTER 10

The Language of Classroom Routines

Without routines, or regular procedures, it would be impossible for classrooms to function smoothly. Teachers would have little or no time to teach if their students did not understand and follow classroom routines such as entering the room, storing belongings in a cubby or cloak room, getting in line, moving in line to the cafeteria, returning from recess, getting coats and books, and boarding the school bus. The repetitive nature and the fact that there are many environmental cues and models help children learn how to perform the classroom routines appropriately.

The language of classroom routines includes both the language used by the teacher, classroom aide, or specialist to teach routines, and the language comprehension and ability to follow instructions of the child with Down syndrome who needs to learn the routines. Having a good grasp of the language of classroom routines should enable your child:

- to learn classroom routines,
- to retain and follow classroom routines,
- to use appropriate classroom behavior.

All children are better at understanding and living up to the teacher's expectations for classroom routines later in the year than they are at the beginning of the school year. These routines are learned by repetition and practice.

It is important to note that teachers have high standards and expectations in this area. A study of a large number of kindergarten teachers found that they placed "the ability to follow classroom routines" as the most important skill that children could bring to school. The ability to follow classroom routines and to behave appropriately in class shape the teacher's opinion of your child, positively or negatively. They contribute to your child's classroom reputation, and that reputation affects the way that the teacher, classroom aide, specialists, and other school personnel view her.

Classroom routines generally fall into five areas:

1. ***Getting ready to learn:*** At all grade levels, students must learn certain routines that are usually done upon entering the classroom in the morning or when returning from lunch. They include arriving on time, entering the room quietly,

hanging up coats, getting needed materials ready for class, putting away unneeded materials, and getting prepared to listen. Other early morning routines may include copying assignments from the blackboard or looking up definitions of words that are on the board.

2. *In class behaviors:* In class behaviors include following all classroom rules, listening to the teacher, not talking or interrupting, and asking for help when needed.

3. *Transitional behaviors:* Transitional skills enable a child to change from one activity to another. These behaviors may involve physical transitions, such as moving from the classroom to the cafeteria, and mental transitions such as moving from the spelling test to a math lesson. Expected transitional behaviors may include lining up, getting coats, organizing books and materials to take with you, and moving to the next subject or the next activity. Unexpected transitional routines may include fire drills, assemblies, school plays or events, and field trips.

4. *Out-of-class routines:* Before and after class/out-of-class routines may include lining up, boarding the bus, following the bus rules, exiting the bus safely, meeting a sibling or friends to walk with, crossing the street when the safety patrol says to, and walking home safely.

5. *At home assignments and learning:* Home routines may include completing homework assignments, taking notices to parents, having forms signed, and gathering materials for the next day.

Getting Ready to Learn

When your child walks into the classroom, there are certain expected early morning routines. When your child is learning those routines, she may need some assistance. A buddy may help her learn the routines. The classroom teacher, special educator, or aide should observe any difficulties that your child has.

Once the "getting ready" routines are learned, your child will probably be able to complete the routines independently, but she may need some adaptations or cues. For example, if cubbies or coat hooks are labeled with names, but she can't read her name, she may need a photograph or a colored dot next to her name to help her locate it. Or, if the names are written in cursive, her name can be printed, if that is easier. Also, learning to read her name in print or cursive can be a goal for special education and/or language therapy.

Picture schedules are another adaptation that may be helpful if your child has difficulty with the sequence of early morning activities, such as what to do after she hangs up her coat. A card could be posted in her cubby or desk, or hung on a belt loop or key chain with pictures showing what she is to do, and in what order.

If saying the Pledge of Allegiance and singing a patriotic song are part of the morning routine, your child may need help participating in the pledge if she can't say/remember all of the words. Actually, many children have difficulty remembering all of the words to the pledge. Your child will do fine as long as she keeps pace with the rest of the class as they say the pledge. You can practice at home using cloze procedure (fill-ins). You say the pledge or sing the song and help your child say the words that she can. For example, "I pledge allegiance" (you)/ "to the flag" (your child)/ "of the United States of" (you)/ "America" (your child). If your child is using an AAC device to communicate, the pledge and a song could be programmed into the device. That way, your child could take her turn leading the pledge. An alternative activity would be for your child to be the flagholder.

If morning announcements are read over a loudspeaker, it will also be important to make sure your child understands announcements that are important to her. If the announcements are read or spoken rapidly, she may have difficulty understanding them. A peer partner or a classroom aide may need to rephrase the information in a shorter, less complex format.

In Class Behavior

LEARNING AND FOLLOWING THE RULES

At the beginning of the school year, the teacher introduces the rules of the class. She should also discuss the consequences that will be enforced when a child in the class violates the rules. Enforcement of the consequences must be fair and consistent in order to be effective. Rules in an elementary school classroom might include:

- Work quietly.
- Always do your best work.
- Complete assignments on time.
- Hand in papers that are neat.
- Listen to the teacher and follow directions.
- Raise your hand if you have questions and wait to be called on.
- Don't interrupt.
- Be respectful to the teacher and other students.

If the teacher does not send a copy of the rules home in the first few days of class, ask for one. This way you can go over the rules and consequences with your

child and help her understand them. You can also let the teacher know if your child might have difficulty following one or more rules due to aspects of her disability that are not under her control. For example, the rules in one second grade classroom included "Follow directions the first time they are given." The parents of a student with Down syndrome in the class thought their child might have difficulty following this rule—first, because she had problems related to attention, memory, and auditory processing documented in her IEP, and second, because she had IEP goals related to improving her ability to follow spoken directions. The teacher agreed to try to make sure she had the child's attention before giving a direction, and, if she didn't immediately respond to directions, to try to determine whether the problem seemed to be due to memory or auditory processing difficulties, or to misbehavior.

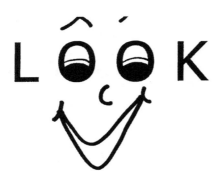

LOOK

Look up and look toward the person talking.

Open my eyes and look at the person's face.

Open my ears and listen.

Keep on looking and listening until the speaker is finished or the conversation is over.

Example of a graphic reminder; this one is intended to help children learn the rules for listening in class.

It might be difficult or impossible for your child to grasp the rules just by listening to them. Speech is rapid and fleeting, and directions are sometimes hard to follow. There are many competing environmental noises in the classroom, including heating and air conditioning noises, fluorescent light sounds, and other children moving and talking. If your child has difficulty hearing or understanding the rules or instructions, a peer buddy may be helpful. Sometimes, new rules or instructions are given which can't be practiced in advance. The buddy could rephrase the rules in shorter, easier to understand language. The teacher needs to be willing to allow the buddy and your child to talk during class to each other.

If your child has difficulty remembering the rules, written or gestural cues can be used to help her remember. A Post-It note could be placed on your child's desk with a reminder, or a sign in the classroom could remind all of the children of the rules. For example, a poster such as the one on the next page could be designed.

A graphic reminder, such as the one at left, may help some children learn the rules for listening in class.

Sometimes children with Down syndrome do not understand the rules due to language difficulties. For rules that are repeated, role playing in language therapy or special education sessions can be used to help children learn the rules. Speech-language therapy goals could be written into the IEP to address this issue:

- Rose will understand the rules of classroom behavior.
- Rose will be able to explain the classroom rules in her own words.
- Rose will be able to follow the classroom rules.

If assistance in the form of practice or cueing strategies for memory are not sufficient to help your child follow the rules, it would be a good idea for an aide to be assigned to her. The aide can both interpret the rules for your child, and help her follow the rules with reminders and direction.

If a child with Down syndrome doesn't follow one or more rules due to behavioral issues, see the section below on "Behavior and Communication."

Classroom Rules

1. Be prepared to work.

2. Begin your work on time.

3. Raise your hand if you need to ask a question.

4. Do not talk while you are working.

5. Keep your hands to yourself.

6. Stay in your seat.

7. When you are finished with your work, raise both hands.

Example of a graphic reminder used to depict the rules of the classroom

In addition to having formal rules, classrooms usually also have a variety of unwritten procedures that students are expected to learn and follow. For example, first graders might be expected to sit in a circle in a certain part of the room for calendar time. Or students might be expected to wait until just before lunch to use the restrooms, or else use a particular signal to request permission to use the restroom. Or, the teacher might expect students to ask nearby classmates for help in certain situations, but not in others.

At the beginning of the school year, the teacher will likely talk the students through these procedures many times. For example, each time before the class begins work on a worksheet, she might tell her students where to put the worksheet once they have completed it, and what they may do while they are waiting for everyone in the class to finish their work. After awhile, however, the teacher will expect the students to know what to do in these routine situations without her telling them.

A buddy or peer partner can be paired with your child to help her learn the routines. If the buddy is seated next to or facing your child, she can provide prompts and reminders, such as "Did you finish your paper? Let's both hand our papers in together." For line up, the buddy can hold your child's hand in the younger grades, or physically prompt her, such as with a hand on her shoulder, in the older grades, to help her learn the routines for line-up, dismissal, etc.

Most children with Down syndrome learn the physical routines such as dismissal very well. At times, they may get distracted, but a physical prompt from a buddy will usually help them get back on track.

A buddy must be chosen very carefully. He or she has to be someone who won't take over for your child, do too much for her, or patronize her. Plus, the buddy needs to know when to back off and see if your child can do the routine herself. Sometimes, a buddy from a higher grade may be used rather than a peer. It takes a great deal of insight and maturity to be a good buddy. (Some of these same considerations apply if your child has an aide. The aide has to know when to step back and see if your child can do things without prompting. The aide needs to support your child, but walks a fine line between assistance and standing between her and her peers.)

If your child is having difficulties learning routines, the speech-language pathologist or the special educator may observe in class to learn what routines are expected. The routines can be practiced at home or in speech-language therapy sessions. It is often effective to role play and recreate the classroom situations. Sometimes, your child can use props such as action figures or stuffed animals to recreate lining up and walking to lunch, or the routine for getting your coat at the end of the day. A classroom aide may also remind your child regarding the routines, or redirect her behavior.

One of the most difficult areas is learning how to request help. Does the teacher want your child to raise her hand? Can she hold up a small sign or use a manual sign to indicate that she needs help? An aide can be of assistance when she sees that your child does not understand or needs help. Children get into trouble for calling out or asking for help at the wrong time. But it is also a problem when children don't ask for help when they need it. That will interfere with the child's ability to successfully complete the task. Refer back to Chapter 7 for more information on requesting help.

Sample Goals Related to Following Classroom Routines

Goal: To improve the ability to follow classroom routines independently.
Benchmark: Lynn will ask permission to use the bathroom by November 15.
Benchmark: Lynn will follow the listening rules by January 5.

Goal: To ask for help when Sean does not understand the instructions.
Benchmark: Sean will raise his hand to signal that he needs help by December 1.
Benchmark: Sean will use his AAC system to request help with assignments by February 10.

Transitional Behaviors

A big part of following a routine is knowing when and how to change, or *transition,* from one activity to another. Most children with Down syndrome have difficulty with transitions unless they are prepared and know what is coming next.

To prepare a child for an upcoming transition such as lining up to leave the room, it can help if the teacher uses a signal such as lights flashing on and off. This is a commonly used signal at shows and concerts and is therefore a good signal to learn. The teacher should use a different signal, such as ringing a bell, when she wants children to prepare for a different type of transition, such as stopping their activity and paying attention. Each signal should be used consistently and exclusively.

In early elementary grades, it can help if the teacher starts each day by going over the scheduled events of the day with the class. For example, the teacher can start by writing a narrative of the day's activities on a large easel, and reading it with the class at the start of the day: "Today is Tuesday, March 8, 2002. This morning we will have reading group from 9:30 until 11:00. Then we will go to Art and finish our spring projects. Then we will go to lunch and recess. After lunch, we will have math groups. Then, at 2:00, we will go to music to practice for our spring concert."

The problem with using this strategy exclusively to prepare your child for events of the day is that this is a lot of language for a young child with Down syndrome to process at once. If your child has an aide or someone who is assigned to adapt materials, a written or picture schedule can be prepared. (See example on the next page.) This schedule can help your child learn the sequence of activities on a particular day. Small stick drawings or photographs of the actual situations may be glued to your child's folder or displayed on her desk in the order that they will occur. Then your child knows that lunch comes after science on Mondays and Wednesdays, and after social studies on the other days. You can include a picture of a bell for dismissal time or any other time a bell would routinely ring in class.

Schedules for routine days can be prepared in advance, but if there are changes on that day, a schedule can be quickly written. Picture cue cards such as Picture Communication Symbols© by Mayer-Johnson (on paper or labels, no gluing re-

Schedule for
Monday, May 7, 2001

Reading

Computer Class

Science

Lunch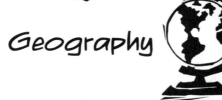

Geography

Art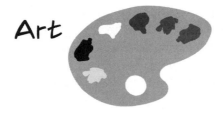

Example of a school day picture schedule used to help a child with class transitions

quired) can be stored in the classroom. Some special education teachers use a tool parts box—a plastic box with many small slide-out drawers—and store stacks of individual picture symbols in the drawers. These pictures can be quickly accessed whenever they are needed for schedules or communication boards. Your child can also be prepared ahead of time for changes to routines, when those changes are known. An assembly, book fair, field trip, or planned fire drill are examples of known changes. Being sent home because of snow or a power outage, or missing art or music when the teacher is absent are examples of unplanned routine changes. The ultimate goal is to enable your child to get down to work, complete work, and plan to transition to the next task as independently as possible.

UNDERSTANDING TIME CONCEPTS

Understanding time concepts is often difficult for children with Down syndrome. The ability to follow a schedule and make transitions independently are functional skills that are needed for adult life. So, we need to teach these skills and practice them over time so they can be learned.

TIME-RELATED LANGUAGE CONCEPTS

There are many language concepts that children need to master in order to be able to understand and talk about what happens when. These include words such as before, after, again, then, next, when, yesterday, tomorrow, first, second, third, etc. For example, teachers often make comments such as: "We will not line up for the bus *until* everyone is quiet." Or, "We need to go back to our seats and *then* line up again."

When these concepts are part of a long string of words spoken quickly, they may be especially difficult for children with Down syndrome to comprehend. It may be helpful to ask teachers to restate these directions more simply: "Everybody quiet down. Then we will line up for the bus."

Time-related concepts can be practiced at home and in the community. For example, when you are in line to buy movie tickets, say "We are in line. *When* we get to the front, we will buy the movie tickets." Or, "This is a long line. *After* we reach the counter, we can take our groceries out of the cart." Or, before you leave the house with your child to run errands, explain, "*First* we are going to get some gas in my car. *Second,* we are going to the store to pick up some milk and eggs. Third, we will go to the video store." Then, while out on your errands, you can talk about what you need to do *next,* or *after* this.

Sample Goals Related to Time Concepts

Goal: To improve understanding of time sequencing concepts.
Benchmark: Teresa will understand the concepts first, second, third, and last by November 15.
Benchmark: Teresa will understand if-then statements by January 30.

CALENDAR CONCEPTS

In the elementary school years, concepts such as the days of the week and months of the year are emphasized very heavily. In many school systems, there are math objectives that children have to pass related to calendar concepts, such as knowing the days and the months; being able to say which day or month comes before or after another one; knowing how many days there are in the week and how many months in the year. There are the issues of memorizing the days and months, and then there are the issues of actually understanding what a day and month are.

Visual activities such as calendars and auditory/verbal activities such as songs can help children learn these concepts. For memorizing days and months, songs work well. For the days of the week, there is a Barney song sung to the tune of "Clementine." There is a classic children's song—"Today is Monday, what do we do

today?" There is a month song which is sung to the tune of "One Little, Two Little, Three Little Indians." It goes: "January, February, March, and April/May, June, July, and August/September, October, November, December/Twelve months in a year!"

Calendar activities might help your child understand the passage of time and relationship between days and months. Try having several fun calendars at home in themes your child likes—maybe a "page a day" calendar, where you let your child rip the page for the day off at the end of every day, and also a wall calendar, where you have your child mark off each day that passes, then change the picture when it's a new month. You could also have your child mark special days with stickers and then count the days until a certain day (like the weekend, or the day your child has karate class, or her birthday.)

If your child has a picture schedule, be sure that it emphasizes which day of the week it is on the schedule. For example, the name of each day of the week might be written in a different color. So, the schedule for Monday, might have "Monday" written at the top in purple, and the activities for the day might also be written in purple. Or, the schedule for each day might have a different sticker or picture at the top to help her distinguish them. As your child begins to be able to distinguish between the schedules for different days, she can be asked at the beginning of the day to get out her schedule for Tuesday, or can learn to look at the blackboard or plan of the day to see what day it is, and then choose the appropriate schedule herself. This way your child will learn that on Monday she has P.E. and speech, on Tuesday, she has music, etc.

At home, you can work with your child on the concept of seasons and which months go with which seasons or holidays. If your child is interested in dolls, talk about summer, read a book about summer, and then dress the doll for summer—for example, with a bathing suit, sun hat, sunglasses, sandals, and a towel. Large dolls can be dressed with regular clothing (12 months-2 toddler), so you can stock up on seasonal gear at yard sales and save clothes from siblings or get hand-me-downs. Seasonal outfits for Barbie-type dolls are also widely available. For older children, you can create a dress-up box or trunk with seasonal clothing. Discuss the seasons and the corresponding months and weather in your area. Ask questions such as, "Would you wear your bathing suit outside in January?" (OK in Florida, but not in Minnesota.)

In class, your child with Down syndrome will undoubtedly encounter worksheets on calendar concepts. As Chapter 5 discussed, there are good worksheets and bad worksheets for kids with Down syndrome. For example, the worksheet on the next page has instructions that are easy to follow: "Fill in the correct 0 for each answer." The Birthday Graph worksheet on page 233 is more difficult. For many children with Down syndrome, it may help to simplify questions such as "How many more birthdays are there in June than July?" by walking the child through the steps needed to figure out the answer. For example:

- How many birthdays are there in June?
- How many birthdays are there in July?
- Which month has more birthdays?
- How many more birthdays? (Hint, use subtraction)

TELLING TIME

The American culture is very time conscious. We expect children to be on time and to follow schedules. We have due dates for homework and projects, and bells that signal the change of periods. Since the culture considers time important, the classroom teacher considers it important that children learn to tell time and to understand time concepts.

There are many time-related language concepts, such as morning, afternoon, night, late, early, hour, minute, a long time, a little while, etc. Times of day which occur every day are often linked to meals. We have breakfast in the morning, lunch in the afternoon, and dinner (or supper) in the evening.

Time concepts involving length of time can be made less abstract through practice at home. You can use a timer at home to help your child grasp the relative length of one minute vs. fifteen minutes. You can tell her she can use the computer for fifteen more minutes, and then set a timer or come in after fifteen minutes to tell her that her time is up. When you are cooking with your child, discuss the times in the recipe—then use the timer to mark the time, such as stirring for two minutes or baking for twenty minutes.

Talk about the time in the course of the day to let your child know some of the uses of knowing what time it is, for example commenting that your child's favorite TV show is on at 4:30 and then turning the TV on at that time. For older children, read the *TV Guide* or the newspaper section with the TV schedule. Look up and make a list of the times that the programs that you want to watch are on TV. In the Sunday newspapers, look up the times that stores open and close. Arrive at a store early and note the time. When it is 10:00 or whatever the opening time is, note the time and watch the activities as the store opens. Do the same for closing times, and note the time of closing.

When you go out to eat, comment on the "Breakfast" menu or "Lunch" menu. Comment, "I wish I could have hash browns now, but they stopped serving breakfast at 11:00." Talk about why you need to serve dinner *early* one evening, or whether Dad is *late* for dinner again. If you turn down your child's request for a snack, let her know that it is because you're going to be eating lunch *soon,* in twenty minutes, or whatever.

Learning to Tell Time. There are many language prerequisites a child needs before she can learn to tell time on an analog clock. They include:

- understanding the concepts of minute and hour,
- understanding mathematical concepts of counting by 5's,
- understanding "before"/"until" and "after"/"past,"

Name _____

Reading a Calendar

♣♣♣♣♣ March ♣♣♣♣♣						
Sunday	Monday	Tuesday	Wednesday	Thursday	Friday	Saturday
			1	2	3	4
5	6	7	8	9	10	11
12	13	14	15	16	17	18
19	20	21	22	23	24	25
26	27	28	29	30	31	

Fill in the correct ◯ for each answer.

A. What is the name of this month?
  ◯ January   ● March   ◯ June   ◯ July

B. How many Tuesdays are in this month?
  ◯ 3   ● 4   ◯ 5   ◯ 6

C. What day of the week is March 18?
  ◯ Monday   ◯ Wednesday   ◯ Thursday   ● Saturday

D. What date is the second Friday?
  ◯ March 8   ◯ March 20   ● March 10   ◯ March 11

Try This! What is your favorite day of the week? Tell why.

FS-32079 Time, Money, and Measurement

Example of a calendar concepts worksheet with easy-to-follow instructions

Name _____

Birthday Graph

Each cupcake on this graph stands for one birthday in Mrs. Wong's class.

Birthdays		
January	🧁 🧁	2
February	🧁 🧁 🧁 🧁 🧁	5
March	🧁 🧁	2
April	🧁	1
May		0
June	🧁 🧁 🧁 🧁	4
July	🧁	1
August	🧁 🧁 🧁	3
September	🧁 🧁 🧁 🧁 🧁 🧁	6
October	🧁 🧁 🧁	3
November	🧁 🧁	2
December	🧁	1

Write the answer to each question below.

A. Which month has the most birthdays? __Sep tember__

B. How many birthdays are there in February? __5__

C. How many birthdays are there in the month after May? __4__

D. How many more birthdays are there in June than July? __3__

E. Which month has no birthdays? __May__

F. Name two months that have the same number of birthdays.
__October August__

Try This! Add a cupcake to your birthday month.

FS-32079 Time, Money, and Measurement

Example of a calendar concepts worksheet with more difficult instructions; children with Down syndrome would be helped by walking through the steps needed to figure out the answers

■ understanding what "quarter" and "half" mean, so that "quarter past" and "half past" make sense.

Sample Goals Related to Telling Time

Goal: To understand language concepts related to time.

Benchmark: Richard will identify times on the clock that indicate breakfast, lunch, and dinner times with 80% accuracy by November 28.

Benchmark: Richard will understand and correctly respond to before and after requests 80% of the time by May 1.

Goal: To use the language of time concepts appropriately.

Benchmark: Sherry will use a picture schedule to tell what activity comes before and after 90% of the time by April 10.

I think that it is better to start with a digital clock so the child gets used to time terminology before she has to apply mathematical concepts to reading an analog clock. Once she understands and has some experience with the times when certain events happen during the day (e.g., she gets up at 7:00 and goes to bed at 8:30), it will be easier to apply this knowledge to make sense out of telling time with an analog clock.

Classrooms may use a lot of worksheets to teach students about telling time, but children with Down syndrome need to spend a lot of time actually looking at and manipulating various types of teaching clocks and real clocks, and reading watches. Clocks with two different colored hands to start, or clocks where the hour hand is noticeably shorter than the minute hand, or clocks in which five-minute segments are marked on the outer borders can help teach the concepts involved in telling time.

On pages 235-239 are some worksheets that are well-designed for helping a child with Down syndrome (or any other child) learn to tell time. These worksheets progress in a systematic manner, first asking for recognition of the time on the clock, and on the most advanced worksheet asking the child to write the time and to connect that time with the appropriate activities. The instructions are well written, some examples are provided, and in some cases, dotted line examples are even provided. The student is asked to:

1. Circle the time represented on the clock out of three choices.
2. Glue on the time represented on the clock.
3. Match the time to the clock.
4. Write the time under the clock.
5. Draw the clock hands to match the time given.

Out-of-Class Routines

Out-of-class routines related to school include transportation by bus or walking to and from school. These routines are generally practiced every day, and are learned well by most children with Down syndrome. Bus drivers and friends and

Name _____

Circle the correct time below each clock.

Row 1:
- Clock 1: (1:00) / 2:00 / 3:00
- Clock 2: 4:00 / 5:00 / (6:00)
- Clock 3: 7:00 / (8:00) / 9:00
- Clock 4: 10:00 / (11:00) / 12:00

Row 2:
- Clock 5: (9:00) / 7:00 / 2:00
- Clock 6: (2:00) / 4:00 / 6:00
- Clock 7: 12:00 / 6:00 / (10:00)
- Clock 8: (5:00) / 12:00 / 8:00

Row 3:
- Clock 9: (3:00) / 7:00 / 1:00
- Clock 10: (12:00) / 6:00 / 5:00
- Clock 11: 8:00 / 1:00 / (4:00)
- Clock 12: (7:00) / 4:00 / 9:00

Worksheet with clear instructions. Child is asked to identify the correct time from three choices.

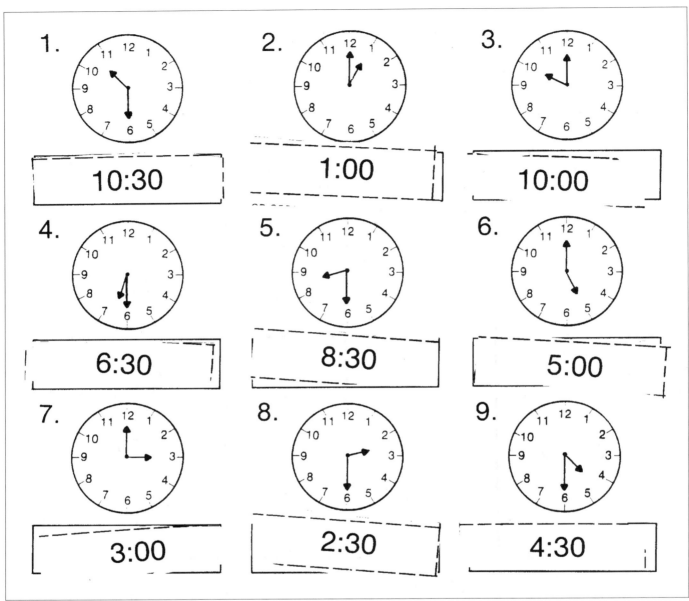

1.

10:30

2.

1:00

3.

10:00

4.

6:30

5.

8:30

6.

5:00

7.

3:00

8.

2:30

9.

4:30

Worksheet in which the student chooses the correct time strip and glues it under the clock

peers usually offer assistance. Difficulties that occur usually result from a change in routine such as a new or substitute bus driver, or other children teasing or provoking your child. Because of speech and language difficulties, especially when your child is upset, it is often difficult to figure out what happened and to help with the situation.

Strategies to help your child learn these out-of-class routines, or to trouble-shoot when problems occur include:

- Request a copy of bus rules and practice these at home with action figures, a toy bus, and a motor map.
- Role play the situation with props.
- Write a story about your child riding the bus or walking home and take photographs of her to illustrate it. You can use the

Name _____ Time to the hour and half-hour

What Time Is It?

Draw a line from each clock to the correct time.

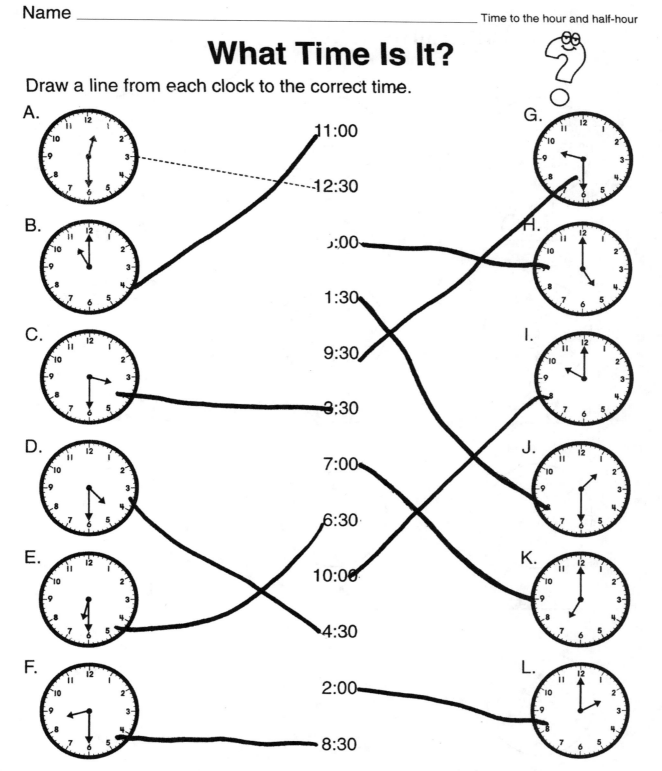

Try This! Name two clocks that show times exactly two hours apart.

FS-32079 Time, Money, and Measurement

Worksheet that requires child to match time to clock

What time is it?

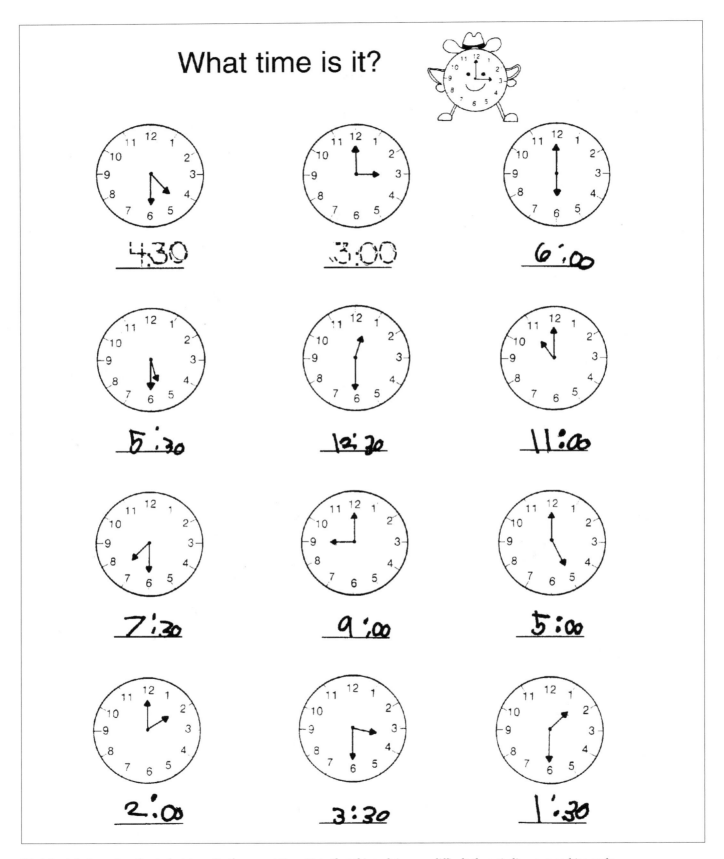

4:30   3:00   6:00

5:30   12:30   11:00

7:30   9:00   5:00

2:00   3:30   1:30

Worksheet that requires the student to write the correct time. Note that this task is more difficult than circling or matching tasks.

Name _____

Complete the Clocks

Draw the clock hands to match each time.

A.   8:00   4:00   1:00

B.   10:00   2:00   5:00

C.   7:00   6:00   3:00

Try This! Finish the pattern: 1:00, 3:00, 5:00, 7:00 9:00, 11:00

FS-32079 Time, Money, and Measurement

A more difficult worksheet which asks child to draw clock hands as well as to complete a number pattern.

story either to help teach your child her routine, or to show her an appropriate way to deal with a problem that she is currently having.

- Read a book about trouble on the bus or walking home, and use the text of the book to open the discussion.
- If your child is having difficulties, ask specific questions to provide a scaffold to help her tell you about what happened: "Did something happen on the bus? Was there a different bus driver? Did someone hurt you? Did you hurt someone else? etc.

At Home Assignments and Learning

Previous chapters have discussed the need to develop a good home-to-school communication system, and to document the need for that system in your child's IEP. An important part of that system should be a method to let you know what needs to be done at home so your child is organized and prepared for school.

Your home-to-school communication system should include information on notices and forms that need to be signed by parents. If you have created a sheet, it can include a line for this information, or the forms can be attached to the sheet, rather than stuffed in a backpack. Check-off sheets to help your child check what she needs to complete or prepare for school the next day can help her learn to monitor her responsibilities. They also can help you know what she needs, so that you don't have to go searching for blue poster board right before the store is closing. Check-off sheets and home-to-school communication logs can also prevent your finding out at 9:30 p.m. that you need to send in a snack or a goody for the bake sale. An example of a sheet is on the next page.

Troubleshooting

When a child has difficulty following instructions that relate to classroom routines, the difficulty is often viewed as problem behavior. In fact, there may be a variety of reasons that a child with Down syndrome does not comply with instructions as the teacher desires:

1. *A language difficulty.* The possibility that language difficulty is affecting your child's ability to follow instructions should always be considered. Difficulties with intelligibility, hearing impairment, expressive language, and word finding can all affect behavior. After all, children who have limited communication may not be able to make their needs known and often have little control over their environment. They may become frustrated because they cannot make their needs understood, and act out.

Homework and School Responsibilities

Day of the Week: _____   Today's Date: _____

Homework assignments:

   Check off the subjects

   ___reading _____

   ___math _____

   ___social studies _____

   ___science _____

   ___other _____

   _____

   _____

Do you have any notices? _____

_____

Do you have any forms that parents need to sign? _____

_____

Do you need to bring anything special to school tomorrow? _____

_____

Example of home-to-school communication form to help parents monitor homework and other responsibilities.

Many children who are unable to communicate effectively act out inappropriately in class. This has sometimes been called the "communication hypothesis" of problem behavior. It states that behavior problems are essentially a form of communication used by individuals who do not have a more advanced form of communication to use to influence their environment (Carr & Durand, 1985, Carlson & Smith, 1999). Many behavioral specialists believe that the speech-language pathologist should be included as part of the team investigating the reasons for the problem behavior and designing the treatment program.

2. ***A disorder that co-exists with Down syndrome.*** For example, attention-deficit/hyperactivity disorder may make it difficult for your child to pay attention to instructions, or she may have metabolic or physiological difficulties that cause fatigue or other symptoms (e.g., sleep apnea, diabetes, allergies). If your child experiences seizures or has autistic symptoms, these, too, could affect her ability to follow instructions.

3. ***Sensory difficulties.*** Some children have difficulty paying attention when there are environmental noises, or need to use movement (finger tapping, squeezing putty or a bean bag) in order to concentrate. There could also be a mismatch between teaching and learning style. For instance, the teacher might use a lot of lecturing, when your child is a visual learner. See Chapter 5 for information on learning styles, multiple intelligences, and adapting materials.

4. ***Cognition and thought processes used for problem solving affect behavior.*** It may be difficult for your child to figure out what to do to solve her problems. If she hates math, acting out, shouting, or running out of the room can get her out of the math class. These are inappropriate solutions, but she may not be able to figure out an appropriate solution. She may need help from special educators and behavior specialists in order to problem solve a solution.

5. ***Medications.*** Side effects of medications could affect your child's ability to listen and follow instructions.

6. ***Fluctuating Hearing Loss.*** If your child is experiencing pain in the ear or fluid in the middle ear, she may not hear the instructions. Even though she usually follows that same instruction, she may not follow it on a day when she is experiencing fluctuating hearing loss.

PINPOINTING THE PROBLEM

Clearly, it is important to identify which, if any, of these factors are causing the problem behavior. Indeed, classroom behavior is directly addressed in IDEA 97. The IEP team is directed to "explore the need for strategies and support systems to address any behavior that may impede the learning of the child with the disability or the learning of his or her peers."

Members of the IEP team may try to informally figure out why your child is having trouble with the classroom routine by observing her and proposing strategies to help. Or they may request a functional behavioral assessment.

FUNCTIONAL BEHAVIORAL ASSESSMENT

A functional behavioral assessment is an evaluation of the causes and functions of a student's behavior. It looks at what the student gets or what the student avoids as a result of the behavior. It tries to understand and document the relation between problem behavior and events in the child's school environment. The ultimate goal is to develop a treatment plan that addresses the reasons a student misbehaves, and effectively helps the student change the behavior patterns through

modifying the behavior and/or the environment. The treatment plan is known as a positive behavioral support plan.

The psychologist is usually the specialist who conducts the functional behavioral assessment. The classroom teacher, special educator, speech-language pathologist, and family should be consulted. They can provide input regarding behaviors that occur at different times in different situations. The SLP can analyze the situations to determine whether there is a component of communication difficulty underlying the behavior, and can suggest appropriate alternative ways for the child to communicate her needs. The goal, if possible, is to prevent problem behaviors in the classroom, rather than to punish the problem behaviors.

Ideally, the support team should be made up of people who are open and willing to share ideas, who know the child well, and who have the power to change the environment and access resources to support the child. Positive behavior support is a collaborative effort, which cuts across disciplines and across settings.

When developing a functional behavior assessment in which the misbehavior is related to speech, language, and communication difficulties, it is important to clearly identify multiple examples of the inappropriate behaviors. Then, for each instance, we must determine:

- the antecedent (i.e., what precedes the behavior),
- the behavior,
- and consequent (i.e., what follows the behavior).

When describing the antecedent event, you want to describe the specific activities, events, or classroom subjects that occur right before the behavior occurs. In what settings does the behavior occur? (Homeroom, therapies, special subjects, lunchroom, playground?) Are there certain times of the day or week when misbehavior is more likely to occur? (Morning, late afternoon, before lunch, after lunch, Mondays, Fridays?) What are the *setting events*—that is, what situations make the behavior more likely to occur for a given child? Examples of setting events in school are: a change in schedule, a fight on the bus on the way to school, or a headache or pain. Who is present when the misbehavior occurs? Who is absent when the misbehavior occurs? Clearly describe the behavior that occurs, providing any details that are observable.

Next, describe the consequents. What happens immediately after the misbehavior? What result does the behavior have? Does this result serve a purpose for the child? What purpose does it serve? Is the behavior gaining attention? Is it helping the child avoid doing a task she does not want to do? Can she escape from a situation that is uncomfortable for her?

Dr. Daniel Crimmins, a clinical psychologist, believes that behaviors we may view as dysfunctional are actually functional for the child. That is, the behavior may be a form of communication. The function of that behavior must be understood so that a replacement behavior that will accomplish that same purpose for the child can be taught. For example, if the behavior results in gaining the teacher's attention, teach the child to raise her hand or to hold up an "I need help!" sign to get attention. If the behavior helps her avoid or escape the task, teach her ways to request a break from her work or to ask for help with a task.

Sometimes the behavior does not appear to be under the child's control. Behaviors such as self-injury, socially stigmatizing rituals, aggression, tantrums, and destruction of property, even though they are not under the child's conscious control, can still serve a purpose for the child. Dr. Crimmins suggests translating the behavior into an "I" message. For example, screaming may mean "I'm confused by what I hear"; running away may mean "I feel scared when my world is not predictable and I am not able to tell you what I need"; repetitive behaviors and self-stimulation may mean "I need to do this over and over to block out a confusing world" (Crimmins, 1996).

Different responses and educational interventions are needed depending on the purpose the behavior is serving for the child. Everyone on your child's team needs to work together to determine the function of the behavior. The two tables on pages 252-254 will help in figuring out the reasons for your child's problem behaviors and in developing strategies to address the problems.

Behavior and Communication in Children with Down Syndrome

Children with Down syndrome who have expressive language difficulties sometimes have inappropriate behavior or "act out" because they can't communicate their needs. Below are some examples of inappropriate behaviors that have underlying communication difficulties.

Shelly is a seven-year-old girl who is sitting in her seat and working independently on an assignment to underline the first letter in each word. Shelly is having difficulty reading the instructions. She circles the first letter in the first three words. She then realizes that she was supposed to underline the sounds, so she tries to erase the circles. The paper rips. Shelly starts banging on her desk. She is unable to ask for another worksheet.

Brendan is a nine-year-old boy who has been having a good day at school. The teacher rewards him by making him the line leader when the class goes to art. Brendan leads the class out the door, but instead of going toward the art room, he goes toward the music room. Brendan likes the music class better. The teacher tries to explain to Brendan that the class needs to go to art. But, she is in the back of the line, and he really can't understand her instructions. There is a lot of background noise in the hall, and Brendan is not easily redirected. By the time the line is redirected, the class is ten minutes late for art class and the teacher is angry. Brendan did not clearly hear the teacher's directions, and did not have any visual cues or anyone else to follow. He is no longer having a good day and will be disciplined by the teacher.

Peggy is a ten-year-old girl who is having a great deal of trouble with math. The teacher hands out a math worksheet. Peggy looks at the sheet, gets up, and says, "I outta here. Time for lunch." She then proceeds to walk into the hall and down towards the cafeteria.

Robert is a twelve-year-old who sits in the back of the room. He looks out the window and sees the school bus driver standing at the door of the bus. It is 9:30 a.m. and the bus driver is usually gone long before this. Robert jumps out of his seat and begins shouting, "I want to go. Nobody told me." The teacher asks Robert to sit down and stop shouting. Robert is noticeably upset and he continues to shout and look angry.

Later, the classroom aide talks to Robert. Through questioning, she finds out that Robert thought that the school bus driver was outside because the class was going on a trip. He didn't know about any trip, and he thought that he would not be allowed to go, because he had not brought a permission slip. The last time, when the class had gone to the space exhibit, the school bus driver had been out there standing by the bus. In reality, the school bus driver was waiting for some students and their teacher to bring out holiday decorations that they had made for the bus. Robert had misunderstood the situation, and was not able to ask, "Why is the bus driver out there?" instead of acting out inappropriately.

Often, although older children and adolescents with Down syndrome signal through their facial expressions, body language, and comments that they are upset, they have great difficulty explaining why they are upset, or asking for help to solve the problem.

Many teachers would see all of the situations above as behavior problems. They would just see the banging on the desk, the running out, or the shouting and not know what provoked it. If this was a one-time occurrence, the child might get disciplined, but the behavior probably wouldn't get analyzed. But if the same or similar situations happened repeatedly, the special educator or a behavior intervention team would be called in to figure out why the child is banging on her desk, shouting, or acting out.

STRATEGIES THAT CAN HELP

Once the function of your child's behavior is identified, intervention consists of:
- short-term prevention strategies,
- educational, instructional, and environmental adaptations, and
- teaching alternative, adaptive behaviors.

Treatment should emphasize teaching your child new skills to replace inappropriate behaviors, as well as a different means of responding to triggers. It should also include changes in the environment, especially the school environment, to decrease the chances that the ineffective challenging behavior will occur and increase the chances that your child will use the new alternative behavior. For each child, the positive behavior support plan is individually tailored to her preferences, strengths, and needs.

When a behavior is linked to communication difficulty, the team can suggest a variety of modifications to help teach and/or reinforce a more appropriate behavior. Some general types of modifications are listed below.

Modify the Physical Environment. Sometimes, the physical environment can be modified to maximize the opportunity for students to follow the rules. Seat children who have difficulty seeing, hearing, or staying on task near the front of

the room, near the teacher, and near other students who behave well and stay focused. Help them keep a clear work surface, free of distractions. Seat students who are having behavior problems away from the windows, away from the doors, noisy air conditioners, etc. Keep distractions to a minimum. Background music or softer lighting might be used in class during certain activities.

Modify the Social Environment. Plan student seating so that children who need assistance will be closer to the teacher. Pair the child with a peer helper or buddy to help her follow the routines. Seat the student who misbehaves at a table with children who can serve as good role models.

One strategy that teachers can use in the classroom is to try to praise children who are near the child with Down syndrome for their good behavior, to give her models of good behavior. For example, the teacher might say, "Sam has his book open to the correct page, he has the heading on his paper, and he is ready to work. Good job, Sam." Or, "Cindy is standing in line quietly, ready to go to lunch. Way to go, Cindy!" This strategy will not work, however, if the child needs to be taught a new behavior skill, not merely provided with a model of good behavior.

Modify Any Antecedent Event Triggers. Using this approach, you look at the events that usually trigger problem behaviors and attempt to modify them so they no longer provoke the misbehavior. For example, if your child always demonstrates problem behaviors right before lunch, have a physician check if low blood sugar or other physical factors are affecting her behavior. If she acts out or is fidgety after lunch, check on what she is eating for lunch. Is her diet affecting her behavior?

Here is an example of changing an antecedent event: Your child is having fun playing during recess. The playground aide says, "Time to come in from recess," and your child throws a tantrum. What could the aide say instead? The aide could give a preparatory prompt to help her transition, such as "Finish playing. We need to go inside in five minutes." Or the aide could use a picture schedule, and show your child that something fun (such as art class) is going to happen once she comes in. Or your child could be given a responsibility that makes her feel important. For instance, she might be asked to hold the door while the other children come in from recess, or be invited to be the Ball Helper and help gather up playground balls at the end of recess.

Modify the Consequent Events. With this strategy, you determine whether the child enjoys the results of her misbehavior, and then change the results so they are no longer satisfying. For example, if your child is gaining attention by her behavior outbursts, use time-out or another procedure that results in decreased attention when she has a tantrum. If your child succeeds in avoiding a low-interest, low performance subject through her behavior, change the outcome so that the behavior does not enable her to avoid the subject.

Provide Teacher Cues to the Child. Teachers can plan with the child to use certain signals to help her before she gets into trouble. For example, if the teacher points to her eyes, it means "Look at me." If the teacher comes over to the child's desk, it means "Settle down." The teacher may also use physical prompting, such as placing her hand on the student's shoulder or on the student's desk.

Provide the Child with Cues She Can Use. If there are certain recurring situations in which communication difficulties lead to inappropriate behavior, provide the child with a cuing system so she can signal what she needs. If she needs a break, she could make the time-out sports signal (hands forming a T shape). If she does not understand the instructions, she could hold up a card that says, "Please help me with the instructions." If her pencil breaks or her paper rips, she could hold up a sign that says, "I need help."

Teach the Child a More Appropriate Strategy. In addition to teaching children cues to use in specific problem situations, the long-range goal should be to give them a communication system they can use effectively in many situations. When a child has significant problems communicating appropriately, the speech-language pathologist should be working to teach her new ways to make her needs known. For example, your child could learn to use sign language to make a request instead of grabbing a book from another child. Or she may use an AAC system that enables her to ask, "Can I have the book?" For more information on these types of nonverbal communication methods, see Chapter 12.

Reinforce the New Behavior. When communication is at the root of the behavior problem, it is important that the replacement behavior or substitute communication get results for the child quickly. For example, if your child's pencil breaks while she is working on an assignment, she can hold up a help sign or raise her hand instead of banging the pencil on the desk. The teacher will come over to her desk and give her another pencil or give her permission to sharpen her broken pencil. If the replacement behavior is ineffective or is difficult for the child to use, she will not use it. For example, if the teacher says, "Put your hand down. You can't ask any questions now," then raising your hand is not an effective strategy. Getting up and sharpening your pencil or grabbing one from another child will seem, to the child, to be a better solution even though the teacher may view it as misbehavior.

Having people respond to their communication efforts is rewarding enough for some children. Other children may need the rewards of verbal reinforcers ("Good job!") or color-coded cards, cards with smiles or frowns, or certificates that commend the child on a positive day.

Still other children may need the motivation of more material rewards to change old ways of communicating. They may benefit from a system that enables them to earn rewards, gifts, or time or access to desired activities for a specific behavior or number of behaviors. For example, if they raise their hand five times

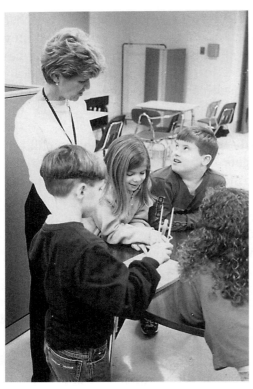

during the day to ask for help, instead of shouting out, they might earn a school privilege such as being at the head of the line, or a home privilege such as going out for pizza. This is known as a token economy system.

In a token economy system, your child might be given stickers, points, stamps or tokens each time she does a desired behavior. Later, she is allowed to use the tokens to purchase items from the school store, privileges, or other meaningful rewards. Parents may be involved in reinforcing the appropriate behavior at home, and in providing rewards for progress. For example, the parent may agree to rent a video at the end of the week if the child has had 4 out of 5 positive charts, or to go out for dinner on the weekend if the child has made a specified amount of progress during the previous week.

Sometimes a point system or color-coded cards may be used when the child misbehaves in class, with each color or a certain number of cards matched with a consequence. For example, if you have three red cards, you don't go out to recess. Fun events, such as a pizza party, or an after school skating session, may be used to promote continued good behavior, or unpleasant events such as detention or staying after school may be used to discourage bad behavior.

It is especially important to reinforce your child for doing things that are difficult or unpleasant for her—for example, if your child is learning to make the transition from P.E. class back to the classroom for math class. It is not hard to transition from one desirable activity to another; it is much more difficult to transition to an activity that you don't like or in which you expect to fail. Learning to transition, in this case, can be approached not from a reward standpoint, but rather from the view of avoiding punishment. Going to math may not be very rewarding to your child, but if she does so, she will avoid being disciplined for not going to math. Your child can be given more tokens for doing things that she would prefer not to, with an explanation that the extra tokens get her closer to her reward. A token system can also be designed so that you take away tokens when your child doesn't do what she needs to. Again, there can be a discussion that she can't go for pizza or go swimming because she doesn't have enough tokens. If she goes to math, she gets tokens that help her reach her goal.

In some cases, parents and teachers may decide to draw up a formal behavior contract that will specify how the child will be rewarded or punished and what she needs to do to succeed.

Home-to-School Communication

Behavior management is most effective when the strategies are used consistently by everyone who comes in contact with your child. Parents, classroom teachers, special education teachers, and therapists should all be aware of your child's behavior goals and the strategies being used to improve her behavior.

Ongoing, timely communication between school and home is important. For young children, sometimes a sheet is used that states what behavior the child is working on. For example, asking for permission or requesting help can be worked on by both parents and teachers. Professionals and families can check off the child's successes. This tally report may be used by the family to determine when the child has earned a reward, should be denied a privilege, etc.

You may want the school to inform you about behavior as part of the same home-to-school communication plan used to communicate about your child's progress toward academic or IEP goals. Or you can use a separate form or report, particularly with an older child. For example, on the next page is a form used to track a second grader's on-task behavior during independent seatwork. For this child, stars were used to indicate "good"; smiley faces to indicate "OK"; and checks to indicate "needs improvement." Her parents let her choose her own reward each Friday when she had received mostly good reports throughout the week. On page 251 is an example of a form that could be used to report a wider range of classroom behaviors.

It is best to designate someone (like an aide) who is to communicate with the family every day/week via a specific modality, such as email or a traveling notebook, about behavior. See Chapter 4 for more information about home-to-school communication plans.

References

Carlson, J. I. & Smith, C. E. (1999). Finding the reason for problem behavior and planning effective interventions: A guide for parents. In Hassold, T. & Patterson, D. *Down syndrome: A promising future together.* New York: Wiley-Liss, 115-125.

Carr, E.G. & Durand, V.M. (1985). Reducing behavior problems through functional communication training. *Journal of Applied Behavior Analysis, 18,* 111-126.

Crimmins, D. B. Positive Behavioral Support: Analyzing, preventing, and replacing problem behaviors. In Hassold, T. & Patterson, D. *Down syndrome: A promising future together.* New York: Wiley-Liss, 127-132.

Durand, V. M. (1993). Functional assessment and functional analysis. In M.D. Smith (Ed.) *Behavior modification for exceptional children and youth.* Boston, MA: Andover Medical Publishers.

Goldstein, S. (1995) Understanding and managing children's classroom behavior. New York: John Wiley & Sons, Inc.

Johnston, S.S. & Reichle, J. (1993). Designing and implementing interventions to decrease challenging behavior. *Language, speech and hearing services in schools, 24,* 225-235.

Kerr, M. & Nelson, C. (1998). *Strategies for managing behavior problems in the classroom.* 3rd ed. New York: MacMillan.

Kincaid, D. (2000). Providing positive behavioral support: Challenges and solutions. National Down Syndrome Congress, Washington, DC.

Reichle, J. & Wacker, D. (Eds.) (1993). Communication and language intervention series: Vol. 3. *Communicative alternatives to challenging behavior: Integrating functional assessment and intervention strategies.* Baltimore, MD: Paul H. Brookes.

Daily Report for
Stephanie

	started work promptly*	on task	completed her work	teacher comments
warm up Early Bird	☆	☆	☆	* passed out papers
Math	☆	☆	☆	* Pre-test on clocks * test on multiplication * listened to book on clocks
Reading	◯	☆	☆	GOOD DAY !!
Science	☆	☆	☆	a little hesitant to pick up her caterpillar now that it is growing, but did complete her work
Social Studies				

* Stephanie must have clear directions. Have her repeat the directions and ask if she understands the task before asking her to work independently.

A home-to-school checklist used to report a student's on-task behavior

Behavior Chart

	Yes	No
1. Prepared to work		
2. Began work on time		
3. Raised hand to ask a question		
4. Did not talk when working		
5. Kept hands to self		
6. Stayed in seat		
7. Raised both hands when finished working		

A home-to-school checklist used to report a variety of classroom behaviors. Teacher may rate or student may use as a checklist to self-monitor behavior

Describing and Analyzing Behavior

The process for changing behavior begins with describing the child's behavior and analyzing the antecedent, behavior, and consequent events (A-B-C analysis). This form can be used to describe and analyze your child's behavior.

1. Can you describe the behavior? _____

_____

_____

_____

2. When does it occur most often? Least often? _____

_____

_____

_____

3. Who are the people with whom the behavior occurs? _____

_____

_____

_____

4. What are some situations and activities in which it occurs? _____

_____

_____

_____

5. Is behavior triggered by social or academic events in class? _____

_____

_____

_____

continued ▶

6. Does the behavior usually occur at the same time each day? _____

_____

_____

_____

7. Does the behavior occur before or after the child has eaten? _____

_____

_____

_____

8. Are there any other regularly occurring events that seem to trigger the behavior?

_____

_____

_____

9. After the behavior has occurred, what happens? _____

_____

_____

_____

10. Does this happen as a result of the behavior? _____

_____

_____

_____

Developing a Behavioral Plan

Once the behavior is better understood in light of the antecedent events (triggers) and consequent events (what happens after the behavior), a positive behavioral support plan can be designed. The following questions will help in developing the plan:

1. What communicative functions does the behavior serve?

___ enables child to continue desired activity

___ enables child to terminate disliked activity

___ gets the help that he/she needs

___ gets him/her out of the situation

___ gets him/her attention

___ other: _____

2. What other systems (gestural, communication board) could be used to help the child reach his/her goal without the inappropriate behavior? _____

_____

_____

3. Would the child respond to a different style of interaction? _____

_____

_____

4. Does the child need a motivational system? What will motivate him/her? _____

_____

_____

5. Does the child need to develop new skills? _____

_____

_____

Following classroom routines involves understanding the instructions, learning the routines, and controlling and monitoring your own behavior. Language plays a role in each of these areas.

CHAPTER 11

Social Interactive Communication

How do children learn to use the language they know in conversations? What are the everyday tasks in which they use social language? How is the language a child uses with peers at lunch different from the language he uses with his teachers in the classroom? Are there hidden rules in certain language situations? Pragmatics answers these questions. Pragmatics is the study of how we use language to interact with others in many different situations in daily life. In school, children use pragmatic language skills to make friends, maintain friendships, and interact with peers, teachers, and school personnel. Pragmatics is a language skill, but it is also, in the broader sense, a social skill.

Most children are not formally taught pragmatics. They learn the social use of language by observing adults and older children and by practice. For example, if they need to greet their teacher or doctor differently than they would greet their four-year-old cousin, they "learn" the differences through practice or through trial and error. If they are too informal or familiar, they are corrected by their parents. But, for the most part, they don't think about it and are not taught pragmatic rules. The skills are generally out of their awareness, but they learn them through situations in daily life.

In contrast, many children with Down syndrome need to work on pragmatic skills directly in therapy sessions. The good news, however, is that in an inclusive school setting, there are many social interactive benefits for children with Down syndrome (Wolpert, 1996). One of the benefits of inclusion in schools and in the community is that there are so many appropriate peer and adult models, more learning opportunities, and more practice with social interactive communication. Researchers have confirmed that children with disabilities gain from socialization with their peers and make many advances in communication, social skills, and skills for daily living (Cullinan, Sabornie & Crossland, 1992; Buckley, 2000).

Pragmatics and Children with Down Syndrome

The goal for all children with Down syndrome is to develop appropriate social interactive communication skills. For some children, this is a realistic goal during the elementary school years. For many others, this goal will be an ongoing one, with social interactive skills continuing to develop well into adulthood. These skills can be developed and practiced in school, at home, in community activities, in recreational activities, in friendships and relationships, and in job settings. Social interactive communication skills can continue to develop throughout life.

There has been a good deal of research on pragmatics and interactional language in typically developing children, but few studies comparing the pragmatic skills of children with Down syndrome with those of typically developing children. What we do know is that children with Down syndrome interact very well socially and can and will communicate with others even before they have speech, through the appropriate use of pointing, facial expressions, gestures, and sign language. In fact, nonverbal social interactional skills are a strength for most young children with Down syndrome (Mundy et al, 1988).

So, although we may need to teach them "how to" use language in certain situations, most children with Down syndrome "want to" interact and to communicate with others. The communication may be through gestures, sign language, a communication board or speech; it is not necessarily through verbal communication.

The Elements of Pragmatics

To identify pragmatic strengths or pragmatic disorders in a child, we need to look at all of the areas of pragmatics, including:

- **intent:** goal of the communication,
- **eye contact:** looking directly at your communication partner,
- **facial expression:** the emotional meaning of the movements of the face,
- **kinesics:** hand gestures,
- **requests:** asking for something through your communication,
- **proxemics:** how you handle distance and space with communication partners,
- **conversational skills:** the social interaction of communication partners, including opening and closing the conversation,
- **topicalization:** introducing topics, staying on topic, shifting topics, and ending topics,
- **stylistic variation:** ability to adapt your speech and language to different conversational partners and audiences,
- **contingent queries and repairs:** asking your conversation partner for information that you don't understand, and providing information that the listener needs
- **presuppositions:** assumptions that you make that may influence a conversation.

As you can see, pragmatics includes verbal and nonverbal communication skills. Nonverbal skills are sometimes difficult for children with Down syndrome, and affect how they fit in with peers, as well as with teachers and school staff. When a child does not use appropriate facial expressions, gestures, or distances, other children will label him "weird" and shy away from him. Although nonverbal

What If Your Child Doesn't Seem Interested in Interacting?

If a child with Down syndrome has difficulty with, and avoids, social interaction, then we need to consider whether there is some other complicating condition. Also, if the child is socializing and then begins to withdraw or seems to lose his ability to use signs or verbal language, we need to consider other diagnoses that may be co-occurring with Down syndrome.

An evaluation by a physician and/or psychologist should consider the possibilities of seizure disorders, autism spectrum disorders (including autism and pervasive developmental disability), or childhood disintegrative disorder. It has been estimated that 5 to 8 percent of children with Down syndrome have a dual diagnosis of Down syndrome and autism spectrum disorder. The major communication signs are: 1) absence or severe delay in using spoken language, 2) lack of communication interaction using speech or gestures, 3) failure to initiate communication with others, poor social relatedness, and a limited repertoire of activities and interests, and (4) poor receptive language skills, which may give the appearance that the child does not hear (Capone, 1999). The child does not seek communication and does not use speech meaningfully to communicate. The child may repeat what you say; this is known as *echolalia.* For example, you say, "What is your name?" and the child repeats "name."

A child with Down syndrome who is very delayed in speaking does not necessarily have autism. A child who is delayed in speech might develop language skills very slowly, or may use sign language, but be unable to speak. Difficulty with sequencing and coordinating movements of the lips, jaws, and tongue may make it very difficult for a child with Down syndrome to speak, but he does not necessarily have autism. A child with Down syndrome alone who is not yet speaking will interact with his environment in many nonverbal ways, including maintaining eye contact, taking turns, and seeking social interaction with his environment. A child with Down syndrome *and* autism would have difficulty interacting with his environment.

Seek out an evaluation if you suspect a dual diagnosis. Ask your pediatrician for a referral to a developmental pediatrician who specializes in this area. This is a co-occurring condition which is not frequently seen, and is difficult to diagnose. The focus of treatment and specific methodologies used for children who have autism in addition to Down syndrome are different, so it is important to determine if autism is present (Patterson, 1999). Two developmental pediatricians who are active in this specialty area are George Capone, M.D., of the Kennedy-Krieger Institute, 707 North Broadway, Baltimore, Maryland 21205, and Bonnie Patterson, M.D., of the Cincinnati Center on Developmental Disabilities, 3333 Burnett Avenue, Cincinnati, OH 45229. If your child does have one of the autistic spectrum disorders, his treatment program will need to be individually designed, and will probably include an augmentative and alternative communication system. For more information on AAC, see Chapter 12.

communication skills are usually not taught in therapy, they can and should be taught as part of a comprehensive communication intervention program. Nonverbal communication information is an ideal topic for SLPs and classroom teachers to collaborate on. The information is important for all children in the class, and can be part of a presentation for the entire class.

Once you understand which skills are included in pragmatics, you will be more aware of which skills your child is using, and which skills may need to be worked on, at school or at home. When your child was young, you probably worked on pragmatic social language skills through a home program or a center program without even realizing you were working on them. For instance, you may have worked on waving bye-bye and turn taking. Now that your child is school-aged, it is important to develop his IEP to include more advanced pragmatic skills based on his needs and strengths in the area.

Intent

Your communicative intent is the purpose of your communication or conversation. What do you want to accomplish through your communication? A child in school might say, "Is it time for lunch yet?" with the intent of letting the teacher know he is tired of doing math or that he is hungry. A child on his way home from school might say, "I'm hungry" right as his mother drives past the Burger King, with his message being, "Let's stop and eat." An adolescent may say, "Everyone is going" (on the school trip to the play), with the intent of convincing his parents to let him go, too.

Linguists use specific terms for the speaker's intent and the listener's interpretation of that intent. The speaker's intent is referred to as the *illocutionary act*, while the listener's perception of that intent is referred to as *perlocutionary act*. When the listener's perception of the speaker's intent is the same message that the speaker intended, we have effective communication (technically, the illocutionary act and perlocutionary act match). When the listener doesn't receive accurately the message that the speaker intended, there is a mismatch (technically, the illocutionary and perlocutionary act do not match).

So, if your child says to his friend in school, "Did you do the reading homework?" with the intent of asking for help, but his friend says, "I did" with no intent of sharing information, there is a mismatch between the illocutionary and perlocutionary act. If your child comes in from playing in the snow and tells you, "I'm cold" and you ask, "Do you want some hot chocolate?" the illocutionary and perlocutionary acts match, if that was your child's intent.

Effective Communication
speaker's message = listener's interpretation

Ineffective Communication
speaker's message ≠ listener's interpretation

People have many different types of intentions when they communicate, including:

- requesting,
- greeting,
- socialization/being friendly,
- protesting,
- regulating the environment, and
- asking for information.

Intents are almost always part of purposeful communication attempts; we usually have an underlying reason for trying to communicate.

Practicing intents in therapy or at home can be very effective. With younger children, the skills can be practiced through play. With older children and adolescents, role playing simulations are good ways to practice intents. In general, it helps if parents, teachers, and others who regularly communicate with your child work with him to help him express his intent more clearly, rather than figuring out what he wants and getting it for him. For example, if your child says longingly "Cindy got chocolate pudding for lunch," you might say, "Oh, would YOU like pudding in your lunch too?" and get your child to verbalize that to you. ("Why don't you ask me to buy some pudding for you?")

If your child is nonverbal, you may sometimes have to interpret his intent for him in a given situation, but then figure out a way for your child to make his intent understood better the next time. For instance, if your child growls at another child for trying to help him do something, you might need to tell that child, "Thomas doesn't want your help right now." But then you should look for something your child can use to replace the grunt when he wants to reject help.

When teachers are preparing students for field trips, there is generally much discussion about the trip. There may be role playing of different situations, such as what happens if you get separated from your buddy at the zoo. The role playing is rehearsal for the real event. This same type of role playing can be used to help your child learn how to use language in different situations to intentionally meet his needs. For example, you can work with him to understand what he should say to communicate that he is lost, or wants a turn shooting baskets on the playground, or wants to sit with someone on the bus.

Asking for help, which is a specific type of intent, is discussed in detail in Chapter 7. Making clearer requests is discussed later in this chapter.

Eye Contact

Looking at someone when you talk or listen is considered very important in many cultures. This is not true in all cultures; in Asian and African-American cultures, it is considered a sign of respect to look away from a teacher when she is talking to you. But, in most American and Canadian and many European schools, if you look away, the teacher will assume that you are not listening. Teachers will say, "Look at me when I talk to you." So, eye contact is important.

Many parents of children with Down syndrome report that their child looks down when someone is speaking to him. Sometimes, a prompt to remind him, such as "Look me in the eyes," may be all that is needed. With an older child or adolescent who is self-conscious, you might agree on an unobtrusive sign to remind your child to look at you. For example, you could point to your eye with your index finger while holding your hand on your cheek. In class, a visual prompt can be used. Prompts could include a Post-It note on the corner of your child's desk with wide-open eyes, or a small photo or picture of a favorite rock star or movie star in which the eyes have been darkened or colored to make them more prominent.

Facial Expression

It is important to the listener that the speaker's facial expressions match what he is saying. Researchers have shown that when the words and the facial expressions or the emotion in the voice don't agree, listeners will assume that the facial expressions and the nonverbal signs are carrying the real message. For example, if I say, "I love art," with a sad or angry facial expression, the listener will assume that I really don't like art, but if I say the same words with a smiling face, the listener will assume that art is one of my favorite subjects.

Help your child tune in to facial expressions. For example, when he brings home a carefully completed school paper and shows it to Grandma, comment, "Look at how Grandma is smiling. She is so proud of how hard you worked on that paper." Or, when your neighbor is standing on the side of the driveway with a scowl on his face, say, "Look at Fred. He is angry that his car won't start." Draw attention to your child's own expressions, too, by saying things like—"Why are you frowning? Did something bad happen today?" or "You are smiling. Did you have lots of fun today?"

Some other ways to help your child learn to "read" facial expressions:

- Cut out pictures from magazines or use family photos and create a dictionary of facial expressions. You can discuss with your child what the person using that facial expression might be thinking.
- Have your child practice making different kinds of facial expressions in the mirror, and talk about what would make someone sad or happy or angry.
- When you are reading books, comment on how the characters feel. Comment on cartoon characters, television show characters, or movie characters. Look at their facial expressions, describe them, and then discuss what makes the characters look happy, sad, or angry.

- Draw faces with your child, and talk about what you do to make them look happy, sad, surprised, etc.
- Use an instant camera or a video camera. Ask your child to make faces that show certain emotions. Then look at the pictures together and discuss the facial expressions.

In school, it is very important to talk about emotions, but this is rarely done, so this may be an area that the SLP will need to address in therapy if your child is having trouble reading facial expressions. Tuning in to facial expressions and voice will help your child better understand when people are experiencing different feelings.

Kinesics

Kinesics is the use of gestures in communication. Examples of kinesics are shrugging your shoulders for "I don't know," or giving a high-five sign, or pointing to the flavor of ice cream that you want to eat. Kinesics are used to accompany speech, and also to replace speech. For example, if I was on the other side of the playground and you couldn't hear me, I could use a "come here" gesture or a "that's OK" gesture to communicate with you. Children with Down syndrome generally use gestures very well, including "instrumental gestures" such as "come here" (Attwood, 1988). Gestures used frequently in school include hand-raising, holding up hands together as buddies, and a quiet sign.

Games are good ways to practice gestures, and to point out that gestures are effective ways to communicate in many situations. These games are also a good way to work on attention skills, eye contact, and socialization skills. In school, games that use gestures are often played at recess or in physical education:

- Play Simon Says with gestures. You say, "Simon Says do this," but what you are asking the child to do is to copy a gesture.
- Play the Hokey Pokey, which involves modeling and copying gestures.
- Practice head gestures (yes, no, I don't know) with a question and answer game. Make some of the questions absurd, so that the game will be fun. For example, "Is your name Suzy?" "Are you a banana?" "Are you a girl?" "Are you smaller than an ant?" "Are you bigger than an elephant?"
- Charades is a more complex game with which to practice gestural skills.
- Teachers can institute a "no talking" time when everything must be communicated through gestures, facial expressions, signs, and body language. This is a time for all children in the class to explore nonverbal communication. Children with Down syndrome can participate fully in this activity, since nonverbal communication is a strength.

Parents and/or SLPs can find out what kind of gestures the teacher routinely uses and make sure your child understands them. For example, do they use the V for victory sign to indicate "peace" (as in "be quiet") or make a zipping motion across their lips to indicate "zip your lip"? Do they have a sign for students to show that they are ready or that they are listening? Do they have a certain sign they want students to make if they need to use the bathroom? You can create a word bank of signs and check whether your child understands the signs. You can make the sign and have your child explain what the sign means. Then change roles; have your child make the sign and you tell what it means.

Requests

In order for your child to get his needs met, he must learn to make requests of people in his environment. Knowing how to request and how to respond to requests are important skills for school. Examples of types of requests at school include:

- **Requesting help:** For example, "I need more time"; "I need help doing this worksheet." Asking for help in a classroom setting is discussed in Chapter 7.
- **Requesting information:** For example, "Do we need to write the date?" "How many lines do we skip between spelling words?" "How much time is left?"
- **Requesting a specific object:** For example, "I need another piece of paper." "My pen is leaking—I need another one."
- **Requesting permission:** For example, "May I go to the bathroom?" "May I stop reading now?"
- **Requesting clarification** of what someone else said (discussed below under "Contingent Queries and Repairs").

REQUESTS FOR INFORMATION

There are two different kinds of questions you can use to ask for information. There are questions beginning with do, can, is, etc., that result in a yes or no answer. And then there are questions beginning with what, who, where, when, which, how words. Clinically, it appears that children with Down syndrome are able to answer yes and no questions earliest. And using verbal requests that result in yes or no answers appears to develop earlier than using "wh" questions.

Parents can work with children to help them learn to answer yes/no and "wh" questions. Reading children's books and asking questions as you read along is a good way to practice answering requests for information. Questions can be serious, "Where is Big Bear? What is he doing?" or funny, "Do we eat dinner when we get up in the morning?" If your child doesn't seem to understand the "wh" word, or confuses "wh" words with each other, try giving him a hint after you ask a question. For example, say "*Where* is the balloon? In the tree? Behind a cloud?" Or, "*How* did he break his glasses?

Sample Goal for Understanding Requests

Goal: To improve skills in answering requests

Benchmark: Joel will be able to respond to "wh" questions with 80% accuracy by Feburary 10.

Benchmark: Joel will answer "wh" questions based on information in his reading books with 80% accuracy by April 10.

Did he drop them? Did he step on them?" Many children with Down syndrome need to work on answering requests, especially "wh" requests, in speech therapy.

It is much easier to teach someone how to answer requests than how to make them. One way to work on making requests is through games. When children are at the stage of asking yes/no questions, there are games that will help learn and practice these skills. I Spy, 20 Questions, and Go Fish are some examples of appropriate games. Other examples include: Secret Square (one player hides a "chip" under one of about 25 picture cards, and the other players ask questions to find out which card it is (Is it something brown? Is it an animal? Can it fly?) and Mystery Garden by Ravensburger (one player draws a card picturing something on the board and the other players take turns guessing what it is).

When you are teaching your child how to use yes/no or "wh" questions to make requests for information, situations that involve following instructions such as cooking and crafts activities can be very helpful. You can set up the activity so your child has to ask "Do we put in the milk now?" "What do we put in next?" "Where is the ___" or "How do I?" Coaching, models, cues, and prompts can be used to help your child learn how to ask questions. The SLP, teacher, or parent may whisper, "Ask me how much sugar we need to put in the recipe," or written cues may be used for the child who can read (how much? how many? when?).

Another way to work on requests is through role playing. With school age children, you can use props such as a hat, a pad and pencil or a microphone, and a button that says Reporter. Role play that the child is interviewing his favorite TV or video star or singer. Or develop a newspaper as a class project, with each child reporting on a different school event or interviewing a member of the school staff. At home, the family can make a family newspaper, or a special holiday newspaper, and your child can interview others for the information to include. For example, he can survey everyone at Thanksgiving to see what their favorite pie is.

Other activities to practice making and responding to requests for information include:

- **Interviewing:** At school, your child could be in charge of collecting information for graphs the class is doing (e.g., if the class is doing a graph of when people's birthdays are, favorite colors, etc.). Or, the class could have an assignment to get to know three classmates by asking them a list of questions. At home, your child could be in charge of asking family members/guests what they want to drink or eat, or what video, DVD, or CD they want to listen to or watch.
- **Playing school:** Who wants to be the teacher? Who wants to be the bus driver? When are we doing spelling? Do you want to do art?
- **Telephone play:** Use toy telephones with younger children, and walkie talkies or real telephones with older children. This may be a play activity or involve real telephone practice. For

example, call up a store to find out when they open or close, or ask whether they have a certain Beanie Baby that you want.

- **Playing Restaurant:** This can be a play activity with props such as a fast food hat, a pad and pencil, and an apron. The children may take turns being the waitress and customer. Or you can practice how to order, and how to ask questions about food: "What drinks do you have?" "Do you have Coke?" Then go out to eat and let your child try out his questioning skills.

- **Play "Mystery Animal":** An adult puts a sticker with the name or picture of an animal on your child's back. He needs to guess what animal he is by asking questions: "What color am I?" "How big am I?" "Where do I live?" "What do I say?" Several children can play the game at once and take turns asking each other questions. Your child can model the other child's questions, if necessary.

- **Barrier games:** See the section on "Presuppositions," below, for more information about barrier games.

- **Sports:** Being a spectator in sports lends itself to asking questions. Who has the ball? What's the score? Who's up? Did the ball go in? When you are a player learning a sport, you may also ask many questions about what to do.

- **Scripts:** See below.

Scripts. Scripts can also be used to practice asking for information. A script is a phrase, sentence, or conversation that you use over and over in daily living. For example, most people have scripts that they use every time they answer the phone. One person says, "Hello?"; another says, "Hi, who's this?" At school, your child may use a script to ask other kids if he can join in their game, or to ask if he could sit next to someone in the cafeteria. If your child uses a AAC device, the scripts may be programmed into the system, so that when he pushes the button with a picture of himself, the speech synthesized voice says, "I'm John, what's your name?" Or when he pushes the button with a picture of children playing, the speech synthesized voice says, "Can I play too?"

Research has shown that children with Down syndrome have better speech intelligibility (can be more easily understood) when they are using scripts in familiar routines. Research has also shown that children with Down syndrome learn and respond well to social scripts (Loveland & Tunali, 1991).

Children learn to use scripts by practicing in real situations and by role playing. Your child can memorize a script so that it becomes almost automatic. Picture cues can also be used to help him remember what to say. The one consideration is that you also need to talk with your child about exceptions to using the script, such as when the person's response doesn't fit in with what he is planning to say next. You would need to practice various ways of adapting the script.

Scripts can also be practiced and mastered by children who use augmentative communication systems such as sign language, communication boards, or high tech systems. All communication systems should enable the user to communicate his needs and requests, and to use scripts for daily conversational interactions.

REQUESTS FOR OBJECTS

At school, your child may need to request school supplies such as paper, the blue crayon, scissors, or tape to complete a project. Requests for objects can be practiced through:

- **Cooking:** You ask your child, "Would you get me a carrot, please?" while making the salad. Or you get your child to ask you for something by asking "What do you need?" For example, when you and your child are gathering ingredients to make chocolate chip cookies, you put the chips out of reach, so he will need to ask you to get them.
- **Dressing:** For example, you misplace your child's gloves so he has to ask for them.
- **Arts and Crafts activities:** You arrange for several kids to share one glue stick or pair of scissors so they have to ask each other for them. Or, you put the construction paper out of reach when you're making valentines, so your child has to ask, "Can I have more red paper"?
- **Pretend shopping:** The "customer" says, for example, "Give me a pound of cheese, please." Using toys or props such as a shopping cart, a cash register, and an apron and hat for the check-out person will make the experience more realistic and more fun.
- **Carpentry or woodworking activities:** The parent says, "Give me the hammer (saw, screwdriver, nail, etc.) please."

Follow up on the practice by planning a field trip to a real place or event (supermarket, library, fast food restaurant) to practice the skills.

When teaching your child to ask for objects, it is important to give him the object right away, even if he doesn't ask perfectly. If he gets frustrated and grabs the object, you have not taught him that asking for things is helpful. If you have a child who is not very verbal or who has difficulty speaking clearly, you should be very liberal in accepting approximations of a request. Work on speech intelligibility should not be combined with teaching requests. They should be two separate activities. If your child grabs things and does not ask, you can take the object away and expect a request question before you give the object to him.

REQUESTS FOR PERMISSION

In school, asking permission for things is often closely tied in with the language of routines. For instance, the teacher may have a set way she wants children to ask for permission to go to the restroom or to get a drink of water. In that case, your child needs to follow the rule. It may be correct to raise your hand or to go up and take a hall pass, rather than verbally request permission. But there are many situations that are non-routine—e.g., your child forgot his project on the bus, or he doesn't feel well. In those situations, he would need to use a request. Some activities for practicing asking permission include:

- **"Mother May I?"** (One person is the Mother and the rest are the kids; one kid asks, e.g., "Mother, may I take one giant step?" Then, the mother responds with: "Yes, you may," "No, you may not," or something like "No, you may not. But you may take two baby steps." The first one to reach the Mother wins.)

- **"Johnny, may we cross your wide blue ocean?"**
  (Johnny stands in the middle of the designated playing area and the other children ask the question, "Johnny, may we cross your wide blue ocean?" Then Johnny might say, for example, "Only if you have red on." Or, "Only if you have blond hair." Or "Only if there is a J in your name." Then the children who have that color on can just walk across to the other side and be "safe," but the other kids have to try to run past Johnny without getting tagged. Kids who are tagged stay in the middle and help Johnny catch the others.)

Proxemics

Proxemics is how people handle space and distance in communication. There are striking differences among different cultures in the use of space between speaker and listener. In some cultures, there is a great deal of touching and hugging. People may speak standing at a very close distance, even with business acquaintances. In other cultures, people stand farther apart, and do not touch each other, even when they are close family members. In some cultures, women can stand close to other women but not to men, whereas in other cultures, men also stand close.

Children also have space and distance issues. There may be some differences from one school to another related to gender and cultural background, but there are some general guidelines as to what is considered appropriate within a school. Typical children generally learn what is appropriate by watching.

Proxemics is often a difficult issue for children with Down syndrome. Many children are affectionate and may have been encouraged when young to give hugs when greeting others. People generally find this adorable in a three-year-old, but may be apprehensive or embarrassed if a fifteen-year-old tries to hug them. The people in your child's environment need to consistently support appropriate behavior. It is important to make sure adults are not encouraging the wrong behavior, such as by asking him for a hug when he leaves speech therapy, or by letting other students hug him for encouragement because he's so little and cute, whereas they wouldn't dream of hugging another classmate. Extended families may also have

varying practices that are confusing to children. For example, the mother's side of the family may hug and kiss in greeting, while the father's side will say "good to see you" and wave from a distance.

The more practice your child gets in how to physically approach people, the better. Talk about who you shake hands with, and who you hug. Talk about how you will greet someone right before you actually greet them. For example, explain, "Ginny is a good friend. We can say hi and hug Ginny." Or, "When we go to the office, let's shake hands with John and say, 'Good to meet you.'" With an adolescent, it's better to err on the side of being more formal and staying at a greater distance when talking with adults. Inclusion provides practice with proxemics, as well as appropriate models.

You also need to evaluate, with the help of the teacher and/or SLP, what's appropriate in your child's school on a yearly basis. From grade to grade, there will be changes. For example, it may be appropriate for two third-grade girls to hold hands or stand close, but not for two boys. On a sports team, physical contact, as well as proxemics will be different than it is in the classroom. It may be appropriate for two guys on the team to jostle each other, or punch each other playfully on the shoulder, but that would probably not be appropriate in class. If your child is having difficulty with issues of space and distance, it may be a good idea to include a line or check-off on the daily home-school communication sheet so that the teacher can let you know if there is improvement, or if these issues need to be worked on at home.

USING CIRCLES TO TEACH ABOUT SPACE

Edward Hall was one of the first to discuss personal space and distance. He talked about four zones:

- the intimate zone (close to 18 inches)
- the personal zone (18 inches to 4 feet)
- the social zone (4-12 feet)
- the public zone (12 feet to long distances)

Sometimes circles marked on the floor with masking tape or chalk lines are used to make the concept of these distances more concrete. These visual aids can be used to make the child more aware of spatial issues and to practice talking and interacting with people at different distances.

Leslie Walker-Hirsch, a specialist in sexuality education, has further developed the circles concept to teach children about appropriate distances as they relate to personal safety (1993). She has identified six circles. They range from the purple private circle—an intimate circle of people close to you who will hug each other and be physically close—to the red strangers space where it is not appropriate to talk to the strangers or to touch them or allow them to touch you.

A specific technique that can be used to teach appropriate distances is to draw concentric circles on the playground or in the gym to represent appropriate distances between people for specific situations. For example, the circle would be larger when talking with the principal than when talking with your brother (each person would stand at the outer edge of a circle). For early elementary school age children, these circles can be used with a dress-up activity. For example, children could choose from office clothes, dressy formal clothes, a fireman's hat, a fast food cap, a gas station attendant's hat, a supermarket cashier's apron, a waitress's apron. When two or three children are dressed in different outfits, you can talk about distances and where on the circle they should stand. For older children and adolescents, the discussion need not involve props. You can suggest roles and then talk about the circle distances that would be appropriate.

If your child uses hugging or other touch inappropriately, or has other problems with proxemics, a positive behavioral support plan can be used to address the problem. (See Chapter 10 for information on positive behavioral support.) The classroom teacher and guidance counselor can provide helpful input when writing the IEP relating to proxemics.

Conversational Skills

Conversational skills is a very broad category that can include speech and language skills as well as pragmatics. Within the area of conversational skills, we can look at specific skills, including:

- starting and ending conversations,
- taking turns in the conversation,
- choosing topics and staying on the topic,
- knowing what information the listener brings with him (putting yourself in his shoes),
- understanding how to talk with different people in different roles, and
- knowing how to get and give more information if there are communication misunderstandings.

Research has usually shown that children with Down syndrome have delays in acquiring conversational skills and typically have short conversations. But, one study found that when young children with Down syndrome were matched with typically developing children by language level, not chronological age, children with Down syndrome "demonstrated significantly greater response abilities than controls" (Leifer & Lewis, 1984). That is, a ten-year-old with Down syndrome who has the language level of a four-year-old would generally have better conversational skills than a typical four-year-old, perhaps because he's had a lot more experience with conversations.

In class, the teacher generally does not want conversations to be ongoing. At lunch and recess, however, children typically engage in conversations with their friends. Using appropriate conversational skills are quite important in making and keeping friends, especially in later elementary school and beyond.

BASIC CONVERSATIONAL SKILLS

Because lengthy social conversations are not usually encouraged within the classroom, conversational skills are best practiced at home and in the community. Some conversational skills, including greeting others and turn-taking, are very basic and can be learned as part of early play.

TURN-TAKING

We learn turn-taking when we roll a ball back and forth, hand a bubble wand from one person to another, or play frisbee. You can practice turn taking through:

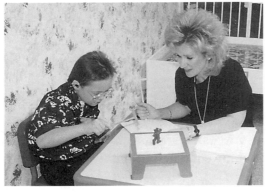

- **Interviewing:** Children take turns asking each their questions about their favorite vacation, their family, their favorite restaurant, etc..
- **Jokes and riddles:** Telling and responding to knock knock jokes and riddles are good ways to practice conversational roles.
- **Crafts projects:** As described above, you can set up activities so children have to share materials such as glue sticks, scissors, and paints.
- **Sequenced story telling:** One child starts telling a story. When he stops, the next child has to continue

the story. A timer or a ball handed from one child to another can be used to signify whose turn it is. A transitional phrase, such as "And then..." can be used to help children get started.

- **Telephone play:** Your child can take turns talking with you or a sibling on a real or play phone or walkie talkies. This is especially good for practicing making responses.

A good source of information on teaching turn-taking and other conversational skills to children with Down syndrome is the Communicating Partners Center, founded by James D. MacDonald, a former professor of speech-language pathology and developmental disabilities (www.jamesdmacdonald.com, 332 Mimring Rd., Columbus, OH 43202).

GREETINGS

What does your child say when he sees the bus driver in the morning? when he leaves the bus in the afternoon? What does he say to the teacher when he first sees her? at the end of the day? How about greeting peers in the same class? older or younger kids at school?

One way to teach your child to use greetings is through the use of *scripts*—repeated phrases that we use in daily life. For example, we all tend to have certain greetings we use in certain situations; we don't plan to say something different each time. We might routinely say, "Hi, how're you doing, good to see you" to friends, and "Hello. How are you?" to new people we meet on the job.

The best way to teach scripts is through role playing, and in real life situations where they occur, such as using the telephone and going to restaurants. For greeting scripts, use stuffed animals or dolls to first practice the greetings, and props such as a toy school bus. For older children you might want to use photographs of fellow students, the teacher, school bus driver, etc. instead. Greet each stuffed animal and doll, "Hi, Paddington Bear" or "Hi, Barbie." You or friends or siblings model the greetings. Look up at the dolls and make eye contact when you say the greeting. Do it as a game and make it fun. You may also give a "high five" sign, or say "How are you?"

When your child is comfortable with the greetings, take the dolls outside in front of your house. Greet each doll and practice some more. Then invite neighbors over to your porch or deck, and let your child practice greeting them, following your example. When those greetings become natural, try going for a walk in the neighborhood or at the shopping center. Greet people who you know in the stores and as you are walking.

If your child is receiving speech therapy in school, ask the SLP to work on greetings. The SLP can take a walk with your child in the school corridors, offices, and cafeteria and practice greeting the school staff and peers. Once your child feels comfortable with greeting people, and has had practice, he will begin to say "hi!" spontaneously. Because the greeting situation occurs so often, he will have lots of practice. When you feel that your child has mastered this skill at home, ask the classroom teacher, SLP, and bus driver to report back to you on whether you child is using the greetings in school with children and adults.

ADVANCED CONVERSATIONAL SKILLS

Other conversational skills are very advanced, such as asking for specific information when you didn't understand all of the information that was given, or understanding what background information you need to provide someone so he can understand what you are talking about.

Practice in using conversational skills is the best way to improve these skills (although we give additional suggestions below). Inclusive school and community settings can promote conversational skills by:

- providing conversational models,
- providing real-life practice and interesting conversational partners,
- providing natural consequences (it's your turn; it's not your turn now).

Some conversational interactions are repeated over and over again in daily life and in school, and can be rehearsed as social scripts, as described above. For example, your child may frequently answer the telephone or greet the bus driver and his friends. Role playing the situations, sometimes using props, is fun for children and adolescents. This may be done as part of the social skills curriculum within the regular classroom, or it may be part of a separate special education life skills class.

TOPICALIZATION

Topicalization involves skills in introducing topics, staying on topic, and changing topics. Maintaining topic (keeping the topic going) and staying on topic (not straying from the topic) are skills that are often difficult for children with Down syndrome. When you have difficulty maintaining the topic, conversations are short. Some children with Down syndrome have longer conversations, but keep changing

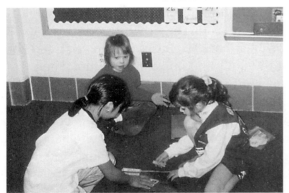

topics and bringing up irrelevant items in the conversation. For example, the teacher is talking about Africa and the habitat of lions. The child with Down syndrome begins answering a question about lions, but then begins to talk about *The Lion King* and his trip to Disney World. When you have difficulty staying on topic, your conversation can seem rambling.

Topicalization skills lend themselves to real-life activities. Having tangible cues, such as photos or videos, can help children learn to develop topics and to stay on topic. Keeping a record of an event in a photo album can form the basis for a conversation, acting as visual cues to keep your child on topic. When you go to a baseball game, a museum, or an amusement park, take many photographs. Mount them in the photo album in sequential order, so that they can serve as cues and can help your child tell the story of the trip. Then ask your child about the excursion. Using the photos as cues, talk about everything that "goes with" the excursion. After several "conversations" about the excursion, when the topics are familiar, do the same activity without the photos.

Visual and graphic organizers (see Chapter 3) can also be effective in helping children understand what is included in a topic. You can help your child complete an organizer (such as a semantic web) with you before you introduce a topic of conversation. Or if your child gets stuck in a conversation, pull out an organizer and help him think of more things to say.

Expanding your child's vocabulary or ability to make associations is another way to help with topicalization. Words that are associated are words on the same topic, so association games are good ways to learn which words go together. Games such as Password, Scattergories, and Pictionary (or Pictionary Jr.) are fun to play and address topicalization skills. Reading books together and discussing what the book is talking about (what topics go with the book) can also help your child master topical skills. For example, if you read a book about the beach, discuss what kinds of things you could tell someone so they could learn about a beach. It is also a good idea to read nonfiction books on topics of interest to your child so he can increase his vocabulary and breadth of knowledge on those topic areas.

Work on lengthening conversations can be done in small groups in the classroom. One suggestion is to use a "Talk" ball, a regular ball, or even a balloon that has lips painted on. One child begins the conversation and then when he is finished hands the ball to the next child, who must continue on the same topic. Another way is to wrap short lengths of yarn or ribbon around a small piece of cardboard. In a basket, place a sufficient number of ribbon cards for each child in the group. A child picks a card. He begins to unwind the ribbon and must continue talking on the topic until the ribbon is completely unwound. A modification might be to let the child with Down syndrome go first so other players don't say everything he was going to say, and so that he does not have to remember what everyone else has said so he doesn't repeat it.

Some other activities to use for practice on topics are:

- **Explaining** how to make a peanut butter and jelly sandwich
- **Guiding** others through an activity
- **Interviewing:** What are five questions that you could ask about baseball?
- **Practicing giving biographical information** in answer to the question, "Who are you?"
- **Shopping:** This is similar to a categorization activity in which you put all articles of clothing or all red things in the shopping cart. In this case, you talk about what items are in different parts of a large discount store—e.g. what would you find in housewares or snacks? This kind of activity also could be done with a newspaper advertising section. When we talk about tools, what can we talk about?
- **Science or nature activity:** Practice staying on topic in a conversation by talking about the zoo or the baseball stadium. What do you find at the zoo? How is it different from the stadium?
- **Simulated restaurant activity:** When you eat out or role play, talk about categories such as beverages or desserts. Practice staying on topic.

At school, topicalization skills might come up if the classroom teacher reports that your child has difficulty responding to questions with relevant information. In this case, you may want to analyze the responses she would like from your child on a specific topic. Let's say the teacher decides that she wants your child to give three major points when he answers a question. Assuming that you have used some of the activities above to practice staying on a topic with your child, you could now practice talking about three things that relate to a given topic—basketball, the Super Bowl, favorite restaurants, animals in the zoo, explorers in Florida, a character in a story. Then create a visual cue to help remind your child to give three pieces of information in his answer and then stop. An example might be an index card that says:

Have your child practice using the cue card to give only three answers. Practice first in therapy, then at home. Then carry over the activity into the classroom. Eventually, you can fade out use of the cue card and have your child count on his fingers, if necessary.

STYLISTIC VARIATIONS

Stylistic variations is the term used to describe an individual's ability to modify and adapt his communication to the audience and the situation. It means knowing you should use a quiet voice in a crowded movie, and that you shouldn't start a conversation while you are participating in a religious service. It means knowing that it's fine to tell a joke at lunch, but not during reading class. It means knowing the differences in how to greet your new baby cousin and your mom or dad's boss, when to be formal and when to be informal, and when to use a quiet voice and when it's OK to be loud and exuberant. Sometimes, these variations are referred to as *registers*.

Children need to learn to use different registers in school. It may be fine to say, "High fives" to the janitor, but not to the cafeteria staff. Teachers may need to be addressed differently than the bus driver. Levels of formality will vary depending on the role of the adult in the school. Stylistic variations involve analysis of the situation and flexibility. They are often difficult for children with Down syndrome to master, but can be learned through practice.

Rehearsal, role playing, and practice in real situations are the best way to learn to use stylistic variations. Inclusive settings within school and the community provide practice in using the skills. Some activities to highlight the variations and practice the skills are:

■ **Doll and action figure play:** Change voices, loudness etc. as you role play superheroes, Barbie, and popular personalities.

- **Explaining how to:** Ask your child to explain how to do xyz as if he were talking to a five-year-old, and then as if he were talking to a teacher or his grandmother.
- **Playing school:** You and your child role play talking with the bus driver, the cafeteria staff, the janitor, teacher, secretaries in the office, and the principal. In practice, use props (baseball cap, a broom, aprons, chef's hats, etc.) and rehearse a situation that may really occur. Then your child will be prepared, and will be able to use stylistic variations where they count—in the real situation.
- **Telephone play:** Have your child pretend that he's telling the same story to a three-year-old cousin and a friend's mother.
- **TV commercials:** As you watch TV commercials with your child, talk about what's appropriate and what's not. For example, "Whazzup" from the beer commercial would not be appropriate to say to the principal but it might be fine with Dad at the football game.

It can be difficult to know how your child is doing with this skill in school. Usually, if your child is using appropriate stylistic variations, the teacher will not mention it. If he is having difficulty, the teacher will often view it as misbehavior, rather than lack of understanding of what's appropriate communication in the situation. It is important for someone who's at school, such as the teacher, aide or SLP, to let you know about which types of interactions your child has trouble with. The SLP has excellent observational skills and a good understanding of stylistic variations. That is one reason that it is important to include the SLP in functional behavioral analyses to help determine whether communication problems are affecting behavior, or if the behavior may actually be a display of difficulty with using appropriate communication. When your child is able to use stylistic variations, but does not always remember to use them, a peer or aide can remind your child of stylistic do's and don'ts.

CONTINGENT QUERIES AND REPAIRS

Contingent queries and repairs are skills that fit with each other. They are both skills involved when there are misunderstandings in communication, known as *communication breakdowns.* As you may recall, the topic of communication breakdowns was introduced in Chapter 7.

Contingent queries and repairs are important skills involved in following instructions and asking for additional information or clarification of instructions. Contingent query is the ability to ask for more information when there is something that you missed or did not understand. Contingent queries are also called clarifications or requests for repair. The use of contingent queries helps the speaker know that you are listening, and keeps the conversation moving along. Examples of contingent queries are "huh?" or "what?" The listener may ask for clarification ("What did you say?") or for specification ("Can you tell me what you mean?") or for confirmation ("Is this what you are saying?").

Repairs consists of the ability to recognize that a misunderstanding has occurred or that your listener did not understand or hear something that was said, and the follow-up, to provide the information needed to "repair" the misunderstanding. In a conversation, it is usually the listener who asks for clarifications and the speaker who makes repairs. Repairs are very specific to the situation. For example, the question might be, "*Who* got a new TV?" The answer might be "Grandpa."

Repairing communication breakdowns is difficult for children with Down syndrome. It is best learned through practice with the speech-language pathologist, and using a peer tutor or aide to model and explain repairs as they are needed in the classroom. Some suggestions of home activities are also provided in Chapter 7.

The SLP can work with your child to increase awareness of different types of communication breakdown, and how to make various types of repairs. For example, if your child said an unintelligible word, she needs to respond to someone's specific request to clarify. Or if someone else said a word very quickly, your child may need to ask for clarification.

Making repairs (responding to others' requests for clarification) is generally easier than asking for clarification. If a listener says, "I didn't understand what you said; can you repeat it?" some possible repairs may be repeating the word, or pointing to the object or person that your child was naming. Other possible misunderstandings are use of unfamiliar words, or giving an impossible command ("Bring me the square" when there are fifteen squares, some red, some blue, some large and some small).

Research with typically developing children and children with language learning disabilities has found that children tend to blame themselves, rather than the speaker, when a communication misunderstanding occurs. As a result, they use fewer requests for repairs. We don't know if this is true for children with Down syndrome, but it is something to take into consideration when working on contingent queries and repairs. In other words, encourage any request for clarification your child makes. Say, "That's a good question! I didn't explain that very clearly, did I?" and the like, to help your child feel good about asking for clarification. If your child uses an AAC system, it is important to make sure that he has ways of expressing "I don't understand" and "Could you repeat."

PRESUPPOSITIONS

Presuppositions are the background information and prior experience that the listener brings to a situation. When we talk about considering our listener's needs or audience analysis (in public speaking), we are talking about presuppositions. Presuppositions involve walking in your listener's shoes, or taking the attitude of your listener. What does your listener know? What do you need to tell your listener?

To provide information and help someone, you need to know what your listener already knows. If you were asked to provide directions to a new restaurant, you would not give the directions in the same way to a native of the area as you would to a tourist who had never been in the city before.

Presuppositions are an advanced pragmatic skill, but you can begin working on presuppositions with young children. One way is to let your child know what you (the listener) need to know. Young children are egocentric, and will tell you about events and children at school, assuming that you know the references. Stop your child, and ask, "Who's Sherry? Is she a girl in your class?" or "When did you make the picture? Was that today in school?" "You need to tell me, because I don't know that."

Other good ways to give your child practice with presuppositions include:

- Have him explain the directions and rules in a board game to someone who has never played that game. In fact, one study found that children with Down syndrome were able to teach the rules of a game to another person well, using gestures and responding to requests for clarification (Loveland et al, 1989).
- If your child is older, you might ask him to describe something that he sees through a Viewmaster or binoculars (where it's obvious that you can't see what he is seeing).
- Play barrier games. See below.

Barrier Games. Barrier games are an effective way to learn and practice giving instructions. There are many possible variations on barrier games. The important elements are:

1. at least two players,
2. an activity to do that requires that one person follow instructions given by another person,
3. a physical barrier that visually separates the two people (or two groups).

The barrier game activity provides a vehicle for practicing how to give directions, and how to ask for help when you don't understand directions. In the barrier game activity, one person gives the instructions and the other person follows the instructions. The idea of the barrier game is to complete a task (such as coloring a picture, or making a sandwich) when you don't have visual models, and must rely on the instructions that have been given to you. The focus is on communication (the process), not on the product.

You can use a series of barrier game activities, and the listener and speaker can change roles. The listener can also have the opportunity to request clarification when he does not understand the instructions that were given. The listener, then, is not only helping the person who is giving the instructions learn how to give clearer instructions, but is also getting a chance to practice how to request more information.

It is important that barrier game activities include lots of pieces with lots of choices, so that the speaker has to be specific in describing how to use the materials, and the listener has to choose from the materials and use them based on the instructions given. The idea is to have items that can be confused if detailed instructions are not given, and items that lend themselves to simple questions to clarify the instructions. Activities that work well include:

- decorating cupcakes or cakes,
- making open-faced sandwiches,
- crafts projects such as making bookmarks with initials of the recipient, or stringing beads of different colors, shapes, and sizes,
- toys that have multiple possible combinations such as Colorforms™ or Legos™.

You will need two matching sets of equipment, one for the two people or two groups of people on each side of the barrier. You can also set the activity up so that one or both of the people has a coach to help him give accurate and detailed instructions—e.g., for the jewelry activity, "Do you want him to use the large or small gold bead? You need to tell him."

Place a physical barrier between the two people or the two groups. A piece of cardboard folded in half or a manila folder works well. Folding photo screens that sit on a table are popular now and can be used for this activity. Study carrels can also be used in school.

One child becomes the instruction-giver. You might have the instruction-giver wear a hat or a badge with lips for talking and the instruction-follower wear a badge or a hat with ears for listening. When the two people change roles, they also change hats or badges.

The person giving the instructions may have a pre-made decorated cake, a picture of the decorated cake, or may decide how he wants the cake decorated as he goes along. Each time he adds something, he needs to describe what he is doing to the other child. The barrier makes it clear that the other child can't see what he is doing, so it is a realistic activity. You can remind the instruction-giver that the other child can't see what he is doing, so he needs to describe everything that he is doing. The instruction-follower can ask questions whenever he needs to. You can coach the giver and the receiver, and can remove the barrier if you need to show what needs to be said or what needs to be asked.

When the decorating is completed, remove the barrier. The goal is for both cakes on either side of the barrier to be the same. If they are not, they can be used as the basis for a discussion of how we need to give directions, and what we need to ask when we don't understand the directions. Refer back to Chapter 7 for more activities to practice giving and receiving directions.

Working on Pragmatics in Speech-Language Therapy

If your child is receiving speech-language therapy at school, a variety of pragmatic skills can be targeted in treatment. Be aware, however, that because of regulations in IDEA 97, pragmatic language issues cannot be addressed at school unless they affect your child's ability to succeed in the regular educational curriculum. So, even though you'd like your child to improve his conversational abilities, the IEP team might not agree that that is an important goal if students at the school are not expected to converse in the classroom.

Some of the social interactional language skills that may be addressed during the school years are:

- interacting verbally and socially with peers,
- participating in peer routines at lunch and recess and in class,
- knowing how to introduce people to each other,
- knowing how to begin a conversation,
- staying on topic,
- understanding turn-taking rules,
- using appropriate greetings for different situations,
- decoding and understanding the teacher's cues,
- decoding and understanding nonverbal cues from peers,

- changing registers to communicate with peers and school personnel,
- sharing information,
- understanding the background that someone brings to communication,
- requesting clarification when a direction is unclear,
- repairing conversational breakdowns.

As previously discussed, many of these skills can be practiced through games or role playing activities. Your child's SLP may also use clinical materials, in the

form of books, videos, and CDs, to set the scenario for real-life situations that can be analyzed and practiced in therapy. For example, the SLP may use the books *Scripting, Ready-to-Use Social Skills Lessons and Activities,* or *A Sourcebook of Pragmatic Activities* (listed at the end of this chapter).

Practice with the SLP can be *skill based*—that is, focused on helping your child learn to use specific social skills such as topicalization or requesting objects. For example, your child can practice how he would greet different people who might come to visit his classroom. Photos can be mounted on tongue depressors or foam core board. One child holds the card, and the other child greets the visitor. Some possible visitors include:

- President of the United States,
- Cat in the Hat,
- The principal of the school,
- children from preschool.

Practice may also be *strategy based*—that is, focused on teaching your child to identify different social situations and discuss and follow through on several different solutions. With this strategy, your child discusses the consequences of each choice, and then selects the best solution for the situation. An example of a CD-ROM that could be used to teach this strategy is *Sanford's Social Skills.* This CD provides situations and allows children to follow through to the consequences. For example, if someone screams out loud that you just kicked him and you didn't, what can you do? Talk to the teacher, kick him now, scream back that you did not kick him? The different scenarios that follow from each response are shown. For children and adolescents with more advanced language skills, this is an innovative approach to promote discussion of social communication skills.

If your child has an aide, it is important for the aide to understand his or her role in helping your child communicate socially with classmates, especially if your child's speech is difficult to understand. The SLP needs to provide knowledge and training for the aide in how best to accomplish the goal of assisting communication for your child, while promoting independent communication and appropriate pragmatics skills. It may be fine for one child with Down syndrome or his classmates to come to rely on the aide as a translator for that child if he cannot be understood. However, it would be damaging for another child with Down syndrome who has different skills.

The aide may need to be very supportive when a child with Down syndrome is beginning to use an AAC device, but the aide may need to gradually decrease the support as the child learns to effectively use the system and his classmates become accustomed to being his communication partners. The aide can be helpful in collecting information on how the child communicates in certain situations and help the SLP and parent identify speech/language goals needed. The aide can also provide valuable feedback on what therapy methods are being carried over into the classroom and what skills are not generalizing to classroom interactions.

Pragmatics and Your Child's Future

Pragmatic skills enable us to use the speech and language skills that we have. When your child is an adult, his pragmatic skills are what he will use to communicate in real life. As your child gets older, it is therefore important to make sure that he is mastering the pragmatics that he will need to accomplish his goals.

Of course, if your child is young now, it is probably too early to make specific predictions about what he might like to do in the future. However, we know in a general way what kinds of goals many adults with Down syndrome have for the future, thanks to a study completed by Mia Pederson, a young adult with Down syndrome, and Dr. Laura Meyer, a linguistic researcher. Among the responses to their survey were:

- have my own apartment,
- improve social skills,
- have friends,
- get married,
- have a good job,
- answer the phone myself,
- go on trips.

As you learn more about what your child wants for the future, he should be included in the decision-making process. What does your child want in the future? What kinds of jobs interest him? What kinds of social and language skills will he need for his job and his life in the community? You and the other members of his communication team can plan individually designed assistance, in the IEP and the transition plan, to help your child with Down syndrome improve his speech and language skills in order to help him reach his goals. Pragmatics or social communication plays a big part in reaching these goals.

References

Attwood, A. (1988). The understanding and use of interpersonal gestures by autistic and Down's syndrome children. *Journal of Autism and Developmental Disorders, 18,* 241-257.

Baran, L. S. (1996). Activity guide to Sanford's social skills. Boulder, CO: Attention Getters Publications.

Begun, R. W. (Ed.) (1995). Ready-to-use social skills lessons and activities for grades 1-3. West Nyack, NJ: The Center for Applied Research in Education.

Buckley, S., Bird, G., Sacks, B. & Archer, T. (2000). A comparison of mainstream and special school education for teenagers with Down syndrome: Effects on social and academic development. *Down Syndrome Research and Practice, 7* (in press).

Cullinan, D., Sabornie, E.J. & Crossland, C.L. (1992). Social mainstreaming of mildly handicapped students. *The Elementary School Journal, 92,* 339-351.

Capone, G. T. (1999). Down syndrome and autism spectrum disorders: A look at what we know. *Disability Solutions 3*:8-15, 1999. Special issue devoted to dual diagnosis. (Can be downloaded from the website www.disabilitysolutions.org.)

Gallagher, T. & Prutting, C. (Eds.) (1983). Pragmatic assessment and intervention issues in language. San Diego, CA: College-Hill Press.

Guralnick, M. J. (1995). Peer-related social competence and inclusion of young children. In Nadel, L. & Rosenthal, D. (Eds.) *Down syndrome: Living and learning in the community.* New York: Wiley-Liss, 147-153.

Hall, E.T. (1966). The hidden dimension. New York: Doubleday.

Johnston, E. B., Weinrich, B.D. & Johnson, A. R. (1984). A sourcebook of pragmatic activities. Tucson, AZ: Communication Skill Builders.

Kent-Udolf, K. & Sherman, E. R. (1983). *Shop talk.* Chicago, IL: Research Press. (pragmatic and work-related communication activities for adults)

Leifer, J. S. & Lewis, M. (1984). Acquisition of conversational response skills by young Down syndrome and nonretarded young children. *American Journal of Mental Deficiency, 88,* 610-618.

Loveland, K. A. & Tunali, B. (1991). Social scripts for conversational interactions in autism and Down syndrome. *Journal of Autism and Developmental Disorders, 21,* 177-186.

Loveland, K. A., Tunali, B., McEvoy, R. E. & Kelley, M. (1989). Referential communication and response adequacy in autism and Down's syndrome. *Applied Psycholinguistics,* 10, 301-313.

Mayo, P. & Waldo, P. (1986). Scripting: Social communication for adolescents. Eau Claire, WI: Thinking Publications.

McConnell, N. C. & Blagden, C. M. (1986). Resource activities for peer pragmatics. Moline, IL: Lingui-Systems.

MacDonald, J. (1989). Becoming partners with children: From play to conversation. Chicago: Riverside.

Mundy, P., Sigman, M., Kasari, C & Yirmiya, N. (1988). Nonverbal communication skills in Down syndrome children. *Child Development, 59,* 235-249.

Patterson, B. (1999). Dual diagnosis: The importance of diagnosis and treatment. *Disability Solutions 3*:16-17. (Special issue devoted to dual diagnosis.)

Walker-Hirsch, L., and Champagne, M. P. (1993). *Circles: Intimacy and relationships* (rev. ed.). Santa Barbara, CA: James Stanfield Company.

Weinrich, B. D., Glaser, A. J. & Johnston, E. B. (1986). A sourcebook of adolescent pragmatic activities. Tucson, AZ: Communication Skill Builders.

Wolpert, G. (1996). The educational challenges inclusion study. New York: National Down Syndrome Society.

CHAPTER 12

Augmentative and Alternative Means of Communication

Most children and adults with Down syndrome use speech as their primary communication system. But, some children and adults cannot use speech to communicate effectively. Their speech may be unintelligible, or they may have great difficulty with language, or they may have a dual diagnosis, such as Down syndrome and autism, that makes it difficult to communicate verbally. These individuals often benefit from the use of augmentative and alternative communication (AAC). AAC is any method that assists and/or supplements speech and language, or, in some cases, replaces speech as the primary communication system.

We all use AAC. In conversations we use our hands and arms to make gestures; we change our facial expressions or move our heads; we point to objects, photos, or people to illustrate our point. All of these things are types of AAC. We use every possible channel to communicate: sound, sight, smell, touch, and even taste.

Children and adults with Down syndrome are no different. Often when speech is difficult to understand or produce, people with Down syndrome are very creative at using alternative methods of getting their message across. For instance, a child who wants a drink, but cannot use the words in a way that is understood, may take you by the hand to the refrigerator, open the door, and point to the milk.

Augmentative and alternative communication merely changes the options of communication methods available, expanding the messages a child can send. For instance, if that same child used sign language for "milk" at the refrigerator door, she would be using AAC. If she has a communication board with snack choices, she may point to a picture of milk as well as cookies on her communication board, expanding her message to "milk and cookies." Or she may have a voice output communication device with snack choices programmed on it. With this device, she could tell you, "I want milk and cookies, please," in a recorded voice from the device. Her message is the same, but using the AAC device enabled her to build a sentence using "I want" and "please." With any of these methods, she may or may not also use her own voice at the same time. All of these methods of communicating, with or without speech, are types of AAC.

AAC for Children with Down Syndrome

Many children with Down syndrome are introduced to AAC before one year of age in the form of sign language or "Total Communication." You and your child's early intervention team may have used and introduced new signs as a communication bridge before your child was able to use speech. If your child began to use speech and was understood by more people, she most likely reduced her use of sign language. If sign language is still an important part of communication as she reaches school age, however, you and the IEP team may need to investigate other forms of AAC or provide for training in sign language for any school staff with whom she will regularly interact.

Most children and adults with Down syndrome eventually use speech as their primary communication system. However, the rate that children with Down syndrome learn to communicate varies. Some children will begin using speech early, while others may not begin to use speech until they are between three and five years old, or later. Research has suggested that only 5 percent of children and adults are unable to use speech at all. Sometimes, even when a child or adult uses speech, it is difficult to understand her speech. She may speak too quickly or the words may not be clear. Or, the child may be capable of understanding and using more complex language, but be unable to "speak" those complex phrases and sentences. For any of these individuals, AAC methods should be considered. Each individual, whether or not she can use speech effectively, wants, needs, and has the right to communicate with the people in his world.

In the past, people with cognitive disabilities have not been given opportunities to use AAC techniques to their full extent in learning to communicate. Studies

Communication Bill of Rights

All persons should have the right:

- to be communicated with in ways that are meaningful, understandable, and culturally and linguistically appropriate
- to be communicated with in a manner that recognizes the individual's dignity
- to be given attention from and the ability to interact with other people
- to request objects, actions, and events
- to be offered choices and to participate in decision making
- to express feelings
- to refuse objects, actions, and events
- to have access to environmental context, interactions, and opportunities that expect and encourage participation as a full communication partner
- to be informed about people, things, and events in my environment

The National Joint Committee for the Communication Needs of Persons with Severe Disabilities, 1992.

show that not only are people with cognitive limitations underutilizing AAC and other assistive technology methods, but they also comprise the greatest number of students who are not using speech effectively in the educational system. This makes it important to ask those working with your child about assistive technology and AAC methods to enhance her opportunities for communication and participation.

Under the Individuals with Disabilities Education Act (IDEA), AAC tools are considered assistive technology. Assistive technology is a very broad category that includes: any tool or item that increases, maintains, or improves the functional capabilities of individuals with disabilities. Remember, IDEA *requires* that your child's need for assistive technology, including AAC, be considered when developing her IEP. This chapter will focus primarily on using augmentative and alternative communication methods to improve language skills and participation in the general education setting. Other types of assistive technology aids are discussed in Chapter 5.

The Purpose of AAC

There are a number of reasons to consider using an AAC system. In general, AAC systems are used as transitional, supplementary, or alternative communication. Each type of system will dictate a different design.

- A ***transitional system*** is typically used as a bridge between language and speech. Many children with Down syndrome are ready to use language at or before one year of age, but are not able to use speech at that time. Many children with Down syndrome use sign language or communication boards as transitional communication systems. The systems will be used to communicate their needs and desires until they are able to speak.

- A ***supplementary system*** adds to the communication abilities of the user by providing vocabulary, sentence structure, and comments that are new or too difficult for her. Sometimes, signs or communication boards or electronic devices are used to supplement speech when intelligibility is a problem for the older child or adolescent who has a lot to say, but is hard to understand.

- An ***alternative system*** of communication serves as the student's primary method of communicating. These systems are often the most complex and time-consuming to design, because they need to meet all of the child's communication needs for learning in school and for communication at home and in the community. *If your child has reached kindergarten age, and speech and/or sign are not meeting her needs to communicate effectively, alternative communication systems should* *be considered.* As your child gets older, AAC should be considered at any time when she is regularly frustrated and unable to communicate to meet her needs. All children have moments when they cannot be understood or can't get their message across, but if this is occurring on a daily or very frequent basis, AAC support should be considered.

Determining Whether Your Child Would Benefit from AAC

As mentioned above, each time an IEP is developed for your child, the IEP team is required to consider whether your child would benefit from assistive technology. Since AAC is a type of assistive technology, this means that your child's needs for AAC must be addressed at least once a year.

An AAC evaluation can determine whether an AAC system would benefit your child. An evaluation can be requested by the family, IEP team (especially the special educator, classroom teacher, or SLP), developmental pediatrician, or other specialists at a comprehensive Down syndrome center who follow your child on a regular basis. Based on the evaluation results, the IEP team should consider whether your child needs AAC as a transitional, supplementary, or alternative system.

If this team determines that your child might benefit from AAC, she will qualify for *Assistive Technology Service* on her IEP. This is defined as any service that directly assists a child with a disability in the selection, acquisition, or use of an assistive technology device. This definition includes:

A. The evaluation of the needs of such child, including a functional evaluation of the child in the child's customary environment. (This should include an assessment of your child's needs at school, and an evaluation of your child's ability to use a variety of communication aids and access devices.)

B. Purchasing, leasing, or otherwise providing for the acquisition of assistive technology devices by such child. (That is, your child's AAC system must be provided at no charge to you, the parents, if the IEP team determines she needs it.)

C. Selecting, designing, fitting, customizing, adapting, applying, maintaining, repairing, or replacing of assistive technology devices. The selection of an appropriate device should be made with the consultation and guidance of a school AAC team, or a center that is a statewide technology center (Tech Act Center), or a participating member of the Alliance for Technology Access. The major consideration is that the center must have a wide variety of devices and equipment, and expertise and experience to enable them to determine what equipment is the best match for your child's needs and abilities (motor and language abilities).

D. Coordinating and using other therapies, interventions, or services with assistive technology devices, such as those associated with existing education and rehabilitation plans and programs. (For example, the SLP will help choose vocabulary but the occupational therapist may need to work on fine motor skills to help the child access the system with switches.)

E. Training or technical assistance for such child, or where appropriate, the family of such child. (That is, the school must teach your child and your family to use her AAC device.)

F. Training or technical assistance for professionals (including individuals providing education and rehabilitation services), employers, or other individuals who provide services to, employ, or are otherwise substantially involved in the major life functions of such child. (That is, the school must provide training for school personnel who will need to communicate with your child.)

Designing an AAC System for Your Child

A wide variety of augmentative communication systems are available today to enable a child or adult to communicate. All of these systems can be customized to meet the needs of their users, as well as to capitalize on their strengths. That is why we refer to *designing* an AAC system, rather than *choosing* one.

Some of the most commonly used types of AAC systems are described in this section. The next section will discuss how to decide whether one or more of these systems might be right for your child, as well as how they can be customized.

TYPES OF AAC SYSTEMS

COMMUNICATION BOARDS

Communication boards consist of pictures, photographs, symbols, alphabet letters, or words organized on a flat piece of wood, tagboard, or plastic in such a way that the child can use it to communicate with others. For a child with Down syndrome, communication boards are usually used as a transitional system to promote the use of language while she is not yet ready to use speech. The communication board may also serve as an AAC system when a child or adult cannot be understood or does not use speech.

Communication boards are designed for specific uses such as school, home, and community clubs. For example, a communication board used at home may enable a child to communicate her breakfast choices, as in the example on the next page. A communication board used at school may include alphabet letters for spelling, names or photos of friends or school staff, favorite activities, or information to share about after school activities. A student may also use more than one board throughout the day. For example, your child may have a board for different academic subjects, after school activities, or for informal conversations with friends. Most communication boards will have a way for the child to request help, ask people to leave her alone, or say "yes" and "no."

PORTABLE BOOKS

Portable books are basically the same as communication boards, but they may have more display space and are more portable, so they give the user a larger

Example of a communication board a child may use to communicate food choices.

vocabulary. Often they are notepad- or pocket-sized books with pages of pictures, symbols, or words. Portable books may also be wallet type, credit card case, mini photo album, or plastic cards on a key chain. The child may wear the key chain on a belt or a loop on her pants. Any of these systems can serve as communication systems for a child or adult.

Sometimes, separate books, albums or key chains are used for different domains and situations. For example, a fast food restaurant book or key chain assists a child or adult who cannot use speech in ordering food at a restaurant. The *Passports to Independence* catalog (Crestwood Communication Aids) has a "School Passport" that includes picture cards designed for school needs, such as student supplies, activities, subjects, and lunch. This is another form of communication system.

Notebooks or photo albums are larger-sized versions of communication books. These are often used in school or in specific situations. Since they are larger, they are a bit less portable, but they can hold more pictures, photos, symbols, or words.

PICTURE EXCHANGE COMMUNICATION SYSTEM (PECS)

PECS is a method of communication developed by autism educators Andy Bondy and Lori Frost. Using PECS, communication partners physically exchange pictures of symbols or words in order to communicate. For example, if a child wants an apple, she physically gives a picture of an apple to an adult (or, in more advanced stages, puts together a picture sentence saying "I want apple").

The system was initially designed to teach communicative intent and communication to children with autism, but students with Down syndrome are using this system well, also. The strength of PECS is that it teaches the process of communication in a way that actively involves a communication partner. PECS can be used with picture symbols, photographs, or objects. Because PECS is a specific method of using objects or symbols, it is essential that it be taught in a specific manner, preferably led by someone who has been trained to teach PECS.

ELECTRONIC DEVICES

Many different electronic devices fall into the broad category of "high-tech" options for AAC systems. Examples are DynaVox™, WOLF™, TouchTalker™, Crespeaker™, and Cheap Talker™. There are two types of voice output for these devices: recorded speech and synthesized speech. Recorded speech or digitized speech output is recorded by another person, preferably a child of the same age and gender as the user. Synthesized speech is an electronic voice created by the device the same way computer programs speak.

GESTURES/SIGN LANGUAGE SYSTEMS

These types of systems rely on movements made with the hands for communication. Sometimes gestures that resemble actual life situations, such as pointing to the mouth for eating or pretending to drink from a cup for drinking, may be used. Formal sign language systems such as American Sign Language (ASL) and Signing Exact English (SEE) may also be taught. (In our center, we use Signing Exact English because the signs are basically translations of English words. In American Sign Language, there is a different grammar, and concepts may be presented in a different word order from spoken English.)

Often, sign language systems are used until a child with Down syndrome develops language. Sign language may also be used as an assistive or alternative communication system for children and adults who do not speak.

VOCALIZATIONS

Vocalizations are any audible sounds someone makes, such as a grunt, laugh, shout or groan, that are not recognizable words. Some children with Down syndrome may use vocalizations to gain a listener's attention, even when they are not using speech. Then after they get attention, they use another system to communicate (e.g., signs or a communication board).

Considerations in Designing an AAC System

The goal of designing an AAC system is to improve your child's ability to communicate and participate in the world around him. So, when designing an AAC system, parents and professionals must work together to ensure the system will be useful and used by your child.

As a parent, you have valuable information about your child's interests and activities, different environments, and family-specific vocabulary, such as the favorite name for "grandmother." Classroom teachers have information about the school environment: projects, curriculum goals, favorite friends, classroom set up, and so on, that are important to consider. Speech-language pathologists and AAC specialists contribute information regarding equipment, methods of presentation, ways to use different systems, and organization of the system that affect usefulness, as well. Last, and equally important, classroom peers have insights about age-specific vocabulary and interactions that are appropriate to consider. All of this information is essential to creating an AAC system that is useful to your child.

AAC systems are dynamic: they change as your child's needs and environments change. This means that many times over the course of your child's childhood, you and the other members of her communication team may need to reevaluate her AAC system. Each time, you should consider the issues discussed below.

CURRENT COMMUNICATION

Any AAC system design should consider the current methods of communication already used by your child, as well as her movement capabilities. This means the team will consider any gestures, signs, speech, or vocalizations your child uses successfully. These include facial expressions, head nodding or shaking, pointing, word approximations ("yah" or "nah"), or even whole hand touches. This information will assist the team in decisions about purpose, content, and the way your child uses the system or makes it work, often called "accessing the system."

ACCESS

Access is the method your child will use to create messages with her AAC system. Whether it is a communication board or a computer, your child's fine and gross motor skills will determine what types of systems will be most effective. For instance, if your child points using her entire hand rather than her finger, then there must either be enough room on the communication board, switch, or keyboard for her to use her hand to access the message, or she must use a different method of sharing her message such as handing cards to her communication partner.

If your child is able to use a keyboard successfully, then computer programs may be considered. If she has difficulty using a single finger at a time, she may need an adaptive keyboard that prevents her from hitting several keys at once. If she cannot point or hit a key with her finger, she may need a scanning system that will scan all of the choices; she will then stop the machine at her choice by hitting a switch, paddle, or other device.

ENVIRONMENT

The target environment for an AAC system has an impact on the design that is developed. For instance, if the goal of the system is to improve vocabulary use or sentence structure in the classroom, the type of language selected will reflect appropriate messages for school. These might include, "I don't understand," "I need a break," or "When is recess?" If the system will be used primarily at home, the messages may include, "I want to watch a video," "When will we go to McDonald's" or "I don't want to go to bed yet." If the system will be used in any or all environments, then it must be able to accommodate the different messages and vocabulary.

CONTENT

It is essential to include messages that are important to your child—the person who is using the system. It is equally important for messages to reflect age-appropriate vocabulary, as well as family values. For instance, when someone is bothering you, do you say, "Please leave me alone," or would you say, "Stop it!" If your child is young, it is more likely she will shout the latter. If that is the case, then your child needs to be able to say that. Another example is greetings. Would a child or teenager say, "Good Morning. How are you today?" Take some time to sit in the hallway at school and notice how children are speaking to each other. Not only does age-appropriate language make sense, it is more inviting to the user and the listeners.

COMMUNICATION PARTNERS

It is also important to consider who your child will communicate with using her AAC system. Not only must she learn to be a competent communication partner, but others must be able to show her how by their example. For instance, if you are considering using sign language as the AAC system, how well will others understand her? Some schools include sign language programs as a part of the school curriculum. This would mean there are children and adults at school who can understand her communicative attempts. However, as children become more sophisticated in their use of sign language, fewer people are able to understand them. It may be more appropriate to use a symbol system in a notebook or simple voice output devices. This helps others understand your child's attempts to communicate more successfully without specific training.

LANGUAGE

When designing AAC systems, "language" means the type of symbol used for the system. For instance, some students use written words or spell with letters to create their messages. Other students may use drawings or photographs to represent an entire message or to build sentences. Language may also include the content—the vocabulary chosen for the system. See page 291 for more information on language considerations.

PORTABILITY

The portability of an AAC system is how easily it can be moved from one place to another. The team must consider whether your child needs, wants, or is able to carry the system with her. The system may be too heavy or cumbersome, even if appropriate in every other way.

If the purpose of the AAC system is to improve intelligibility, vocabulary, or language skills, it will probably be used in specific environments such as the classroom or at home for homework. In this case, it may be acceptable if the system is not very portable. However, if your child needs to use an AAC system throughout the day in all environments, then it must be easy for her to carry from place to place and use. It must also be sturdy enough to hold up in different environments. A system that is movable between classrooms, such as a laptop computer, would be difficult to use at recess while playing with friends.

LAYOUT AND DESIGN

The layout and design is the way the components of the messages are organized and displayed. That is, are symbols or words for different types of foods grouped in one place, while symbols for different types of activities are grouped in another? Or are the symbols your child uses most often grouped in one place, with less frequently used symbols somewhere else?

The type of message your child needs to create is an important part of the layout and design. With electronic devices, the layout and design is often determined by the design of the computer keyboard. However, even in this instance, a specialized computer keyboard such as IntelliKeys could be used so the layout and design can be customized to your child's needs. The success of AAC systems that use symbolic representations for words or phrases is greatly affected by the layout and design of the system.

TRAINING

Successfully using AAC systems to teach language takes training. Not only does your child need training to use the system, but everyone involved with your child, including her friends, must have some training to be a good communication partner (see "Communication Partners, below"). When choosing an AAC system, the IEP team must consider who needs training and how much they may need. Needed training for school personnel should then be written into the IEP as a program modification or support. IDEA 97 includes training under Assistive Technology Services.

TEACHING STRATEGIES

Regardless of the type of AAC system used, any student using AAC must be taught how to use it. It is important for your child to understand how the AAC system will affect her communication with others, classroom participation, or quality of homework. How will she be taught and encouraged to use the new system? If teachers or support personnel are aware of the purpose of the system and how to use it in their classroom or for assignments, they will look for and encourage your child to use it.

UPDATING THE SYSTEM

Communication is a dynamic process: lesson plans change, classrooms change, friends change, hobbies change, and so on. Someone on the team must be ready and able to anticipate and respond to changes in the messages your child needs. There must be someone who is readily available to update, maintain, or create new messages for the AAC system. This person should be identified in your child's IEP.

In addition, for the AAC system to be successful, the team must meet regularly to discuss what is working and what is not working. Open and frequent communication regarding the AAC system reduces frustration for your child, the person updating the system, and everyone involved in communicating with your child.

STORAGE AND MAINTENANCE

It is important to agree where the AAC system will be kept. If it is for use at school only, everyone needs to know where it will be so they can use it. For instance, if your child will be using speech-to-text software for writing projects, will the program be on the computer in the computer lab, in the classroom, in the library, or in the resource room? If your child needs to use the program during an unexpected time, will she be able to or will it be disruptive to another class?

Some systems also require maintenance to ensure they are working correctly. This means that someone on the team needs to be able to check the system regularly, as well as fix the system if there are problems. For instance, if a child is using a communication notebook in a three-ring binder, someone needs to be responsible for fixing the binder if it breaks. If your child is using a voice output communication device, someone needs to be responsible for replacing batteries or fixing the system if the voice mechanism begins to speak gibberish. The person responsible for the maintenance should be specified in the IEP. An AAC system will not be an effective language support for your child if it does not work.

Making a Decision as a Team

As your child's team gathers the information above, they can begin to design a system that will meet her needs. For some children, this process is more involved and formal than for others. You can help by keeping the categories above in mind when you listen to the discussions. Ask questions that reflect your child's personality for each category. Fill out the worksheet on pages 306-307. You have information about your child that others may not think of at the time. Your input is invaluable for the AAC system to be effective and used by your child.

As the team, including you, gathers information about how your child communicates, they will consider the different types of AAC systems that will meet your child's needs. In a formal evaluation, the team will gather all the information in the previous section prior to discussing the types of systems that fit your child's situation. However, many teams discuss possible systems throughout the process.

Before the decision about an AAC system for your child can be finalized, there are two primary decisions that must be made regarding the system: the language of the system and the level of technology of the system.

WHAT LANGUAGE IS RIGHT FOR YOUR CHILD?

The type of language used for your child's AAC system will, to some extent, reflect her literacy skills. For instance, if your child is not reading yet, the system will need to use more than words and letters. In this situation, the team will discuss the use of symbols, photographs, or objects.

Speech-language pathologists use a guideline for the progression of symbolic systems for language:

- objects
- photographs
- colored pictures or colored picture symbols
- black and white drawings or picture symbols
- abstract symbols
- alphabet
- words

See the sidebar on pages 292-293 for a detailed description of each category.

While this is the general progression of language development, there are a few important points to remember:

- *Words must always accompany pictures.* This is important for developing and expanding literacy skills.
- *Your child may not follow this continuum as listed.* The list is generally the order in which things are learned, but is not intended to be a rigid process. A child does not need to show expertise at one type of language to "progress" to the next. For instance, some children with Down syndrome have what is called "splinter skills." This means skills in one area are at a different developmental age than other skills.

Symbolic Systems Used for Language

OBJECTS

Objects are the most direct, or least abstract, method to identify the language concept. With this system, objects are used to communicate the message. For instance, if your child wants a drink, she would point to, touch, or take a cup. You would then respond, "You would like a drink? OK, Let's go get a drink." Obviously, it is impossible to represent large things with an exact replica of the object such as cars, trucks, and buildings. However, smaller representations such as toy cars, trucks, or buildings can be used to send the same message.

PHOTOGRAPHS

Photographs are next on the symbolic continuum. Generally color photographs are best because they represent the object or place with the most accuracy. When using photographs it is helpful to remove any other objects or people in the picture that are not a part of the message. The greatest benefit to using photographs is how specific they are. For instance, if your child wants to say "I" using a photo, she points to a picture of herself, rather than a general picture of a girl or child. If she wants to say, "go home," she uses a photo of her own house (a colonial townhouse), rather than a photo of a house that does not look like hers (a contemporary individual house).

Not all of the concepts children want to communicate involve objects. Photographs can also show people, events, seasons, and holidays. A common problem with using photographs is that they are so specific. For instance, if your child chooses a photo of *Doritos* to indicate her snack, she may not be happy when you give her BBQ potato chips instead.

COLORED PICTURES

These may be cut from magazines or picture dictionary books, or printed out from software packages. Although the pictures are representational, the colors provide additional cues that help a child identify the object from the picture. Most standardized language and intelligence tests use colored pictures or black and white drawings. So, using pictures helps children learn skills that they will need for test taking.

- *Your child may need a blend of different language systems.* For example, a child using picture symbols may not understand the symbolic representation of a new concept or word. In this case, she may need a photograph for a period of time before using the symbolic representation. Picture symbols are also available that show a person using the manual "sign" for the word or concept.
- *Be consistent.* If you choose a symbolic representation for a phrase, object, or activity, use the same one each time. It is confusing to your child if the symbol for "I want" changes with the environment or situation.

DRAWINGS

Symbols and drawings can be hand drawn or computer generated. Colored symbols are usually introduced before black and white symbols. There are a variety of symbol systems available, many of which can be printed out using software packages. Sources of these symbols are listed in the Resource Guide.

ABSTRACT SYMBOLS

Abstract symbol systems are closer to language than pictures, in that they do not resemble what they represent. For instance, a picture of a glass of milk looks exactly like an actual glass of milk. A rebus, Bliss symbol, or other symbol does not look like the actual object. It is more representational.

ALPHABET LETTERS

Letters may be used for direct selection or for various types of scanning. For instance, if your child is able to choose letters directly by pointing and can spell words, she can point to the appropriate letters. This might be done with a communication board, a computer with a talking word processor such as *IntelliTalk,* or with a voice output communication device. When she is finished writing, the speech synthesizer will speak the words that she has written. A system can also anticipate the word that your child will use based on the first few letters she selects and the vocabulary that is stored in her system.

If your child cannot point to individual letters or press specific keys, there are systems that can scan all of her choices by letter and number. For example, the system sweeps a light across line 1 and she stops the system at the letter F.

WORDS

Words are used to build sentences or as a representation for phrases or sentences. For example, a communication board or computer system may have the individual words for "thank you." Your child points to those words whenever she wants to communicate "thank you." She may also point to a single word, such as "have," to activate a phrase such as, "May I have" or use "pizza" to access the phrase, "Let's order pizza."

The idea of choosing a language system for your child can be daunting, but it is essential that you, as your child's best resource, stay involved in the process. While you may not have the educational expertise of the team, you do have important insight about what your child understands.

A common problem in this process of language selection is to try to choose only one system. Keep in mind that learning is a process. Your child may need different types of language representation for familiar messages or literacy skills than for new ones that she is learning. Focus the attention on *teaching* your child rather than *testing* her. Keep an open mind when you observe her using various options for communication, and note which options meet her communication needs best.

WHAT TECHNOLOGY LEVEL IS RIGHT FOR YOUR CHILD?

The second main category you will consider when selecting the AAC system with the team is the technology level. You will hear words such as "high-tech" and "low-tech" used during this discussion. Obviously, unless certain equipment or programs are readily available for your child to try, the "low tech" system is the least expensive. However, decisions about assistive technology are not supposed to be driven by cost. Rather, if your child's IEP team determines that a particular system is necessary for your child to progress at school, the school system is required to provide it.

Regardless of cost, both types of systems can be time-consuming to set up and individualize. To avoid wasting time and money on a system that will not work for your child, make sure that the evaluation provides the opportunity to assess the appropriateness of a variety of systems for your child. It is needlessly expensive to purchase a system that will not meet your child's needs, and will therefore not be used. A high tech system needs to be designed by a team of assistive technology specialists in consultation with the family and the IEP team.

LOW-TECH SYSTEMS

Low-tech systems use "low technology" or no technology. They include categories such as communication boards, the Picture Exchange Communication System, notebooks, sign language, and other gestural systems. Generally these systems are designed for your child to take with her from place to place. The advantages to low-tech systems include their cost, durability, and portability. They can be redesigned easily, and new vocabulary can be added as needed, as long as your child can handle a larger number of symbols. However, they are not foolproof. They can be bulky to carry around, especially at recess or lunch, the content of the system is limited and, like all systems, they can be lost.

Sign language is the system closest to spoken language, since the child generates the signs spontaneously using her own body. There are no boards, books, or other aids that need to be carried around.

HIGH-TECH SYSTEMS

High-tech systems refer to those systems that use computers or voice output devices. High-tech systems are changing all the time. They include specialized software for word prediction; single switch voice output devices (which can be programmed to "speak" a variety of messages when one key, button, or switch is pressed); and intricate voice output systems such as a *Liberator* (a high-end expensive system that enables the user to create an almost endless number of messages using digitized speech sound bits rather than words and phrases).

High-tech systems can range from a hundred dollars to thousands of dollars. As you can see, it is essential to try out expensive systems before investing in them. Most vendors selling expensive systems have a loan period. In some states, the technology center has equipment to lend for trial purposes (see Resna and ATA in the Resources at the end of this book). Choosing an intricate and expensive system without thoroughly investigating the purpose, interests, abilities of your child, or utilizing a trial period, may result in a device that sits on the shelf unused. However, the process of choosing an AAC system must not exclude more expensive systems merely because they are expensive. An expensive system that enables your child to communicate is better than an inexpensive system that does not meet your child's needs and sits unused.

When the system is being designed, families are an essential part of the process, but it is best to work with a team. Just as you cannot design the system on your own, the team will have difficulty designing an appropriate system without your input. One family told me that they had not known where to get an AAC evaluation. They contacted a manufacturer and purchased a system on their own. After spending over $3,000 for the system, they discovered it was not a usable system for their son. In all fairness, however, if the process is not thorough or if the child is not the center of the evaluation process, professionals also can and do make costly mistakes in selecting and implementing AAC systems. Do not let the potential cost or the fear of making a mistake prevent you from advocating for an AAC system for your child. Especially if trial of the system is included, the opportunity for mistakes can be reduced.

AAC systems must fit your child's motor and cognitive abilities, as well as meet her communication needs. When considering a high-tech system, you need to consult a professional who designs AAC systems on a regular basis and has many different types of systems that your child can try. Most school systems have AAC teams, though access to trial equipment varies. If your school system does not have an AAC team or adequate equipment to try in a reasonable time frame, seek out a statewide center from the Alliance for Technology Access or RESNA. Contact information is provided in the Resource Guide at the end of this book.

Learning to Use the System

Once the system is chosen, obtained, and designed, the *real* work begins: learning to use and respond to it. It is important to continue to work as a team, sharing information about successes and struggles when using the AAC system.

There are a number of people who need to know how to use the system besides your child. Classroom teachers must understand the system in order to adapt or design classroom instruction that is appropriate. The SLP must know how to individualize therapy to encourage progress in AAC-related goals. School personnel must know how to communicate with a child using an AAC system. Classmates need to know how to respond to the person using the AAC system. Some students may want to be involved in the maintenance and design of the system. Family members need to know how to include new vocabulary from home, as well as communicate with or encourage appropriate use of the AAC system to improve language skills.

In short, everyone who will come in contact with your child when she is using her AAC system needs to understand how to respond naturally and encourage your child's communication or language skills.

Whenever we communicate, we are sending a message to another person. Communication isn't successful if there is a problem with how the message is sent or received. So, your child cannot communicate using her AAC system unless there is someone to receive and respond to her message. Communication partners are those people with whom your child communicates.

Most of us have not had an opportunity to be around other people who use AAC systems. People may be uncomfortable or unsure of how to respond to your child's attempts to use her new system. Training for communication partners (classmates, teachers, librarians, parents, siblings, and related service providers) should be included as a part of the AAC implementation process. Key elements to this training include:

- **Responding:** Communication partners may need coaching in how to respond to messages sent by your child using her AAC system. It takes practice and encouragement to become adept at responding to an AAC user.
- **Waiting:** Communication partners must wait for your child to construct her response using her AAC system. The most common struggle for communication partners is listening without anticipating or interrupting the person using the AAC system.
- **Opportunities:** Early success with AAC systems sometimes requires shaping opportunities. The team must meet to discuss how to create natural opportunities for your child to learn and become an expert using her AAC system.

There are many ways to train communication partners. Probably one of the most effective methods of teaching classmates about being a communication partner is through a *Circle of Friends*. A circle of friends is a group of peers who agree to support the student with disabilities in a variety of situations. The format of a Circle of Friends discussion provides an easy, comfortable environment for friends to ask questions and share their successes with the student.

Learning to Use the AAC System: Issues at School

Researchers and clinicians working with children who have Down syndrome estimate that only 5 percent will need an AAC system in their lives. However, the percentage would be much higher if students who use AAC (such as sign language) as a transition to speech or to improve language and communication skills were included in those numbers.

There is a wide range of possible communication needs for students with Down syndrome. Therefore, it is impossible to create one quick and easy method for including students using AAC systems in the classroom. However, by considering the individual student's needs and the opportunities in the school environment, it becomes easier. Basically, there are two areas to consider:

- **Academic opportunities:** group discussions, homework, report giving, and individual work
- **Social opportunities:** recess, lunch, before and after class, transitions between class, and after school activities.

Ideally, the system will be individualized and team members will know how to encourage the student to use the AAC system to enhance these opportunities. There will be a time of learning for the student and all team members, including family, while the system is designed, refined, and implemented. This time can feel a bit confusing, but if the team communicates what is successful and what is not, it will come together.

A group of students huddle around the table engaged in a group activity. They must create three characters for a character web and use them in a simulation of life during colonial days. The conversation is animated and colorful. However, if you look closely, the group is orderly. Each student chooses a different aspect of a character created in the group. One child uses symbols to provide input: "Joe, what color should her hair be?" asks one boy. Joe pulls a symbol of the color brown out of his communication notebook and hands it to the child who asked the question. "OK. She has brown hair," he says as he returns the symbol to Joe. These students have been coached to modify their brainstorming session to include a child with Down syndrome who does not use speech. All the children in the group contribute.

The classroom teacher and the special education teacher are the team members with the most input regarding academic opportunities for communication. At first, it may be necessary to review lesson plans and activities with the team. Once the classroom teachers become comfortable with how the AAC system can be included in lesson plans and activities, adaptations will become second nature for them. It is important to remember it takes everyone time to learn. Here are some areas to consider when adapting lesson plans:

- If a student is using an AAC system to supplement or replace speech at all times, look for opportunities to use that system to improve participation.
- Allow extra time for the student using an AAC system to answer questions or give reports. She is learning her system too.
- Give her a "heads up" that she will be asked for the answer to a question (and tell her the question) after two more students answer theirs. This gives her time to compose the message or practice it with a peer mentor or educational assistant using her AAC system. This method not only gives her time, but is time efficient for your classroom.
- Use AAC systems for report-giving. If a student is learning new vocabulary or language skills using text-to-speech and word prediction software, she can also present her report using the computer and talking software.
- If the student is using AAC systems to replace or produce intelligible speech, consider use of a tape recorder or special interface with the voice output system. A peer can record the report for the student using the AAC system. The student with the AAC system must operate the tape recorder or voice output system to present the report. For example, James, a

fourth grader with Down syndrome, took part in a classroom sharing session by pushing a button on his tape recorder to play back a prerecorded account of his weekend while he showed his classmates the illustrated story below.

If your child is using a symbol or pictorial based language system, there are specially designed materials available commercially that can be used to help your child learn at school. An example is *News-4-You,* a symbol-based weekly subscription newspaper activity that uses the Picture Communication Symbols© made with Boardmaker™ software (Mayer-Johnson Company). It enables children to understand the current news stories, and to be able to work on activities that relate to current events. It also enables them to write their own stories or summaries of news events using the Boardmaker symbols. See example on page 300.

AAC SYSTEMS AND SPEECH AND LANGUAGE SERVICES

When designed and implemented properly, AAC systems provide a means of communicating for a student. As such, they supplement or replace speech. However, they do not instantly provide language; the student is not immediately able to use the system to communicate with others. Students must be taught to use the systems. In turn, the systems must be part of a greater language development program. The system should be used *in* therapy, not *instead* of therapy.

Thursday there was no school so we took a trip to Bonneville Dam

Thursday

school

trip

Bonneville Dam

to see salmon go up the fish ladder.

salmon

fish ladder

The lifecycle of the salmon

life cycle

The underwater fish ladder

An example of a sharing sheet used in conjunction with a tape recorded story

Sometimes when students are provided with an AAC system to use for communication, speech and language services are terminated. This is equivalent to providing someone with a piano and then not providing music lessons. Some parents have been told that since their child now has a way to communicate, her language abilities are commensurate with her mental abilities and therefore speech services are no longer necessary.

The fact is, all of the language development "speaking" children learn also has to be learned by the child using AAC. This requires thought, planning, and speech and language services. The child first needs to learn how to use the device or to make the signs. Then she has to learn vocabulary, sentence production, and conversational skills using the system. It is very important to continue speech and language therapy in order to use the AAC system to help your child progress in language.

It is also important to consider where or how speech and language services will be delivered to your child. Many schools remove the student from the classroom or separate her from the class activity to provide direct instruction. However, studies show that best practice for delivering speech and language instruction for students who have cognitive disabilities and are using an AAC system is in the classroom or activity as it is happening. In other words, the most effective instruction will be done in the classroom at the time your child will be using the AAC

The salmon go up a fish ladder to lay their eggs

in the bottom of the stream where they were born.

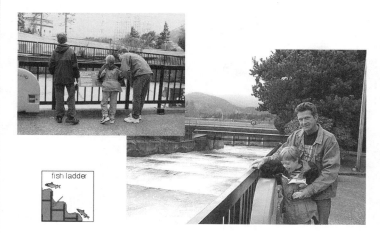

The outdoor fish ladder

We had a great time!

Continued from p. 298

MORE NEWS

 **What**

?

SUPER BOWL

Football players wear helmets and pads.

They play on a football field with a goal post at each end.

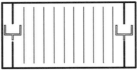

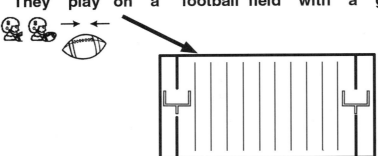

Football fields are in stadiums.

Many people go to the stadiums to cheer their teams.

Sample page from News-4-You

system. This can be a challenge. However, especially if the AAC system is to be used throughout the day and across environments, it can be done. SLPs will need to vary the time of service delivery throughout the day in order to individualize direct instruction for different situations between your child and her classmates.

WRITING IEP GOALS FOR STUDENTS USING AAC SYSTEMS

There are two main categories to consider when writing IEP goals and objectives for students using AAC systems:

1. competence in learning to use the system, and
2. targeted language and communication skills.

That is, like other children with Down syndrome, your child should have goals designed to help her improve her communication skills (e.g., receptive language skills, pragmatic language, syntax). But she also needs goals focused on helping her learn to use her new system.

If an objective is written for communication skills, but your child has just been introduced to an AAC system, it is important that the goal be geared to her proficiency using her system rather than language development. Once she is proficient and understands *how* to use the system, progress on the targeted language goals is appropriate. This can be accomplished by using graduating steps toward the overall communication goal.

If your IEP team is in the process of designing an AAC system for your child, multiple devices or methods can be listed in the IEP goal. For instance, "Using a variety of electronic devices (tape recorder, IntelliTalk, voice-in-a-box, talking photo album), Sierra will make 3 presentations to the class throughout the academic year."

As with all IEP objectives, it is important to include any information that is crucial to your child's success. For instance, you may want to define whether or not she will receive a verbal, visual, or physical cue or assistance to accomplish the goal. For example, she might receive hand over hand assistance to point to an answer if she is having difficulty. Remember, it is important for your child to become independent using her system, so there must also be a reduction of these prompts in the IEP objectives.

Common topics to consider for IEP goals and objectives related to your child's AAC system include:

- initiating conversation,
- sustaining conversation,
- asking questions,
- making appropriate requests,
- socially appropriate comments,
- classroom presentations,
- working in small groups,
- expressing basic needs,
- expressing feelings,
- using carrier phrases such as "I want to" or "Let's go."

Training for staff, family, and classmates also needs to be defined in the IEP. In most cases, this is included with accommodations and modifications. You can also suggest language within the IEP objectives to highlight the importance of this training such as, "Jamie will sustain a 10-minute conversation using her AAC system with friends who are trained communication partners during her lunch buddy time."

Another area to consider when writing the IEP is including time for teachers and related services personnel to communicate. This can be addressed in the accommodations and modifications section. An example might be: "general education teachers and special education teacher will meet weekly to discuss instruction and adaptations for AAC system use." Goals and objectives can also be written relating to staff members' involvement with the AAC system.

Sample Goals for AAC System Use

Goal: To use the Touch Talker to participate in classroom activities.

Benchmark: Using the Touch Talker, Antonio will use greetings with classmates and teachers 80% of the time by the end of the first report card period.

Benchmark: Antonio will spontaneously ask for help on classroom assignments, when appropriate, using the Touch Talker, once a day by December 15.

Goal: To use a communication board for classroom communication.

Benchmark: Susan will use a communication board with 4 picture symbols to answer yes/no/maybe/I don't know questions with 80% accuracy by November 30.

Benchmark: Susan will use a communication board with 4 picture symbols to make requests at least twice a day by the end of the first marking period.

Goal: To use sign language to communicate in class and at home.

Benchmark: Margie will use Signing Exact English (SEE) signs for the phrase, I need to ___ with 6 verbs 80% of the time in class by May 30.

Benchmark: Margie will use Signing Exact English (SEE) to ask for help with class assignments at least twice daily by the end of the first marking period.

Learning to Use AAC Systems: Issues at Home

Once your child has an AAC system to try or to use, it is essential to encourage her to use it at home the same way she uses it at school. For instance, if your child is using word prediction and text-to-speech software to complete assignments at school, she should do the same at home with her homework if you have a computer. If your child uses symbols to answer worksheet questions that are read to her at school, she needs to do this with her homework, too. Taping or gluing picture symbols or typed words on the worksheet to complete sentences not only helps her participate in homework, but also provides information for a student portfolio to show her progress in learning the curriculum and how to follow instructions.

To support your child's use of any AAC system, you need training, encouragement, creativity, and patience. Training for you and other family members should be included in the process of creating an AAC system. However, this needs to go beyond how to use the actual device, software, or symbol system. It must also include training to be an effective communication partner.

Once you begin to use the AAC system at home, there are some key elements to success:

1. *Ask everyone to use the system with your child.*
2. *Be responsive.* If your child uses an AAC system to augment her speech, respond to sentences created on a board or by a voice output device just as you would any other conversation. Don't be afraid to say, "What? I wasn't listening carefully. Can you tell me again?" Try to avoid asking for too many repetitions, but it's important to understand the message rather than guessing.
3. *Be honest.* If your child is an emerging communicator and asks for something you don't have, don't ignore her. Tell her the truth. "I'm sorry, we're out of apples. Can I get you something else?"
4. *Reward your child's communication attempts after you have answered her question or responded to her comment.* Wait until the conversation has ended and then praise her for how well she is using her AAC system. Tell her how much you enjoy communicating with her.
5. *Include the AAC system in family games.* This means teaching siblings to be patient while your child communicates her message, "I want to buy Park Place."
6. *Be consistent.* Do not use the AAC system only when it is convenient. You will be rewarded for your hard work over time.
7. *Wait.* No one likes to be second-guessed or interrupted. Remember that it takes longer to create a message when using any AAC system. Give your child time to respond. Avoid guessing what word she is going to choose. Wait for her to choose it before you repeat it or respond. And always let her finish her sentence!

It takes time to integrate an AAC system into the everyday life of a family. Be patient with yourself, your family, and friends. Begin by implementing the system in parts of the day your child seems most motivated to communicate. Remember that communication and AAC system design is ever-changing. Share what is working and what is not working with the team working with your child and listen to what is working at school. A frequent and consistent home-school communication plan enables you to work together and build on each other's successes. This, in turn, will help your child generalize the use of her AAC system across environments and into the community.

Computers for Literacy Skills

Using computers as part of an AAC system is a relatively new practice and already rapidly evolving. As mentioned earlier, computers are considered a part of a broader category called Assistive Technology (AT). One method of enhancing language or vocabulary skills is the use of word prediction and text-to-speech software. Depending on your school's team and how the software is used, this may be considered AAC or AT. Regardless, these are powerful methods of building literacy skills.

In today's world, children are introduced to text-to-speech software early in the form of talking computer books such as the *Living Books* series. As the computer reads the story out loud, the words are highlighted on the screen. Additionally, the program allows children to repeat sentences or single words over and over and over by highlighting or clicking on them. This repetition can be tough to be around, but it is an active learning process. Listening to the synthesized voice of the computer may be helpful because:

- It says words the child cannot.
- It doesn't scold the child for incorrect pronunciation when she tries to repeat something.
- It will endlessly repeat words without getting tired or bored.
- The words and phrases are highlighted, which encourages the connection between the written words and speech.

There are myriad software programs available that can encourage and enhance your child's literacy, language, and communication skills. In addition, there are many less expensive assistive technology techniques and tools that may accomplish the same goals, depending on your child's strengths and weaknesses. See the Resources at the back of the book for a list of companies that produce and/or distribute communication, literacy, and educational software.

Parent Comments

We purchased our first real computer when our son was seven years old. When I saw the *Living Books* CD programs at school, I knew these would be helpful for him, and they were. He could work on these independently, which he liked a lot. He could repeat something for the 200th time if that was what he wanted or needed. While crayons and pencils could be difficult for him to manipulate, he became adept at using a mouse. Computer software is still a big part of our son's assistive technology support at school.

Alex knows *so* much, and now has a way to express it. Verbal communication may be rough and most people cannot read his handwriting, but he has a lot to say. Using Co:Writer® [a talking word prediction program] and Write:OutLoud® [text-to-speech word processing software] have been a great help to him. He still needs some assistance in getting a direction or idea organized, but once he does he is off and running. I really like working on his homework with him. I've learned a lot more about "Alex, the person" by being involved in his creative writing. I think it also has helped his relationships with teachers. It's been a learning experience for many, seeing what Alex can do with the right supports and opportunities.

Conclusion

At the beginning of the book, we made an important distinction between communication, language and speech. It is important to provide an effective communication system for all children that will meet their educational and daily living needs. These needs change as your child grows and develops.

Sometimes parents are reluctant to use AAC with their child because they fear it will prevent her from learning to speak. This is not true. Because a two year old uses sign language, it does not mean that the same child, at five years of age, will not be able to speak. The sign language helps the child to continue to learn language, at the same time that the signs are enabling her to communicate her needs. Research has shown that children who use sign language increase their vocabulary.

Parents may also be reluctant to try an alternative communication system because they feel as if they have failed somehow if their child begins to use a communication board or device. But when a child cannot communicate what she needs to with the people in her environment, she may not continue to try to communicate.

Low- and high-tech devices can help children progress in language learning and enable them to continue to communicate with those around them. They will be less frustrated and more independent. Your child can learn many kinds of language skills, such as combining words and composing sentences, while using AAC. Using a speech synthesizer, the child who is unintelligible can be more understandable to peers, and thus begin to form relationships and feel more included.

AAC provides a powerful kind of language support system. It is another tool that we can use to help children learn language and to enable them to communicate with family members, peers, teachers, and other people in the community.

Worksheet for Designing an Augmentative Communication System

Name: _____ Age: _____

Current Needs

____ Transitional Pre-Speech System

____ Clinical/Educational Learning System

____ Alternative Communication System

Team Members (including parents, the user, peers, and AAC specialists): _____

_____

_____

_____

Type of System

Unaided:

____ Sign Language

____ SEE

____ ASL

____ Other: _____

Aided:

____ Communication Board

____ Communication Notebook

____ Picture Exchange Communication System (PECS)

____ Electronic high-tech system (specify)

____ Other: _____

Symbol System:

____ Objects

____ Photographs

____ Pictures

____ Letters

continued ▶

_____ Words

_____ Other: _____

\# Symbols Used: _____

Content of System: _____

_____

Settings

_____ Classroom

_____ All School Settings

_____ Home

_____ Community

_____ Other: _____

Purposes

_____ Social Communication

_____ Learning

_____ Behavior Prompts

_____ Other: _____

Organization of Information: _____

_____

Training Needed

_____ Child

_____ Parent

_____ Teacher

_____ Other: _____

Maintenance of System: _____

_____

Funding of System: _____

_____

Final Thoughts

We now know a great deal about the way that children with Down syndrome learn best. In some schools, information on learning styles and multiple intelligences is used regularly to help all children learn in the particular way that they learn best. But, in most schools, there is a prescribed way of teaching and learning the subject areas of reading, writing, language arts, math, science, social studies and other subjects in the curriculum. In the curriculum and in classroom interactions, there is a heavy reliance on language skills. In the early grades, there may be more visual models and examples. But, in the later elementary school grades and middle school, there is an emphasis on verbal instructions and complex verbal or written responses.

Because children with Down syndrome are visual learners, this approach does not usually match their learning styles. Fortunately, when a child is eligible for special education services, accommodations, modifications, and special services can be used to develop a good match between the way that the child learns and the way that the material is presented. Special education teachers and speech-language pathologists can work with the classroom teacher and the family. Together, they can explore and use methods, adaptations, modifications, and additional assistance through aides and peer tutors that can help children with Down syndrome succeed in school. Families, teachers, researchers, and speech-language pathologists can form a powerful team to help children with Down syndrome achieve in school.

In the childhood years, school is such a major part of your child's life. Successful experiences in school lead to improved self-esteem and a "can-do" attitude. Improved communication skills help not only in achieving success in school. Improved communication abilities can also help your child succeed as he or she grows to adolescence and adulthood and makes the transition to the world of work and community. There are many opportunities in school to practice and use language skills, and children with Down syndrome continue to learn and improve their communication skills throughout the school years.

Knowledge and information empower you as parents and as professionals as you journey through the educational process. We can walk together on this path. Together, we can make a difference for school-aged children with Down syndrome!

Appendix

This appendix includes a variety of forms that can be used in planning your child's speech-language treatment program, as well as his Individualized Education Program. Below are short descriptions of the forms and how to use them.

COMPREHENSIVE LANGUAGE TREATMENT: A LONGITUDINAL PLAN FOR THE SCHOOL YEARS

Many parents say that they don't know what to ask for in speech and language services. This comprehensive treatment plan outlines all of the areas that have an impact on communication function during the school years. Your child may already have mastered some of these skills. Other skills may be worked on in school speech-language therapy. For areas such as speech skills and intelligibility, you may need to seek SLP services from a center outside of school. All of these areas should be observed and/or tested by the SLP so that she has a comprehensive evaluation of your child's strengths and needs.

IEP CHECKLIST FOR COMMUNICATION: INFORMATION NEEDED FOR PLANNING MEETINGS FOR SPEECH, LANGUAGE, AND HEARING

This checklist is a "packing list" for your trip to the IEP planning meeting. This is the material that you want to bring with you. These are the records of what was included in the IEP, and whether that level of service was actually provided. If your child was supposed to have speech sessions twice weekly, how many did he actually have? What accommodations were used for testing? What adaptations to curricular material? Were they used? If you do not have copies of reports, request them before or at the IEP meeting. If testing was not done, request that it be done. The records that you bring, and the checklist items are designed to help you check whether the program is being implemented and whether changes are needed.

IEP PLANNING GUIDE FOR SPEECH & LANGUAGE

Your school system will have its own official IEP form that will be used for recordkeeping. The speech-language section will be very brief. This form is designed to help you flesh out the official form. It is a way of reframing the information so that you are sure that all of the relevant information is written into the IEP. It can be used at the IEP planning meeting, or can be used after the plan is designed, but before you actually sign the IEP. The SLP can help you fill this form out, or you can use it as a guide for planning. It can be used every time the IEP team meets for planning sessions.

Comprehensive Language Treatment

A LONGITUDINAL PLAN FOR THE SCHOOL YEARS

I. **Preschool Through Kindergarten**
    A. Receptive Language Skills
        1. Comprehension
        2. Semantics/Concept Development
    B. Expressive Language Skills
        1. Semantics
        2. Syntax
        3. Mean Length of Utterance
    C. Pragmatics Skills
        1. Social Interactive Skills
        2. Communication Activities of Daily Living
        3. Requests

II. **Elementary/Middle School Years**
    A. Receptive Language Skills
        1. Comprehension
        2. Semantics
        3. Morphology/Syntax
        4. Literacy
    B. Expressive Language Skills
        1. Semantics
        2. Morphology
        3. Syntax
        4. Mean Length of Utterance
        5. Reading
        6. Writing
        7. Narrative Discourse
    C. Pragmatics Skills
        1. Social Interactive Skills
        2. Communication Activities of Daily Living
        3. Requests
        4. Clarification Strategies/Repairs

IEP Checklist for Communication

INFORMATION NEEDED FOR PLANNING MEETINGS FOR SPEECH, LANGUAGE, AND HEARING

Testing Information

___ Speech (includes articulation, intelligibility, voice, rate, and fluency)

___ Oral motor evaluation

___ Language (includes receptive and expressive language, semantics, morphosyntax, and pragmatics)

___ Hearing (includes pure tone, speech audiometry, central auditory testing)

___ Augmentative communication

___ Any independent evaluations

___ Countywide (or district-wide) tests

___ Statewide tests

___ Are any accommodations being used for testing?

   List the accommodations: _____

Treatment Information

___ Copy of previous IEP

___ Attendance and service records (how many sessions did child attend and receive services?)

___ Samples of worksheets used in treatment

___ Audio- or videotaped samples of present communication ability

___ Summary of progress achieved for each speech & language objective

   How was progress measured? _____

Classroom-Based Information

___ Language of the curriculum

___ Language of instruction in the classroom

___ Language of the hidden curriculum

___ Language of testing (classroom)

continued ▶

___ Language of classroom routines

___ Social interactive communication

___ Assistance in the form of adaptations

___ Assistance in the form of support personnel

___ Assistance from peer tutors or buddies

List assistance provided: _____

_____

_____

List accommodations currently provided: _____

_____

_____

Home-School Communication

___ Information on how the SLP and family have maintained communication

Other Information

___ Copies of relevant correspondence

___ Any additional information needed to plan the IEP: _____

_____

_____

IEP Planning Guide for Speech & Language

Child's Name: _____

Educational Placement: _____

Present Level of Performance in Speech & Language:

_____
_____
_____
_____
_____
_____
_____
_____
_____

Annual Goals:

_____
_____
_____
_____
_____
_____
_____

SHORT-TERM OBJECTIVES/BENCHMARKS *(List objectives in each area as needed)*

For each area listed in the IEP, how will progress be measured? How will we know if the student has achieved his/her goals? _____

_____
_____
_____

continued ▶

Communication Area / Measure of Progress

Speech: _____

_____

_____

_____

Language: _____

_____

_____

_____

Hearing: _____

_____

_____

_____

Augmentative Communication: _____

_____

_____

_____

Curriculum Based Language: _____

_____

_____

_____

Language of Instruction: _____

_____

_____

_____

continued ▶

Language of Routines: _____

_____

_____

_____

Language of Hidden Curriculum: _____

_____

_____

_____

Social Interactive Communication: _____

_____

_____

_____

Other: _____

_____

_____

_____

_____

Speech-Language Pathology Services:

Frequency per week: _____

Length of each session: _____

Location of each session: _____

Individual or group size: _____

continued ▶

Supplementary aids and services (program accommodations and modifications) to support speech and language needs:

1. Time and schedule

___ untimed tests or assignments

___ extra time

___ child permitted to take breaks: ___ as needed   ___ scheduled breaks

2. Curriculum-based materials

___ language organizers

___ pre-teach subject vocabulary

___ copy of teacher's notes

___ summary of important information

___ peer takes and shares notes

___ reduce reading difficulty of unit material

___ present material via audiotape, videotape, or computer (can be replayed)

3. Equipment

___ augmentative communication device

___ word processor

___ audiotape recorder

___ video recorder

___ camera

4. Modifications in language used in presentation of instructions

___ shorten directions

___ reduce language level

___ provide demonstrations

___ provide picture cues

___ provide written instructions

___ read directions to child

continued ▶

___ tape record directions for child (can be replayed)

___ aide interprets directions

___ provide oral cues or prompts

___ provide organizers and modified worksheets

___ complete task in cooperative learning group

___ provide alternate activity

___ child restates directions to demonstrate understanding

5. Modifications in language channel, mode, length child uses in response

___ student gives answer verbally; aide writes down

___ word processor

___ augmentative communication device

___ child uses picture communication board

___ child writes sentence instead of paragraph

___ child responds in writing

6. Language impact on behavior. Does language difficulty have an impact on the child's behavior?

Situations where language is related to behavior: _____

_____

_____

Child's intent when that behavior occurs (e.g. frustrated and does not want to do math):

_____

_____

Results of a functional behavior evaluation (attach or briefly summarize): _____

_____

_____

_____

continued ▶

Can child use a communication board or augmentative communication device to make needs known? _____

_____

_____

Is there a positive behavior support plan in effect? _____

_____

_____

7. Supports/training for school personnel in speech and language

	School Personnel	Training needed (e.g. augmentative communication)
Classroom teacher:	_____	_____
	_____	_____
	_____	_____
Classroom aide:	_____	_____
	_____	_____
	_____	_____
School staff:	_____	_____
	_____	_____
	_____	_____
Bus driver:	_____	_____
	_____	_____
Other:	_____	_____
	_____	_____
	_____	_____

Resources

DOWN SYNDROME

Canadian Down Syndrome Society
811 – 14 St. NW
Calgary, Alberta T2N 2A4
Canada
800-883-5608; 403-270-8500
dsinfo@cdss.ca
www.cdss.ca

Down Syndrome Educational Trust
The Sarah Duffen Centre
Belmont St.
Southsea, Hampshire
PO5 1NA
United Kingdom
+44 (0)23 9282 4261
enquiries@downsed.org
www.downsed.org

Down Syndrome: Health Issues website
www.ds-health.com
    Information on health and medical issues related to Down syndrome, as well as links to hundreds of other Down syndrome-related websites

National Down Syndrome Congress
7000 Peachtree-Dunwoody Rd., NE
Suite 100
Atlanta, GA 30328
(800) 232-NDSC
NDSCcenter@aol.com
www.ndsccenter.org

National Down Syndrome Society
666 Broadway
New York, NY 10012
(800) 221-4602
info@ndss.org
www.ndss.org

GENERAL SPEECH AND LANGUAGE ISSUES

American Speech-Language-Hearing Association
10801 Rockville Pike
Rockville, MD 20852
(800) 638-8255
actioncenter@asha.org
www.asha.org

National Institute on Deafness and Other Communication Disorders
National Institutes of Health
31 Center Dr., MSC 2320
Bethesda, MD 20892-2320
www.nidcd.nih.gov

ASSISTIVE TECHNOLOGY AND AUGMENTATIVE AND ALTERNATIVE COMMUNICATION

Sources of Information and Support

For assistance within the United States in finding a center that provides evaluations for Assistive Technology and Augmentative Communication, contact the Alliance for Technology Access or RESNA, below.

In Canada, technology issues are administered through the Ministry of Health, Assistive Devices Branch, and includes Hugh MacMillan Rehabilitation Centre in Toronto, ON and Bloorview Children's Hospital in Willowdale, ON. More information is available from the Canadian Down Syndrome Society at the address above.

Alliance for Technology Access
217 East Francisco Blvd., Suite L
San Rafael, CA 94901
(415) 455-4575
www.ataccess.org

On the Internet, you can find a complete list of all centers affiliated with the Alliance for Technology Access organized by state. This national network of technology resource centers provides information and resources and demonstration. Some centers will analyze your child's computer needs and provide free or low-cost evaluations. Others will lend or provide computers and software.

Apple's People with Special Needs website
www.apple.com/disability

Has a searchable database of hardware, software, and other products for people with disabilities that are compatible with Apple computers. Also links to helpful organizations.

Center for Special Education Technology
1920 Association Drive
Reston, VA 22901
(703) 620-3660

Council for Exceptional Children center which publishes a monthly newsletter about technology and children with special needs

Closing the Gap
P. O. Box 68
Henderson, MN 56004.
(612) 248-3294
www.closingthegap.com
Resource center for technology information. Publishes bimonthly newsletter and holds annual conference. Website provides library resources, article summaries, and a list of upcoming conferences.

IBM Accessibility Center
www-3.ibm.com/able
The website has links to information on AT products (IBM) and solutions for people with disabilities.

International Society for Augmentative and Alternative Communication (ISAAC)
49 The Donway West, #308
Toronto, ON M3C 3M9
Canada
(416) 385-0351
www.isaac-online.org
ISAAC's mission is to improve communication and quality of life for people with communication impairments. They have publications, conventions, and, on the website, links to resources.

National Easter Seal Society
230 W. Monroe St., #1800
Chicago, IL 60606
(312) 726-6200
www.easter-seals.org
Among services offered by local chapters is assistance with assistive technology, including computers.

RESNA (Association for the Advancement of Rehabilitation Technology)
1101 Connecticut Ave., NW, Suite 700
Washington, DC 20036
(202) 857-1140
www.resna.org
Offers information on state Technology Assistance Projects that will provide hardware and software support. The Resna website provides a complete list of state centers that are funded under the Technology-Related Assistance for Individuals with Disabilities Act of 1988 and 1998.

TASH
29 W. Susquehanna Ave.
Baltimore, MD 21204-5201
410-828-8274
www.tash.org
This organization, which advocates for "equity, quality and social justice for people with disabilities," has information and an annual conference.

Trace Research & Development Center
University of Wisconsin-Madison
5901 Research Park Blvd.
Madison, WI 53719-1252
info@trace.wisc.edu
www.trace.wisc.edu
This web site provides information about assistive technology, including augmentative and alternative communication.

United Cerebral Palsy
Assistive Technology Funding and Systems Change Project
1660 L Street, NW, Suite 700
Washington, DC 20036
202-7765-0406
www.ucp.org
UCP's website includes articles on assistive technology, on topics such as choosing AT and finding funding sources.

The U.S. Society for Augmentative and Alternative Communication
c/o Barkley Memorial Center
University of Nebraska
Lincoln, NE 68588
(402) 472-5463
website under construction
Information and resources regarding augmentative communication, hardware, and software.

Sources of Equipment and Supplies

These companies can provide information on hardware and software to support assistive technology. Many design and sell augmentative communication devices. Some also provide picture symbols or picture systems for communication. Picture symbols can be used for communication boards, notebooks, and other communication systems. They are also helpful in creating adaptive material, such as learning worksheets, for classroom inclusion. The picture symbols are often used in language therapy. Many of the companies have software with picture symbols, and those programs are noted below. The major products that could be helpful in assistive technology for children with Down syndrome are also noted,.

For information and catalogs, contact these companies directly, or contact CAMA (The Communication Aids Manufacturers Association) or ATIA (The Assistive Technology Industry Association), the associations which include the major companies.

Industry Associations

CAMA
P.O. BOX 1039
Evanston, IL 60204
(800) 441-CAMA (2262)
www.aacproducts.org
CAMA holds local/regional conferences for professionals and/or families throughout the country where you can learn about various communication devices.

ATIA
526 Davis Street
Suite 217
Evanston, Illinois 60201
(877) 687-2842
ATIA@northshore.net
www.ATIA.org
ATIA holds an annual conference where you can learn about communication devices, software, and learning aids. Speakers address a wide range of topics on assistive technology equipment, techniques, and research intiatives.

Companies

Ability Research
P.O. Box 1721
Minnetonka MN 55345
(612) 939-0121
www.skypoint.com/~ability
> They produce the *Action Voice* and *Hand Held Voice*.

ABLENET
1081 Tenth Ave. SE
Minneapolis, MN 55414
(800) 322-0956
www.ablenetinc.com
> Resources include *Language Master* (card replay system); *Let's Go Activity Pack; Can Do Recorder, Quick Start Communication Kit; Big Mack* recorder switch; *TalkTrac; Step by Step Communicator, One Step* and *All Turn It Spinner.*

Academic Software
331 W. Second St.
Lexington, KY 40507
(859) 233-2332
www.acsw.com
> Specializes in AT and computer access for individuals with disabilities.

Adaptivation
2225 W. 50th St., Suite 100
Sioux Falls, SD 57105
(800) 723-2783
www.adaptivation.com
> *VoicePal Max*; switches and interfaces to create activities; *Recipes for Success, Volumes 1 and 2.* Website includes links to sites with information on AT.

AlphaSmart
20400 Stevens Creek Blvd., Suite 300
Cupertino, CA 95014
(888) 274-0680; (408) 252-9400
www.alphasmart.com
> The *AlphaSmart* is a portable keyboard that stores typed information and then easily sends it to any type of computer. Simple editing and printing may be done directly from the *AlphaSmart.*

Assistive Technology, Inc.
7 Wells Ave.
Newton, MA 02459
(800) 793-9227; (617) 641-9000
www.assistivetech.com
> They sell the *Freestyle*, a tablet-type Macintosh computer with a touch window and companion software. They also sell the *LINK*, a "smart" keyboard that talks; *EvaluWare*, assessment activities for augmentative communication; *Emerging Language Software* (cause & effect, language readiness, early concepts, advanced concepts); Assistive technology photos for daily life; Computer funding guide; *Gemini* computer.

Attainment Company
504 Commerce Parkway
Verona, WI 53593-0160
(800) 327-4269
www.attainmentcompany.com
>*Go Talk-36* message voice output communication system; *Teaching Social Competence; WordWise* (functional litreracy program); *Picture Cue CD; Writing with Symbols; Ready Set Read.*

Cole Educational
P.O. Box 1717
Pasadena, TX 77501
(713) 944-2345; (800) 448-COLE
www.edumart.com/teacherstore
>They sell the *EIKI Portable Card Reader, the Language Master,* and blank cards.

Communication Devices, Inc.
421 Coeur d'Alene Avenue, Suite 5
Coeur d'Alene, ID 83814
(800) 604-6559; (208) 765-1259
www.comdevices.com
>They sell the *Holly.com* and *Holly.com E-lite* augmentative communication devices with built in disk drives for changing vocabulary.

Communication Skill Builders
313 North Dodge Blvd., Box 42050-H
Tucson, AZ 85733
(602) 323-7500
www.psychcorp.com/catg
>Picture Symbol Systems including *Peel and Put, Pictures Please Stickers, Communicards, Photo Sticks, Photo Cue Cards,* as well as games and activities for communication skills.

Consultants for Communication Technology
508 Bellevue Terrace
Pittsburgh, PA 15202
(412) 761-6062
www.concommtech.com
>Equipment for turning a laptop into a communication device in British English, American English, Spanish, and German.

Crestwood Communication Aids
6625 North Sidney Place
Milwaukee, WI 53209
(414) 352-5678
www.communicationaids.com
>Speaking aids such as *The Crespeaker* and the *Crespeaker MAXX* use alphabet letters. Talking picture frames and recorded card machines are excellent for practice. Talking pictures and passports can be used as picture communication systems including, *Passport to Independence, School Passport, Sign Language Pictures.*

Developmental Equipment
P.O. Box 639
Wauconda, IL 60084
(800) 999-4660
>*Picsyms, Oakland Picture Dictionary.*

Don Johnston, Inc.
26799 West Commerce Dr.
Volo, IL 60073
(847) 740-0749; (800) 999-4660
or
Don Johnston Special Needs Ltd
18 Clarendon Ct., Calver Rd.
Winwick Quay, Warrington,
England WA2 8QP
info@donjohnston.com
www.donjohnston.com

Talking word processor (*Write:Outloud*) and word prediction software. Adapted as well as other Macintosh and Windows products and a variety of other communication and computer products, including books and other resource materials: *Core Picture Vocabulary; PixWriter; Clicker 4* (writing software with picture support); *Discover Literacy; Start-to-Finish Book Club; Discover Board, switch, and screen; PCA Checklist; ATI Assessment.*

DynaVox Systems, Inc.
2100 Wharton St.
Suite 400
Pittsburgh, PA 15203
(888) 697-7332
www.dynavoxsys.com

Communication devices in English and Spanish: *DynaMyte 3100; Dynamo-digitized; DynaVox 3100.*

Edmark
P.O. Box 97021
Redmond, WA 98073-9721
(800) 362-2890
www.edmark.com

Software for typical and special-needs learners available in English and Spanish. Critical thinking, early learning, language arts, math, science and social studies software. Website has curricular correlations which match curriculum objectives with Edmark software products. Curricular objectives and the matching products are provided for each state, and for curricular programs that may be used in more than one state, such as the Stanford 9 Instructional Objectives and the Texas Essential Knowledge and Skills. Company has excellent customer support.

Educational Resources
1550 Executive Dr.
Elgin, IL 60123
(708) 888-8300
www.edresources.com

A discount supplier of software and hardware from many companies.

Electronics Technology Group
9333 Penn Ave.
South Bloomington, MN 55431-2320
(800) 480-4384; (612) 948-3100

A discount supplier of software and hardware from many companies.

Enkidu Research
247 Pine Hills Rd.
Spencerport, NY 14559
(800) 297-9570
www.enkidu.net
info@enkidu.net
They sell portable *IMPACT* dynamic display augmentative communication devices that come in three different hardware versions: The Palmtop, the Handheld, and the Tablet. Also, *DeCtalk,* speech synthesis, letter-based and symbol based communication systems.

Feelings, Inc.
P.O. Box 574
Virginia Beach, VA 23451
(757) 363-9585
Communication vests and toys made from Tempo Loop Display fabric.

Frame Technologies
W681 Pearl St.,
Oneida, WI 54155
(414) 869-2979
cframe@netnet.net
www.frame-tech.com
Inexpensive digitized voice-output devices: *Voice-in-a Box, TalkPad, Book Talker,* and *MicroVoice.*

Freedom Scientific Learning Systems Group
NASA-AMES Moffett Complex, Bldg 23
P.O. Box 215
Moffett Field, CA 94035-0215
(888) 223-3344
www.freedomscientific.com
WYNN (text to speech software).

The Great Talking Box Company
2245 Fortune Dr., Suite A,
San Jose, CA 95131
(408) 456-0133; (877) 275-4482
www.greattalkingbox.com
inquire@greattalkingbox.com
They sell the *E-Talker, Dynamic Display Augmentative Communication device,* the *EasyTalk,* and *Digicom-2000.*

Gus Communications
P.O. Box 4362
Blaine, WA 98231-4362
(604) 279-0110
www.gusinc.com
They sell a dynamic display communication software for IBM compatibles.

Imaginart
307 Arizona St.
Bisbee, AZ 85603
(800) 828-1376; (520) 432-5741
www.imaginartonline.com
Pick 'N Stick Fast Food, Pocket Picture Holder, Touch 'N Talk Communication Board /Notebook, Pick 'N Stick Color Packs.

IntelliTools, Inc.
1720 Corporate Circle
Petaluma, CA 94954
(800) 899-6687; (707) 773-2000
www.intellitools.com

They sell *IntelliKeys* (specially designed limited choice and adaptable multiple choice program-mable keyboards); keyguards; *Overlay Maker; IntelliTalk II* communication system; *IntelliPics* picture library; *Access Pac* (curriculum adaptation tool). They also have an activity exchange on their website.

Laureate Learning Systems
110 E. Spring St.
Winooski, VT 05404
(800) 562-6801
www.laureatelearning.com

Extensive variety of well-designed language software for learners with special needs, including *First Words I & II, First Verbs, Exploring First Words I & II, Talking Nouns, Talking Verbs, First Catego-ries. Simple Sentence Structure, Early Emerging Rules: Plurals, Negations, Prepositions, Adjectives & Opposites, Words & Concepts I-III, Language Activities of Daily Living: My House, My Town, My School,* the *Sentence Master 1-4.*

Mayer-Johnson Company
P.O. BOX 1579
Solano Beach, CA 92075
(800) 588-4548
www.mayer-johnson.com

Mayer-Johnson sells a wide variety of AAC systems and tools, including *Picture Communication Symbols,* which can be photocopied or printed by computer with *Boardmaker* software (available in ten languages). Mayer-Johnson also sells *Speaking Dynamically Pro,* an AAC software program; inex-pensive digitized voice output devices; curricula augmented by symbols and other resources; *Com-munication Board Builder; Print 'n Communicate; Print 'n Learn Thematic Units for Boardmaker; Print 'n Learn Community Units for Boardmaker; Speaking Dynamically Pro; Speaking Academically; TALK Boards; Language Exercises for You and Me; Hands On Reading; Curriculum Experiences for Literacy, Learning and Living.*

Pyramid Educational Consultants
226 West Park Place, Suite 1
Newark DE 19711
(888) PECS INC (888-732-7462)
pyramid@pecs.com
www.pecs.com

They offer training and sell products to assist with the Picture Exchange Communication System.

Prentke-Romich Company
1022 Heyl Rd.
Wooster, OH 44691
(800) 262-1984
www.prentrom.com (in the U.S.)
www.prentromint.com (outside the U.S.)

They sell a wide variety of augmentative communication devices, and have extensive customization options and customer support services. Website includes links to summer camps for people who use AAC.

Saltillo Corporation
2143 Township Rd., #112
Millersburg, OH 44654
800-382-8622; 330-674-6722
aac@saltillo.com
www.saltillo.com
> They sell the *ChatPC,* the *ChatBox, Message Box, VocaFlex,* and a variety of other AAC devices.

Sammons Preston
AbilityOne Corp.
4 Sammons Ct.
Bolingbrook, IL 60440
(800) 323-5547 (in U.S.)
(800) 665-9200 (in Canada)
www.sammonspreston.com
sp@sammonspreston.com
> *Communication Sheets,* many self-help daily living aids.

Slater Software
351 Badger Lane
Guffey, CO 80820
(719) 479-2255
www.slatersoftware.com
> AT for pre-readers and beginning readers, such as *Picture It, Tool for Teachers; PixReader; PixWriter; T.A.L.K. (Take Along Language Kits); Interactive Book Kits.*

Softtouch
4300 Stine Rd., Suite 401
Bakersfield, CA 93313
(877) 763-8868
softtouch@funsoftware.com
www.funsoftware.com
> Software for children with special needs, including: *Teach Me to Talk; Companion Activities for curriculum adaptation; Learning software;* overlays for *IntelliKeys; Picture This: Nouns & Sounds, Learning for Teens; Concepts on the Move; Print, Play & Learn; Teach Me Phonemics.*

Synergy
68 Hale Rd.
East Walpole, MA 02032
(508) 668-7424
www.synergy.qpg.com
> They sell Macintosh PowerBook and Windows systems with built-in touch screens for use as a portable communication devices and other AAC devices.

Technology for Education
1870 E. 50th, Suite 7
Inver Grove Hts, MN 55077
(800) 370-0047
www.tfeinc.com
> AT and learning products from a variety of manufacturers.

Turning Point Therapy and Technology
P.O. Box 310751
New Braunfels, TX 78131-0751
(877) 608-9812; (830) 608-9812
www.turningpointtechnology.com
 Custom keyguards and protectors for computer keyboards.

Words+
40015 Sierra Highway
Building B-145
Palmdale, CA 93550
(800) 869-8521
www.words-plus.com
 Communication software, communication systems, speech devices. Website has online newsletter with news about AAC issues.

Zygo Industries
P.O. Box 1008
Portland, OR 97207-1008
(800) 234-6006; (503) 684-6006
zygo@zygo-usa.com
www.zygo-usa.com
 Specializes in high-tech AAC systems: *Optimist* (augmentative communication device); *Winspeak* (symbol based communication system); *PICTOCOM SE*; software programs; *MACAW* communication device.

Education

ERIC Clearinghouse on Disabilities and Gifted Education (ERIC EC)
Council for Exceptional Children
1110 N. Glebe Rd.
Arlington, VA 22201-5704
(800) 328-0272
ericec@cec.sped.org
http://ericec.org
 Offers many fact sheets and digests on the education of children with disabilities. Many publications available in Spanish. Documents may be downloaded free of charge from the website. If you do not have Internet access, you may write or call for documents in print form. One copy of each document is available free of charge; additional copies of most publications cost $1.00 each. Website provides access to the ERIC database of publications on disabilities.

NICHCY
P.O. Box 1492
Washington, DC 20013-1492
(800) 695-0285
(202) 884-8441 (fax)
nichcy@aed.org
www.nichcy.org
 The National Information Center for Children and Youth with Disabilities (NICHCY) has many publications on special education issues and other disability issues available. They can be downloaded free from the website or ordered for a nominal fee by phone or mail. Some publications available in Spanish.

Office of Special Education Programs Website
www.ed.gov/offices/OSERS/OSEP
    Fact sheets and other online publications about U.S. special education regulations and laws are available here.

SERI website
http://seriweb.com
    SERI (Special Education Resources on the Internet) provides many links to sites with information on special education laws, inclusion, and the education of children with specific disabilities.

Wrightslaw website
www.wrightslaw.com
    A great deal of information for parents interested in being their child's educational advocate. Website includes many informative articles on IEPs, inclusion, etc., and the option to subscribe to a free online newsletter.

Index

About the Author

Libby Kumin, Ph.D., CCC-SLP, is the Director of the Graduate Program of the Department of Speech-Language Pathology/Audiology at Loyola College in Baltimore, Maryland, where she founded the Down Syndrome Center for Excellence. She is the author of *COMMUNICATION SKILLS IN CHILDREN WITH DOWN SYNDROME* (Woodbine House, 1994). Dr. Kumin has been and continues to be active in scholarly research, with many publications and presentations to her credit.